Introduction to Leisure Services:
Career Perspectives

Richard Kraus
Elizabeth Barber
Ira Shapiro

Temple University

Sagamore Publishing Inc.
Champaign, Illinois

© 2001 Richard Kraus, Elizabeth Barber and Ira Shapiro
All Rights Reserved.

Production Manager: Janet Wahlfeldt
Book Layout: Jennifer Polson
Cover Design: Charles Peters
Front Cover Photo by PhotoDisc

ISBN: 1-57167-482-9
Library of Congress Catalog Card Number: 00-107471

SAGAMORE PUBLISHING
804 North Neil Street
Champaign, Illinois 61820
www.sagamorepublishing.com

Contents

Preface vii

Chapter 1
Recreation and Leisure in American Life 1
Introduction 1
Leisure Participation Today: An Overview 2
Recreation and Leisure: Underlying Concepts 2
Recreation in Earlier Eras 4
Growth of Support for Organized Recreation 4
Benefits of Leisure: Recent Findings 8
Leisure Trends at the Begininng of the 21st Century 12
Changing Patterns of Work and Free Time 13
Impact of Multiculturalism 14
Growing Influence of Technology 14
Commodification of Leisure Services 15
Benefits-Based Management 18
Leisure Services and the Future 20

Chapter 2
The Organized Leisure-Service System 23
Why Focus on Organized Services? 23
Leisure Services as a System 24
Models of the Organized Leisure-Service Field 25
Public, Governmental Agencies 27
Nonprofit Community Agencies 27
Commercial Recreation Businesses 27
Armed Forces Recreation 28
Employee Services and Recreation 28
Campus Recreation 28
Private-Membership Organizations 29
Therapeutic Recreation Service 29
Sports Management 30
Tourism and Hospitality 30
Functions of Leisure-Service Agencies 30
Other Elements in the Leisure-Service System 32
Dynamics of the Organized Leisure-Service System 35
Scope of Employment in Leisure Services 37

Chapter 3
Public Recreation, Park and Leisure-Service Agencies 42
Government's Role in Recreation and Parks 43
Federal Government Agencies 43
State Leisure-Service Agencies 45
Legal Basis of State and Local Programs 46
Park District Operations 47
County Recreation and Park Agencies 49
Municipal Recreation and Park Programs 50
New Business-Related Approaches in Government Service 57
Employment Patterns in Public Recreation 58

Chapter 4
Nonprofit Leisure-Service Agencies: The Voluntary Sector 64
Scope of Nonprofit Organizations 65
Youth-Serving Agencies 65
Religion-Affiliated Leisure-Service Organizations 71
Special-Interest Organizations 76
Other Types of Nonprofit Organizations 77
Employment Practices in Nonprofit Organizations 80

Chapter 5
Commercial Recreation Businesses 87
Commercial Recreation Defined 87
Types of Commercial Recreation Businesses 88
Outdoor Recreation Businesses 89
Water-Based Commercial Recreation 95
Fitness Centers and Health Spas 97
Family Play Centers 101
Employment Perspectives in Commercial Recreation 102

Chapter 6
Armed Forces and Employee-Service Programs 107
Recreation in the Armed Forces 107
Goals of Military Recreation 108
Organization of Armed Forces Recreation 108
Newer MWR Management Strategies 115
Employment and Career Development 116
Employee Services and Recreation 119
Shifting of Program Emphasis 122
Changing Employee-Services Identity 123
Professionalism in Employee Services 123

Chapter 7
Campus and Private-Membership Recreation 128
Overview of Campus Recreation 128
Goals of Campus Recreation 129
Recreational Sports Programs 131
College Union Programs 132
School-Sponsored Recreation 136
Private-Membership Organizations 138
Country Clubs 140
Residence-Based Memberships 140
Staffing Patterns in Private-Membership Clubs 144

Chapter 8
Therapeutic Recreation Service 148
Early Development of Therapeutic Recreation 148
Legislation Assisting Persons with Disabilities 149
NTRS Leisurability Model 149
Therapeutic Recreation Today; Two Models 150
The Clinical Approach 151
Patient-Client Assessment 151
Development of Treatment Plan 152
Documentation of Outcomes 154
Factors Promoting Special Recreation 156
Examples of Community-Based Special Recreation 157
Employment and Professional Development 163

Chapter 9
Sports Management Today 169
Sports in American Life: Scope and Variety 169
Growth in Participation 172
Gains for Girls and Women in Sport 173
Minority-Group Participants in Sport 173
Nonprofit Organizations Promoting Recreational Sports 175
Economic Importance of Sport 177
Career Development in Sport 179
Special Aspects of Sport Management Field 182
Need for Ethical Values in Sport 184
Career Opportunities in Sport 184

Chapter 10
Travel, Tourism and Hospitality 189
Basic Concepts of Travel, Tourism and Hospitality 189

Scope of Tourism Today 191
Trends Promoting Tourism 192
Structure of Tourism Industry 194
Theme Parks 197
Cruise Lines 200
Special Destinations and Leisure Interests 202
Social and Environmental Effects of Tourism 207
Jobs and Career Opportunities in Tourism 210
Future Perspectives in Travel, Tourism and Hospitality 211

Chapter 11
Career Perspectives in Leisure-Service Agencies 216
Leisure Services: Their Rewards and Demands 217
Personal Qualities of Leisure-Service Professionals 217
Need for Self-Assessment 218
Making Career Choices 221
Key Characteristics of Agencies 221
Analyzing Job Opportunities: Five Factors 223
Examples of Present-Day Employment 224
Position Descriptions and Job Notices 225
Career Development Planning 236
Career Advancement and Professional Development 238

Bibliography 243

Appendix A
Listing of Organizations and Societies 245

Appendix B
Suggested Class Assignments and Student Projects 249

Author and Subject Index 251

Preface

Most college and university departments of recreation, parks, and leisure studies offer one or more introductory courses designed to acquaint students with this field of community service.

However, since the field has been dominated by the public recreation and park movement, most such courses and textbooks have focused primarily on the work of public, tax-supported leisure-service agencies and have paid little attention to other types of specializations.

Gradually, this pattern has changed, as therapeutic recreation service, sport management, and tourism and hospitality have become increasingly important areas of professional practice. Today, no fewer than ten different types of leisure-service sponsors offer significant recreation programs throughout the United States. They represent an important source of employment for young men and women entering the overall field.

This text presents a detailed, comprehensive picture of these ten different types of leisure-service agencies and pays special attention to their personnel practices, goals, and programs and the career potential they offer to college students. Based on materials submitted to the authors by dozens of organizations of every type and supplemented by a systematic search of relevant Web pages through the Internet, this book presents detailed, up-to-date profiles of all types of leading leisure-service organizations.

While it is not possible to credit all of the individuals or organizations that responded to our search, credit should be given to the directors of public recreation, park, and leisure-service departments in the following communities: in California, the cities of Long Beach and San Mateo and the East Bay Regional Park District; in Arizona, Phoenix and Scottsdale; Westchester County, New York; Sarasota County, Florida; Prince George's County, Maryland; Vail, Colorado; and in Canada, Vancouver and Kamloops, British Columbia, and North York, in Ontario.

Numerous nonprofit youth-serving and special-interest organizations were helpful, including the Boys and Girls Club of America; the Police Athletic League, the Boy Scouts and Girl Scouts; the YMCA, YWCA, and YM-YWHA; the Catholic Youth Organizations; Campfire Boys and Girls; the American Camping Association; the National Outdoor Leadership School; and Woodswomen, Inc. Among commercial recreation sponsors, several outdoor and adventure recreation companies provided materials, including Pocono Whitewater

Adventure and Whitewater Vacations in California and Chuck E. Cheese (CEC) Entertainment, Inc. which provided information on family play centers.

Therapeutic recreation agencies included Special Olympics, RCH Inc. in San Francisco, and the South East Consortium in New York. Campus recreation materials were provided by Northern Colorado University, Southern Illinois University, Virginia Commonwealth University, and Concordia University in Montreal, Canada. An abundance of other brochures, reports, planning studies, and personnel guidelines was received from armed forces, private-membership, and major recreational sports organizations.

Supplementing the printed materials gathered from these sources are numerous illustrations, photographs, brochure covers, organization charts and similar visual materials—that should help students become more intimately familiar with all the different kinds of leisure-service agencies described in the text.

As a single example, recruitment Web pages and job descriptions drawn from a number of organizations help to illustrate the various and diverse job opportunities available in this field today. One thread that runs through the book is that recreation represents far more than simple "fun and games"—as it might have been thought of years ago. Instead, recreation is widely recognized as an important health-related field that is closely linked with other human services and is often responsible for key areas of community development.

It is our hope that Introduction to Leisure Services: Career Perspectives achieves its goal of helping students to understand this field and to become motivated to enter it professionally. Chapter-ending questions; a listing of important national organizations; suggested class assignments and student projects; and a comprehensive, up-to-date bibliography all should help it to achieve this objective.

Richard Kraus
Elizabeth Barber
Ira Shapiro
School of Tourism and Hospitality Management
Temple University
Philadelphia, Pennsylvania

Chapter 1

Recreation and Leisure in American Life

Introduction

Recreation and leisure represent a major force in American life today. This chapter begins with a brief history of the field and an explanation of its key concepts. It outlines the growth of participation in various forms of leisure activity, including sports and games, hobbies, social pursuits, travel and tourism, and outdoor recreation.

This chapter also examines the motivations underlying participation in leisure activities, along with the important personal, social, environmental, and economic values and benefits derived from constructive forms of recreation.

Several important trends affecting recreation and leisure today are presented: (1) shifts in the amount of available free time for people in different socioeconomic groups; (2) demographic change, in terms of age trends, racial and ethnic shifts in the population, gender related and evolving family needs; and (3) the related forces of innovative technology, commercial development, and privatization as they affect the delivery of leisure opportunities and services.

Finally, the chapter shows how recreation in its varied forms has become the responsibility of a huge array of different types of organizations and program sponsors, and has become a major source of employment for men and women throughout North America.

Leisure Participation Today: An Overview

If a visitor from the 25th century or from a distant planet were to pay a sudden visit to the United States or Canada today, he or she would probably be impressed by the degree to which men, women, and children were taking part in a host of playful pursuits—hobbies, video games, parties and social events, sports, hunting and fishing, visiting theme parks and enjoying sightseeing trips, engaging in the arts or other cultural pastimes, and other varied forms of entertainment.

This space-and-time traveler might also discover that many thousands of different kinds of organizations provide facilities, leadership, and program services to facilitate these nonwork experiences.

Our extraterrestrial visitor might ask, "What do you call all this activity? It's not work. People don't have to do it to survive; Why do they *do* it?"

The answer, of course, is that people are voluntarily taking part in recreation and leisure pursuits for a host of reasons. In some cases, their primary motivation is the pleasure or fun they gain from taking part in a competitive sports activity or watching a skilled performer in the arts. In other cases, their goal may be to improve their health and fitness, to enjoy the companionship of others, to express themselves creatively, to experience new environments, or simply to relax and enjoy a change of pace.

Recreation and Leisure: Underlying Concepts

If, finally, our space traveler were to question the essential meaning of recreation and leisure, it might be helpful to explain that recreation and leisure have long been recognized as important elements in human society.

Recreation is a form of human activity, carried on in one's free or discretionary time. It is voluntarily chosen and was traditionally intended to help participants recover from the stress of toil and to restore themselves for renewed work. Today, it is often considered to be not only participation in an activity, but also an important kind of human experience, marked by a sense of accomplishment, self-discovery and creative growth, oneness with nature, or rewarding social contact.

Leisure, usually defined as time that is free of work or work-related tasks or family or other civic responsibilities, provides the setting in which recreation is carried on. Like recreation, leisure is often thought of as a state of mind, a transforming experience marked by freedom of choice and personal enrichment. In a sense, leisure is broader than recreation in that it may be used for other nonplay purposes, such as continuing education, volunteer work in the community, religious involvement, or other cultural pursuits (see Figure 1-1).

Finally, both recreation and leisure may be regarded as social institutions because they are studied by economists, sociologists, and other social scientists and are provided or served by a huge network of governmental, voluntary, educational, commercial, and therapeutic agencies. This text is concerned with the *leisure-service system* that these agencies constitute, and it deals primarily with their role in providing recreational programs and facilities.

Figure 1-1
This brochure cover from Scottsdale, Arizona, conveys the important message that recreation and leisure are an important part of one's lifestyle.

Recreation in Earlier Eras

Throughout humankind's history, people in all societies have enjoyed varied forms of play and recreation. In earlier human cultures, religious rituals often included contests of various kinds, song and dance, and artistic pursuits, which ultimately were transformed into play.

Similarly, over time, survival-related activities such as hunting, fishing, or even warfare lost their original purposes and became recreational experiences. Today, rodeos, lumberjack contests, archery and riflery, yacht racing or fishing competitions all are modern-day vestiges of what once were serious occupations.

In ancient Greek and Roman civilizations, contests that ranged from track-and-field to boxing or wrestling to chariot racing and slaughters of wild beasts in huge arenas were carried on—originally as part of religious festivals and ultimately to entertain the masses.

During the Middle Ages and Renaissance in Europe, the wealthy and powerful nobility sponsored the arts—music, drama, and ballet—or hosted spectacular entertainment as royal celebrations. Knightly jousting, gambling, village fairs, folk crafts, and rustic pursuits also entertained people of all classes.

In the late 18th and 19th centuries in Europe and America, hours of work in factories, mines, mills, and on farms continued to be long and hard. Religious disapproval tended to condemn many forms of play and entertainment through much of the 19th century. Gradually, however, work hours were reduced—both through laws and the efforts of labor unions—and religious leaders and civic officials realized that there was an important need for organized forms of play.

Growth of Support for Organized Recreation

During the second half of the 1800s and the early decades of the 20th century, there was growing support for organized leisure programs and facilities. It took several forms:

Cities, states, and the federal government in both the United States and Canada set aside major tracts of land as parks, both to preserve their natural beauty and, increasingly, as places for camping, wilderness exploration, and a host of other outdoor recreation pursuits.

Municipal governments and school systems built networks of playgrounds and established day camps and summer play programs—first serving children and youth and ultimately all age groups with diversified play activities.

Major national organizations, such as the Boy Scouts and Girl Scouts, the Boys Clubs and Girls Clubs, the Young Men's and Young Women's Christian Associations, and other religious and secular youth-serving and character-building groups, initiated recreation, camping, and social programs and helped to serve other educational and citizenship functions.

In the years following World War I, often referred to as the Jazz Age or the Roaring Twenties, there was an explosion of interest in varied forms of popular recreation. Movies and radio offered new means of entertainment, and college and professional sports became national obsessions. During the 1930s, the United States, like the rest of the world, was challenged by widespread unemployment, bankruptcy, and foreclosures on homes and farms, But even this situation helped to promote public support for organized recreation, as

President Franklin Roosevelt's New Deal provided jobs helping to build thousands of new parks, playgrounds, community centers, and sports fields and hired recreation leaders, writers, artists, and cultural performers in an effort to boost public morale.

Following the Allied victory in World War II, both the United States and Canada saw recreational interest and involvement reach new heights. In both nations, millions of young families moved from city streets to suburban or small-town settings, where they supported newly established park and recreation departments, joined the Parent-Teacher Association, formed Little Leagues, and engaged in a host of popular pastimes.

Factors Supporting the Growth of Mass Leisure

Several factors were responsible for the emergence of recreation and leisure as key elements in national life during the 1950s and 1960s. First, there was steady growth in population numbers as the baby-boomer generation matured and was supported by a brisk economy during the post-World War II decades.

Growth in the Nation's Free Time

Next, there was a striking increase in the amount of free time available to most Americans. The workweek had been cut sharply in the years before the war, and labor union contracts continued to reduce the average number of hours worked in many businesses. The increased number of holidays and expanded availability of vacations additional free time, as did Social Security and company pension plans that made earlier retirement possible for many older citizens. Labor-saving devices made many forms of work more efficient.

Concern about the Natural Environment

Growing concern about the nation's natural environment led to a major research study and the report of the Outdoor Recreation Resources Review Commission to Congress and the president in the early 1960s. The report highlighted the damage done to the nation's wildlands and waterways by overcrowding, pesticides, and pollution and led to a host of legislation and funding programs to reverse environmental decay, acquire and protect wilderness areas and create major new parks.

Recreation as a Social Instrument

In the so-called "War on Poverty" initiated by President Lyndon Johnson in an effort to overcome both urban and rural unemployment and social pathology, recreation services became a key element in such national agencies as Job Corps, Model Cities, Volunteers in Service to America (VISTA), and Comprehensive Employment and Training Act (CETA) programs.

Expansion of Popular Participation

The most striking evidence of recreation's new popularity was shown in the explosion of participation in varied forms of play, as shown by the statistics of involvement and leisure spending. In May 1977, *Newsweek* described the "dazzling world of play" that characterized American society:

> Almost unnoticed, leisure-time activities have become the Nation's No. 1 industry, as measured by people's spending. Latest figures... show that Americans will spend more than 160 billion dollars on leisure and recreation in 1977. By 1985, the total is expected to climb to 300 billions. The expenditure is a clear indication, sociologists say, of how avidly Americans pursue "the good life" beyond the bounds of work and home.[1]

Newsweek reported that sports involvement, including boating, tennis, golf, archery, jogging, hunting, bowling, and other active forms of play, drew more than 700 million participants a year, with attendance at sporting events rising to 314 million annually. Participation in cultural activities had also increased dramatically, with hundreds of new opera, theater, and dance companies and symphony orchestras being formed. Over 78 million Americans visited museums annually, and 62 million attended at least one performance of live theater.

Growth of Employment in the Leisure-Service Field

Inevitably, as recreation and leisure became key components in our national lifestyle, attention was focused on recreation's important contribution to the economy and on its emergence as a major new source of employment. Thanks to hundreds of new, government-sponsored recreation and park agencies, plus the manufacture and distribution of play-related goods and equipment and the expansion of travel and tourism ventures and other forms of new leisure enterprise, millions of Americans had begun to find jobs.

Higher Education

In the early years of the 20th century, a number of colleges and teacher-training institutions had offered scattered courses in play leadership, and the National Recreation Association had also sponsored short-term training programs for recreation and park administrators. Beginning in the 1930s, a few institutions began to offer degree options in this field, with an emphasis on leadership and programming.

When the recreation and parks movements merged in the mid-1960s, with the formation of the National Recreation and Park Association in the United States and the Canadian Parks/Recreation Association, the accompanying linking of formerly separate local recreation and park departments gave a new impetus to the field. Several hundred new curricula ware established, including hundreds in two-year community college programs.

Diversification in the Leisure-Service Field

Inevitably, the growth in the overall field and in its separate areas of program service led to a trend toward diversification among several different types of leisure-service agencies.

One of the most obvious areas in which professionals and educators have broken fairly sharply from the mainstream of recreation and park service is *therapeutic recreation*. This field not only developed a clearly defined philosophy and set of professional goals in the 1970s and 1980s, but also established its own certification process at an early stage.

Other specialized leisure-service areas that gained separate identities in the 1970s and 1980s included *employee services, armed forces,* and *commercial recreation,* seen as an umbrella area that included a number of different program fields.

Linked to commercial recreation, but far from simply being an offshoot of the recreation and park movement, were *sports management* and *tourism* and *hospitality*. Today these areas of professional service involve multibillion-dollar annual expenditures, dozens of specialized types of jobs, employment for millions of men and women and the development of a considerable number of trade associations or professional societies that promote their needs.

Common Elements: Leisure Motivations and Outcomes

To better understand the nature of the complex leisure-service field, it is helpful to examine the reasons why people engage in recreation, as well as the outcomes and benefits that come from participation.

Motivations for Participation

Clearly, the urge to play is a widely shared phenomenon, shared by animals of every kind and people in every culture and throughout history.

Ethnologists who specialize in the study of animals and birds report that every species—including cats, dogs, giant carnivores, primates large and small, and even insects—appears to engage in play activity, which is defined as behavior that includes competition, teasing, make-believe, exploration, and role-playing. Play seems to be instinctive, particularly among the young of each species, where it serves important functions related to learning social skills, defining one's place in the social order, and later, courtship rituals.[2]

However, not all recreation consists of play. Many forms of involvement, such as hobbies, serious and dangerous forms of outdoor recreation, commitment to artistic creation and performance, literary pastimes, or health-related and fitness activities, are not really playlike experiences. It is therefore helpful to recognize that researchers have identified a number of other important personal motivations for recreational participation.

Adult Motivations. In 1980, Rick Crandall developed a list of seventeen factors identified by a cross-section of American adults as reasons for taking part in varied forms of leisure activity, including

> . . . enjoying nature and escaping civilization; escaping from routine and responsibility; physical exercise and health-related benefits; social contact and companionship; creativity and aesthetic expression; gaining a sense of power and influence; altruism and being of service to others; excitement or thrillseeking; enrichment of one's personality or self-actualization; and escaping boredom.[3]

Other Age and Gender Factors. Subsequent researchers have found that motivations for recreational involvement vary not only in terms of one's age group, but also with respect to gender and the type of activity one selects.

For example, research on the elderly and recreation shows that they value (1) the opportunity for creative self-expression; (2) companionship with others; (3) power, expressed as the need to feel competent in social situations; (4) compensation for lost abilities, including the need to develop new outlets; (5) security in taking part in safe and familiar activities; (6) service in volunteer roles that help others; (7) intellectual and aesthetic stimulation; and (8) a sense of self-sufficiency and the ability to spend time alone comfortably.

Sexual Identity Factors. Canadian researchers Bolla, Dawson, and Harrington examined the basic meanings of leisure for several thousand adult women. They found that these included such positive elements as gaining a feeling of competence, security, or playfulness and the expression of serenity, femininity or assertiveness.[4]

Clearly, too, as many women seek to overcome the barriers that have limited their full participation in daily life, recreation represents an area in which they can engage in what were traditionally considered masculine roles and activities-particularly the area of sports (see Figure 1-2).

It has become increasingly clear that taking part in varied forms of recreation represents much more than simply having "fun" or "relaxing." Instead, leisure pursuits satisfy important human needs and interests and often require deep commitment and self-discipline, as well as the willingness to risk one's safety in challenging sports and outdoor recreation pursuits.

Benefits of Leisure: Recent Findings

Within the past decade, a number of comprehensive research studies have identified the significant benefits and outcomes of recreation—particularly those stemming from organized leisure-service programs.

Driver, Brown, and Peterson, for example, defined the positive impacts of recreation, particularly government-sponsored recreation and park agencies) summarizing numerous professionally sponsored studies.[5]

Similarly, in the mid-1990s. a task force sponsored by the National Recreation and Park Association initiated a systematic study that identified the contributions made by community recreation programs in terms of such problems as ethnic or racial relations, environmental protection, serving disabled persons, strengthening family life, and overcoming poverty.[6]

A detailed study funded by the U.S. Department of Education documented the positive effects of therapeutic recreation service carried out in medical and rehabilitational settings.[7]

Another report issued by the Parks and Recreation Federation of Ontario and several other cooperating Canadian organizations described the benefits of community recreation under four major headings: *personal, social, economic,* and *environmental* outcomes.[8]

Personal Benefits of Recreation

The personal benefits of leisure involvement involve several important categories, all documented by research in recent years.

Health Benefits
The physical rewards of active recreational pursuits are critical. The positive effect of regular, vigorous physical exercise—such as that gained through sport or outdoor activity—in terms of maintaining cardiovascular health, combatting obesity and reducing the incidence of such diseases as diabetes, certain forms of cancer, and stress-induced strokes, has been clearly shown.

Emotional Benefits
Beyond its physical benefits, recreation can yield important emotional outcomes for the individual, helping to relieve boredom, tension, or depression. Through it, participants may

Figure 1-2
Summary of sports values for women. Compilation of research by Women's Sports Foundation (1999)

25 Years of Making a Difference

In celebration of the Women's Sports Foundation's 25th anniversary, we want to remind everyone why the Foundation was established: to give more girls and women the opportunity to play! If you need to explain why this is so important, here are:

25 Benefits of Playing Sports

1. Sports are FUN!
2. Girls and women who play sports have a more positive body image than girls and women who don't participate.
3. Girls who participate in sports have higher self-esteem and pride in themselves.
4. Research suggests that physical activity is an effective tool for reducing the symptoms of stress and depression among girls.
5. Playing sports teaches girls how to take risks and be aggressive.
6. Sport is where girls can learn goal-setting, strategic thinking and the pursuit of excellence in performance and other achievement-oriented behaviors — critical skills necessary for success in the workplace.
7. Playing sports teaches math skills.
8. Sports help girls develop leadership skills.
9. Sports teach girls teamwork.
10. Regular physical activity in adolescence can reduce girls' risk for obesity.
11. Physical activity appears to decrease the initiation of cigarette smoking in adolescent girls.
12. Research suggests that girls who participate in sports are more likely to experience academic success and graduate from high school than those who do not play sports.
13. Teenage female athletes are less than half as likely to get pregnant as female nonathletes (5% and 11%, respectively).
14. Teenage female athletes are more likely to report that they had never had sexual intercourse than nonathletes (54% and 41%).
15. Teenage female athletes are more likely to experience their first sexual intercourse later in adolescence than female nonathletes.
16. High school sports participation may help prevent osteoporosis.
17. Women who exercise report being happier than those who do not exercise.
18. Women who exercise believe they have more energy and felt they were in excellent health more often than nonexercising women.
19. Women who are active in sports and recreational activities as girls feel greater confidence in their physical and social selves than those who were sedentary as kids.
20. Women who exercise miss fewer days of work.
21. Research supports that regular physical activity can reduce hyperlipidemia (high levels of fat in blood).
22. Recreational physical activity may decrease a woman's chance of developing breast cancer.
23. Women who exercise weigh less than nonexercising women.
24. Women who exercise have lower levels of blood sugar, cholesterol, triglycerides and have lower blood pressure than nonexercising women.
25. Regular exercise improves the overall quality of life.

gain needed satisfactions and a sense of accomplishment, freedom, and control of their lives, leading to improved psychological well-being.

Social Development

Clearly, games and sports, clubs and parties, involvement with others in creative arts programs, and other shared experiences are important ingredients in helping children and youth develop well-rounded, resilient social personalities. They learn to place group needs above their own, to accept rules and discipline, and to value traits of good sportsmanship and working toward common goals.

Cognitive Values

Many forms of recreation may also contribute to cognitive or intellectual development. Studies have shown that physical activity tends to be linked to mental performance. For young children, play becomes a means of exploring the environment and gaining problem-solving skills. Puzzles, quizzes, and computer and table games and kits help participants to develop their powers of observation and analysis and improve their decision-making skills.

Societal Benefits

In addition to the positive values of recreation for individuals that have just been summarized, leisure activities may also provide important benefits for the community at large.

From a social perspective, recreation often provides a focal point around which neighborhood residents may mobilize in an effort to improve their shared lives. Through holidays, community celebrations, neighborhood cleanup campaigns and similar events, or the volunteer management of youth sports programs, families are brought closer together, and community residents gain a strong sense of pride.

Similarly, recreation may provide a useful tool in overcoming racial or religious prejudice and in helping to provide fuller understanding of the customs, traditions, and cultural backgrounds of others. Recreation is also part of the spectrum of social services needed to improve the lives of individuals with varied forms of physical or mental disability.

Economic Benefits of Recreation

From an economic perspective, the most obvious benefit of recreation is that it represents a giant diversified industry with hundreds of billions of dollars spent each year for the purchase of various goods and services (see Table 1-1). The leisure services and enterprises listed here provide jobs for millions of men and women in American and Canadian society. However, the economic picture presented here is incomplete in that it does not include other major forms of spending on recreation.

For example, the huge amounts spent each year on building, maintaining, and staffing a host of different types of leisure attractions and structures—from theme parks or cruise ships to ski centers and multiplex theaters—represent enormous leisure-related expenditures.

Table 1-1
Annual Personal Spending on Recreation: 1985 to 1996

Type of Product or Service	1985	1990	1996
Total Recreation Expenditures (billions of dollars)	116.3	281.6	431.1
Percent of Total Personal Consumption	6.6	7.3	8.3
Books and maps	6.5	16.5	23.2
Magazines, newspapers, and sheet music	12.0	21.5	26.5
Nondurable toys and sport supplies	14.6	31.6	45.4
Wheel goods, sports, and photographic equipment	15.6	29.8	42.0
Video and audio products, computer equipment, and musical instruments	19.9	53.8	89.7
Radio and television repair	2.5	4.2	5.1
Flowers, seeds and potted plants	4.7	11.1	14.9
Admissions to specified spectator amusements	6.7	15.1	22.1
Motion picture theaters	2.6	5.2	6.3
Legitimate theater and opera and entertainments of nonprofit institutions	1.8	5.6	9.3
Spectator sports	2.3	4.4	6.4
Clubs and fraternal organizations except insurance	3.1	8.9	13.0
Commercial participant amusements	9.1	23.0	46.2
Parimutuel net receipts	2.3	3.4	3.5
Other (includes lottery receipts, pets, cable TV, film processing, sports camps, video rentals, etc.)	19.4	62.7	99.6

Sources: Statistical Abstract of the United States U.S. Department of Commerce, 1999.
See this source for a fuller explanation of product and service categories.

Table 1-1 does not include several hundred billions dollars a year spent on tourism and travel, hunting and fishing, and a variety of gambling other than parimutuel racetrack betting.

Taken all together, estimates of leisure spending in the United States are well over a trillion dollars annually, vividly underlining the critical importance of recreation in the nation's economy.

However, recreation's economic benefits extend beyond its contribution to the overall employment picture.

Well-designed and beautifully maintained park systems, beaches, and other facilities for play help to make cities and towns appealing and attractive both to potential residents and to companies that are considering new sites for relocation. Cultural institutions and facilities such as museums, library systems, theaters, and concert halls or opera and ballet companies have a similar value.

Some of the economic values of recreation and leisure cannot easily be measured. However, having a network of impressive cultural resources, professional sports teams, and nearby outdoor recreation attractions clearly contributes to the positive image of cities—and thus to the volume of tourism that helps to sustain a city's economic well-being.

Environmental Benefits of Recreation

In its linkage with the parks movement, recreation accepts an important responsibility for protecting millions of acres of wildland, rivers, streams and beachfronts, historic monuments, and scenic areas.

Major government agencies such as the National Park Service and the Forest Service provide the opportunity for varied outdoor recreation pursuits and commit themselves to preventing the overuse of natural resources. Numerous other public agencies on federal, state and provincial and local levels in the United States and Canada have struggled to overcome pollution, restore damaged waterways, and reduce air pollution.

Many nonprofit organizations such as the Sierra Club, the Audubon Society and Nature Conservancy promote environmental values and causes today, encouraging ecological policies and uses of the wilderness for constructive recreation purposes.

Leisure Trends at the Beginning of the 21st Century

In the very last days of 1999, an editor of the *New York Times* commented that during the past 100 years, most Americans had experienced a "wild ride"

> ... from rural isolation and industrial drudgery to communities and comforts once unimaginable. The country's population grew from 76 million to 275 million, but that only hints at our dizzy metamorphosis. Consider instead how 14,000 motor vehicles in 1900 exploded to more than 200 million in 2000, with vast reverberations of density or dispersion. Or consider the psychic dislocations that occurred as a day's travel was redefined from 10 miles by horse to 10,000 by jet.
>
> And how can we grasp the effects of the 100-year surge in the typical American's life span from 42 years to 76? Or the growth of the over-65 population from 3 million to 35 million, even as the workweek has shrunk from 60 hours to 38 . . .[9]

Clearly, the past century represented an era of immense growth and change in every respect—dramatic population expansion, the shift from rural to urban environments, and business development. The 1900s saw a steady improvement in educational opportunity, the elimination of many aspects of racial and gender- discrimination, a growing environmental concern, and steady improvement in the quality of life for most Americans.

Leisure has been an important element in this progress, as this chapter has shown. Today, increasing numbers of individuals and families take part in recreation on every level: sports, hobbies, entertainment and cultural activities, social programs, and travel and tourism (see Table 1-2).

Numerous other research reports by the U.S. Department of Commerce and other agencies confirm that public participation in varied leisure pursuits—including the purchase of books, musical recordings, and lawn and garden supplies; the care of pets; outdoor recreation, cultural arts, and tourism—also climbed steadily in the final years of the 20th century.

At the same time, a number of significant economic and social trends that gained momentum in the recent past seem certain to influence the role of organized leisure services in the years ahead.

Table 1-2
Growth of amusement and recreation services
Statistics summarize annual receipts of selected categories of leisure-service enterprises in millions of dollars.

Type of Business	1980	1996
Motion pictures	$39,982	60,205
Production, distribution, and allied services	28,888	46,223
Theaters	6,088	7,035
Videotape rental	5,006	6,946
Amusement and recreation services	50,126	85,769
Dance studios, schools, and halls	626	1,036
Theatrical producers, bands, orchestras, and entertainers	10,735	19,679
Bowling centers	2,800	2,719
Commercial sports	8,636	14,632
Professional sports clubs and promoters	3,702	8,877
Racing, including track operation	4,934	5,755
Miscellaneous services	27,329	47,702
Physical fitness facilities	3,623	4,970
Public golf courses	2,254	3,976
Coin-operated amusement devices	2,146	3,486
Amusement parks	4,922	6,775
Membership sports and recreation clubs	4,825	7,439

Source: Statistical Abstract of the United States, 1998.
U.S. Department of Commerce, p. 260.

Changing Patterns of Work and Free Time

Until the latter decades of the 20th century, all reports indicated that the workweek was growing shorter and shorter and that free time would continue to expand for all Americans. Then, in the mid-and late-1980s, Harris polls and a number of other studies concluded, on the basis of extensive interviews, that employees throughout the nation were working longer and harder hours and that leisure time had declined dramatically.

While this trend was generally accepted as factual, other research by social scientists at the University of Maryland and the University of Michigan concluded that for the bulk of workers, free time had actually increased from the 1970s through the 1990s. The U.S. Bureau of Labor Statistics, which regularly monitors 400,000 nonfarm businesses and thousands of randomly selected households, found that

> ... the average workweek in the companies studied "trended down" from 38.8 in the mid-1960s to 36.1 in the mid-1970s, 34.9 in the mid-1980s and 34.6 in 1998.[10]

Other studies have confirmed these findings. However, it is clearly the case that for a segment of the population—chiefly business managers and executives, successful professionals, and other high-level personnel—the hours of work *have* lengthened, along with the increased stress and pace of work, due to the use of computers, e-mail, fax machines, and other job pressures. Also, for the growing number of individuals holding two jobs, or for single parents who must work *and* maintain a family, leisure hours are sharply limited.

Ultimately, the challenge to the leisure-service movement will be to serve both groups in the population: those who are overworked and will require restorative forms of play in their limited free time, and the larger group which who, many economists believe, may be underemployed and may not be able to afford expensive forms of leisure activity.

Impact of Multiculturalism

All demographic and census reports make it clear that the population of the United States has become increasingly multiracial and multiethnic over the past half a century. Due to increased immigration from so-called Third World countries and nations close to us in the Caribbean and Central American regions and because of a higher birth rate among these groups, the proportion of those of non-European descent in America has grown steadily.

As of the early 1990s there were in the United States 30 million African Americans, 7.3 million Asian Americans, 22.4 Hispanic Americans, and 2 million Native Americans—with these numbers rising steadily. In a comprehensive report on population change, *Time* magazine described the "browning of America" and predicted that within a few decades, the Caucasian population would be outnumbered by racial and ethnic minority groups.

Responding to this trend, many public recreation and park agencies have introduced special programs of workshops, holiday events and multicultural festivals to increase understanding among different populations and to celebrate the nation's growing diversity as a source of future strength and cultural richness.

Growing Influence of Technology

Technological innovation will continue to have a mayor impact on every element of American society, including business, education health care, and government. Within the recreation, parks, and leisure service field, it will have two primary kinds of effects: (1) the creation of new and exciting forms of recreation, made possible by scientifically-based invention; and (2) the use of technology within the operation of leisure-service agencies, to deliver and manage recreation programs.

New Leisure Experiences

The history of recreation and leisure during the past century has been one in which technology created entirely new kinds of play and entertainment possibilities. The invention of radio, motion pictures, television, sound recordings, tape recorders and players, CDs, and similar devices clearly expanded the leisure lives of Americans young and old.

Outdoor recreation was radically influenced by technology, with the creation of snowmobiles and off-road vehicles, scuba diving equipment, Jet Skis, gliders, and sky-diving equipment. Downhill skiing expanded with the creation of chair lifts and snow-blowing systems, and artificial ice rinks made it possible for cities in the Deep South to host ice hockey teams and enjoy recreational skating.

During the past two decades, video games and other computer-based pastimes have become a major preoccupation, with the Internet giving millions of individuals the opportunity to explore new hobbies and interests or engage with others in chat rooms that provide contact at a moment's notice. Figure 1-3 shows how computer technology has been adapted to create new forms of childhood play.

Computers and Agency Management

Similarly, electronic forms of analysis and communication are widely used by public, commercial, and other types of leisure-service agencies. Computers are invaluable in planning and information-management processes and also in monitoring financial functions, facility maintenance operations, personnel performance, and a host of other management tasks.

Increasingly, computers are also used in contacts with the public in terms of public relations, informing participants about program opportunities or counseling them, registering for classes, courses and leagues, and similar tasks.

Commodification of Leisure Services

Commodification—meaning the systematic commercialization of given types of agencies, professions and services—has become an increasing reality in American life.

Leading professions, such as medicine or law, have become heavily commodified through the development of managed care chains, the linkage of professional societies with commercial products, and the establishment of major chains that advertise heavily and promote their services nationally.

The degree to which many forms of recreation have become "big business" is illustrated in Figure 1-4, an advertisement of a huge travel, sport and outdoor recreation exposition, typical of hundreds of such events held each year throughout the United States.

Many public recreation and park agencies, initially designed to be free service departments, similar to highways or public education, today make extensive use of programs and services that rely heavily on fees and charges. Classes, courses, fitness and aquatic centers, day-camp registration, equipment rental, and a host of other publicly sponsored leisure activities come at a price—and clearly must satisfy bottom-line revenue expectations.

Similarly, many nonprofit organizations have adopted a forceful marketing orientation, in terms of developing public support and involvement, gaining sponsorship, "target" marketing, sophisticated advertising and pricing methods, and similar commercial strategies. While sandlot baseball or schoolyard basketball were once viewed as casual, spontaneous, and free play activities for American youth, today almost every form of organized sport requires a fee for participation, as shown in Figure 1-5.

While youth-serving public or nonprofit organizations often provide scholarships, fee discounts, or other waivers for those lacking financial capability, too often individuals or families in the poverty population are unable to enjoy the rich range of leisure opportunities available to their wealthier neighbors. This problem promises to present a severe challenge

Figure 1-3
Catalog advertisements for children's computer play products.

Figure 1-4
Example of outdoor recreation trade show, Winter 2000.

to public and nonprofit leisure-service agencies in terms of the widely accepted mission and social goals of community recreation organizations.

Meeting Social Needs

Responding to this challenge, many public and nonprofit leisure-service agencies in the 1990s initiated vigorous new programs designed to counter negative trends in American society.

Organizations of all types today sponsor family-oriented programs to combat the fragmentation of American family structures that had occurred during the second half of the 20th century. Nonprofit agencies such as the YMCA and YWCA and Boys and Girls Clubs, developed services to assist girls and women in coping with their new roles in economic, family-related, and other spheres of American life.

Through the 1990s, there was growing concern with the major episodes of gun-related violence by at-risk youth that culminated with the tragic slaughter at Columbine High School in Colorado. Witt and Crompton sum up the growing concern with teenage needs, writing that there was a remarkable resurgence of elected officials' interest in issues involving youth:

> . . . a series of events—drive-by shootings, increases in gang membership, and rising teenage-pregnancy, school dropout, single-parent family, and drug-use rates—coalesced to force teen issues to the forefront of the political agenda.[11]

Major national and regional conferences were held to revitalize programs that would serve youth from high-risk environments. Sponsored by the American Academy of Park and Recreation Administration, these conferences and other national meetings encouraged local recreation and park agencies, in particular, to combat delinquency and other antisocial behavior. For example, a list of program services offered by the member agencies of the California Park and Recreation Society included such elements as

> . . . programming for latch-key children; juvenile curfew support; gang prevention and intervention; academic support, vocational training and career counseling; youth mentoring and youth leadership programs; substance abuse prevention; individual and family counseling; teen pregnancy; and physical and mental rehabilitation services-all linked to appealing and positive youth recreation programs.[12]

Benefits-Based Management

This final important trend affecting the delivery of leisure services gained momentum during the latter part of the 20th century. Essentially, it represented a determined effort to validate the value and social contribution made by recreation, park, and leisure-service organizations in concrete terms, rather than with vague platitudes and claims.

Traditionally, many public recreation and park departments had justified their existence through general statements about the importance of recreation in community life and by statistical summaries of attendance or participation in programs and the use of facilities.

In the 1980s and 1990s, when tight government budgets meant that many forms of public service had to reduce staffing, programming, and maintenance operations, it was

Figure 1-5
Example of Little League bulletin.

Attention all boys 5-18, and all girls 5-12:

if you live in the area bounded by Tennis Avenue, Welsh Road, Fort Washington Avenue, Highland Avenue and Bethlehem Pike,

you are now eligible to play officially sanctioned Williamsport Little League and Senior League Baseball!

Congratulations! You are now eligible to participate in Lower Gwynedd Little & Senior League Baseball. This means that you now have the option of playing officially sanctioned Williamsport Little League Baseball and Softball, or Senior League Baseball in the Lower Gwynedd Baseball program.

Our program is one of the finest in the area, and includes:

Tee Ball - Boys & Girls ages 5 & 6
Machine Pitch - Boys & Girls ages 7 & 8
Softball - Girls only, ages 8-10
Minors - Boys & Girls ages 9 & 10
Majors - Boys & Girls ages 11 & 12
Seniors - Boys ages 13 - 18

Fees are $70 per player age 5-12 (includes $25 purchase of opening day raffle tickets, which can be resold), and $110 per player age 13-18.

Our season runs from April through June for Little League, and through July for the Senior League. It includes a lot of fun, family activities as well as great Little and Senior League Baseball.

HOW TO SIGN UP: Just bring your parent, a copy of your birth certificate and insurance company name and policy number to any of the following registration sessions:

Sat., Jan. 8, from 9 to 11 AM
Sun., Jan. 9th, from 1 PM to 3 PM
Wed., Jan. 19th, from 7 to 9 PM
Sat., Jan. 22nd, from 1 to 3 PM

WHERE: Come to the Lower Gwynedd Township Building, 1130 North Bethlehem Pike, Spring House.

---

recognized that more convincing kinds of evidence were needed to maintain public support. At this point, a *benefits-based management* approach was adopted, containing four key elements. Leisure-service managers needed to do the following:

1. Establish a clearly defined *mission* or *philosophical statement*, leading to the precise listing of *agency goals* and *objectives* that could realistically be attained, and that were capable of measurement.

2. Plan and carry out *programs* and other *services* specifically designed to achieve these goals and objectives, within agreed-on time frames.

3. Rigorously and systematically *monitor* and *evaluate* program outcomes to identity the actual benefits derived from programs.

4. *Report* and *publicize* their findings in order to familiarize civic officials and the public at large with the positive value and contribution of recreation, park, and leisure services.

By focusing not only on the numbers of participants, but also on the documented benefits of recreation in such terms as reduced incidence of juvenile delinquency or school dropout or improved health statistics and measures of fitness, the benefits-based approach became widely accepted throughout the leisure-service system in the United States and Canada by the turn of the century.

Leisure Services and the Future

Having examined the past and the present, we must now ask: What are the prospects for the recreation and leisure-service field in the 21st century that lies ahead?

Social scientists and futurists are generally agreed upon a number of the changes to be expected and the social and economic trends that are likely to continue in the coming decades. They foresee the continuing reliance on information technology and the development of an "interactive society" in which electronic communication dominates many aspects of business, government, and social life.

They expect the continuing diversification of our society in racial and ethnic terms, with changing patterns of family and gender relationships. Increasing globalism of the business and entertainment world, environmental concerns, and radical shifts in the world of work are also likely to develop.

One author speculates grimly about tomorrow's urban society, in *The Futurist*:

> Imagine a world with almost twice the current population. Imagine cities with 40 or 50 million inhabitants. Think of urban strangulation; overwhelmed buses, trains, and highways; lung-choking pollution; ranks of unemployed; alienated families; overstressed individuals; escalating crime; chronic terrorism.
> Nightmarish fantasy? No. These images reflect current trends and portray what big-city life may well be like only a generation from now.[13]

On the other hand, many social scientists are highly optimistic about the future, envisioning a world of economic and agricultural abundance, in which many of our current problems are solved by technological and social-policy innovations. They predict

> ... a new "macroindustrial era"—an age of abundance and prosperity. Within this oncoming period of turbocharged economic and technological growth, it is expected that there will be general improvement in the human condition on a global scale marked by increased ability to direct the course both of nature and of human societies.[14]

Whichever scenario comes to pass, it is safe to predict that recreation and leisure will play increasingly important roles in the social and economic lives of Americans in the years ahead. Given this certainty, it is appropriate to systematically examine the total leisure-service system today in terms of its agencies, processes, and career-related potentials.

Suggested Questions for Class Discussion or Essay Examinations

1. What were the most important social and economic factors and trends that led to the growth of leisure involvement in the United States after World War II? What role did the government play in developing recreation and leisure programs or policies at that time?
2. People in the past tended to think of recreation as "fun and games." What arguments would you cite to broaden their view of the leisure-service field? In your discussion, you might include information from the text, as well as your own personal experiences or observations.
3. The chapter outlines four major areas of benefits derived from organized recreation and leisure services which have been documented by research in recent years. Select any two of these and explain them in full detail.
4. Following a long period in which the workweek was reduced steadily, reports in the 1980s indicated that Americans were working significantly longer hours, and leisure hours had been reduced. In your view, is this true, or is the work-leisure relationship more complex than this research suggests? In today's society, who has more free time, and who has less?
5. Three major trends of the 1990s that seem certain to continue into the 21st century and that affect leisure services are multiculturalism, commodification, and evolving technology. Explain these trends and show their implications for the leisure field.

Footnotes

[1] The boom in leisure: Where Americans spend 160 billions. (1977). *Newsweek*, May 23, p. 62.
[2] Brownlee, S. (1997). The case for frivolity. *U.S. News and World Report*, Feb. 3, p. 45.
[3] Crandall, R. (1980). Motivations for leisure. *Journal of Leisure Research*, 12(1), pp.45–55.
[4] Bolla, P., Dawson, D., and Harrington, M. (1993). Women and Leisure: A study of meanings, experiences and constraints. *Recreation Canada, 51*(3), 223–226.
[5] Driver, B.L., Brown, P., and Petersen, G., eds. (1991). *Benefits of leisure*. State College, Pa: Venture Publishing.
[6] New study reveals recreation, parks' impact on serious social issues. (1994). *Dateline: NRPA*, Dec., 1-2.
[7] Coyle, C., Kinney, W., and Shank, J. (1993). *Effect of therapeutic recreation and leisure lifestyle on rehabilitation outcomes for individuals with physical disability.* Temple University and U.S. Dept. of Education.
[8] Parks and Recreation Federation of Ontario, Can. (1993). The benefit of parks and recreation. Summarized in *Programmers Information Network*. NRPA. 4 (4), 1.
[9] Frankel, M. (1999). Only yesterday. *New York Times Magazine*. Dec. 26, 20.
[10] Scott, J. (1999). Working hard, more or less. *New York Times*, July 10, B-7.
[11] Witt, P., and Crompton, J. (1999). A paradigm of the times. *Parks and Recreation*, Dec., 66 - 75.
[12] Parks and recreation goes beyond "fun and games." (1995). *Phoenix Report*, California Park and Recreation Society.

[13] Hager, L.M. (1997). The non-stop city and other heretical notions about time. *The Futurist*, May-June, 39.
[14] Zey, M. (1997). The macroindustrial era: a new age of abundance and prosperity. *The Futurist*, Mar.-April, 9-14.

Chapter 2

The Organized Leisure-Service System

Introduction

We now turn to an analysis of the overall recreation, park, and leisure-service system. This chapter shows how the diversified range of organizations that provide leisure-service organizations may be seen as having three key elements:

(1) ten types of agencies that take major responsibility for providing leisure programs to the public; (2) several other different types of organizations and associations that play a supportive role within this overall effort; and (3) professional societies and educational institutions that contribute to the effectiveness of leisure-service sponsors.

Following a detailed analysis of these elements, the chapter examines their interaction, including both competition and cooperation, the growth of partnerships among different groups, and the career possibilities they offer.

Why Focus on Organized Services?

Not all forms of recreational involvement are *organized* in the sense of being provided or sponsored by some outside group that schedules activities, provides leadership or equipment, and maintains physical settings for participation.

A great deal of leisure involvement is *unorganized*, in that it is carried out voluntarily and spontaneously by individuals and their families without any sort of formal guidance, structure, or outside sponsorship.

People read books, watch movies or television, plan picnics and parties, walk or jog for exercise, swim at a nearby beach, care for their pets, enjoy gardening or other personal hobbies, listen to music, or chat with friends on the telephone or through e-mail or the Internet—often without any sort of formal guidance or outside assistance.

Hidden Forms of Assistance. Yet, even in such independent and spontaneous: forms of leisure involvement, certain kinds of assistance are often necessary for satisfying play.

Watching movies or television depends on producers who create the entertainment product or those who manufacture the equipment or manage the theater or network. Jogging for exercise often requires a safe and attractive trail, free from the gasoline fumes of the highway, and this is often found in a public park. Pet care depends on breeders who sell pets, stores that offer food and other equipment, and veterinarians who protect the health of dogs and cats, birds, and other pets.

Similarly, gardening may be promoted by gardening clubs, classes in various aspects of horticulture, nurseries that sell plants, flowers and seeds, and other kinds of establishments. Music, dance, theater, and other creative and performing arts also depend on a variety of organizations that offer instruction; the opportunity to play, sing, or perform in a public setting; or the chance to exhibit one's artwork or craft products.

Beyond the sphere of unorganized activity, a vast amount of recreational participation *is* carried on through the assistance or direct sponsorship of organized groups or agencies that are usually referred to as the leisure-service system.

Leisure Services as a System

What does it mean when we describe recreation, park, and leisure services as a system? This term is usually used to identify any set or assembly of elements that are directly or indirectly related to each other and that involve a shared set of purposes and processes.

There are several different types of systems, including those that exist in nature and operate independently of human intervention, and others that are artificial in the sense that they are created and modified by human beings. In the most advanced sense, the term *system* suggests that all of the elements within a given structure are closely interrelated, with each having a specific part to play, and with each having deliberately designed effects on other elements. Arthur Laufer writes:

> Any group of things which are interrelated and combined so as to form an integrated whole can be called a system. It is not the individual parts that are important, but it is the connecting together or the interrelationship of these parts which is important to the making of a system.[1]

Within the organized leisure-service field, such individual enterprises as a water-play park, a country club, or a cruise ship might be regarded as systems that include elements of staffing, facilities, fiscal operations, participants, and environmental factors. On a larger scale, armed forces recreation or therapeutic recreation services might also be seen as systems—and, indeed, the whole complex structure of all types of leisure-service agencies also constitutes a system.

Interrelationships of Leisure Agencies

Realistically, the varied organizations that comprise the overall leisure-service system are not fully interdependent. They do not have clearly assigned functions that relate to each other, and there is relatively little joint planning or coordination to ensure that recreational opportunities are offered to the public in a fully efficient and comprehensive way.

However, leisure services *do* function as a system in three important ways: (1) all of their component parts are basically concerned with one important task—providing or promoting leisure programs and opportunities to meet human needs; (2) different elements within the system constantly interact with each other, often competing in the struggle for support and growing numbers of participants; and (3) there are steadily growing examples of partnerships and developing networks among different parts of the system, which promote its overall integration.

Finally, leisure services must also be perceived as a part of other, major systems in national and community life. Clearly, they operate as an important element of government responsibility, of neighborhood life, of commercial enterprise, of health care and social services and of the total physical environment in which people live.

Models of the Organized Leisure-Service Field

Numerous authorities have suggested that there are three primary elements in the organized leisure-service field that constitute the major sponsors of recreation programs and facilities in American communities, as shown in Figure 2-1.

This model, however, is incomplete, because it does not include a number of major types of leisure-service sponsors that do not fit under the three headings they identify. Instead, a fuller listing of agency types would include *ten different major categories,* as well as several other different kinds of organizations that promote varied areas of leisure involvement; serve as advocates, lobbyists, or publicists for recreational pursuits, or promote professional development in leisure services. These ten categories and other support organizations are shown in Figure 2-2. They are described briefly in the following section of this chapter and in much fuller detail in the next eight chapters.

Figure 2-1
Community recreation and leisure-service system[2]

Public Subsystem	Private Nonprofit Subsystem	Commercial Subsystem
City recreation and parks departments	Youth-serving agencies (YMCA, Girls Clubs, Boy Scouts)	Amusement parks Theaters
City recreation commissions		Tennis, golf, sailing centers
School-sponsored recreation	Church-sponsored recreation	Hotels
	Social and fraternal organizations(country clubs, Kiwanis)	Resorts

Figure 2-2
Major elements in the leisure-service system

(Note: The same program elements, facilities, leisure needs, and outcomes may be found in all ten types of agencies. Each column should be read vertically, rather than across the page)

Types of Recreation Sponsoring Organizations	Assisted by Support Groups and Services	Provide Leisure Programs Consisting of	To Satisfy Public Needs For	Yielding Major Benefits in Four Areas
Government recreation and park agencies	Trade associations	Direct program Leadership	Full spectrum of involvement in: Games and sports	Personal values (health, emotional wellness, mental development)
Nonprofit community organizations	Professional societies	Provision of facilities for undirected public use	Outdoor recreation Cultural activities Creative arts	
Commercial recreation Businesses	Special-interest Groups	Education for leisure	Hobbies Special events	Social and Community-based Outcomes
Employee service and Recreation programs	Sponsors of Special programs Or events	Information- Referral Services	Club and other social groups Other social services	
Armed forces morale, Welfare, and recreation	Professional preparation institutions	Enabling- Facilitation	With needs Influenced by: Age group	Economic benefits, employment, taxes other fiscal returns
Private membership Organizations			Gender	
Campus recreation Programs	Private groups that subcontract leisure functions	Advocacy and leadership in special areas	Socioeconomic status Racial/ethnic factors Educational background	Environmental values, both natural and urban settings
Therapeutic Recreation service	Other civic agencies and citizen's groups	Jointly sponsored campaigns and events	Residential and regional factors Physical and emotional health	(As discussed in Chapter 1)
Sports management Organizations			Family status	
Tourism and hospitality Industry				

1. Public, Governmental Organizations

On all three levels of government (federal, state, and local), recreation and park departments, bureaus, or commissions provide networks of parks and other facilities; offer directed activities for all age groups and special populations; and promote varied forms of leisure involvement—often in cooperation with other community organizations.

While supported mainly by tax funds, governmental recreation agencies also depend heavily on revenue sources, such as fees and charges, grants, contributions, and other sources of income. In general, their purpose is to meet the basic needs of the public at large, particularly in the field of outdoor recreation, and to serve important social and environmental goals.

Beyond recreation and park agencies as such, local government often assists or directly supports other community organizations that provide important leisure outlets: libraries, museums, performing arts groups, theaters and concert halls, youth boards, commissions serving the elderly, and similar groups.

2. Nonprofit Community Agencies

A second major component of the overall leisure-service system consists of nonprofit community organizations that offer recreation, usually as part of a total multiservice approach that includes education, citizenship development, and other social functions. Often called voluntary agencies because they represent the voluntary efforts of community residents, nonprofit organizations depend on a number of different fiscal sources: membership fees and charges for participation, community-wide fund-raising drives, foundation grants, sales of merchandise, and, in some cases, contracts with government to carry out much-needed social programs.

They include a variety of youth-serving organizations such as the Police Athletic League, Boys and Girls Clubs, Salvation Army, and Boy and Girl Scouts, as well as other groups serving broader age categories. In some cases, they focus on meeting special social needs, such as programming for persons with disabilities. They may promote a given area of sport, outdoor recreation, or hobby activity and include both church-related and nonreligious sponsorship.

3. Commercial Recreation Businesses

It is generally agreed that for-profit recreation enterprises represent the most diversified area of leisure-service sponsorship, involving by far the greatest amount of public participation and annual expenditures.

Recreation businesses are of many types. They include varied forms of outdoor recreation pursuits, commercially operated bowling alleys, billiard parlors, ski centers, golf courses, and tennis clubs. They involve video game arcades, children's gymnastic centers, and family party facilities. They include various forms of sociability, including bars and nightclubs, dance studios and ballrooms, dating services and singles groups. In the realm of travel and tourism, they encompass travel agents, hotels and other resorts, cruise ship lines, theme parks, and a host of other attractions.

In a broad sense, the manufacture of toys and games, sports equipment, television sets, CD players, and video cameras are also part of commercial recreation, along with the sale of boats and boating equipment and the operation of private marinas. While for-profit recreation entrepreneurs do not usually regard themselves as part of the main body of

4. Armed Forces Recreation

Another massive sphere of leisure-service program delivery is carried on within the Morale, Welfare, and Recreation (MWR) branch of the armed forces in the United States.

Operating with fiscal support allocated by Congress as an integral part of the U.S. Department of Defense, and with additional "nonappropriated" funding from post exchanges and other revenue-yielding services, the major segments of the armed forces, such as the Navy, Army, Air Force, and Marine Corps, assign thousands of uniformed personnel and civilian employees to recreation responsibilities.

Programs include a wide range of sports, hobbies, outdoor recreation, entertainment, and special events. They are designed to achieve important defense department objectives, such as maintaining physical health and fitness, supporting military morale, combating such negative attractions as drug or alcohol abuse, and offering a positive quality of life that encourages reenlistment by both enlisted men and women as well as officers. The needs of family members also represent an important priority for armed forces MWR units, both in peacetime and when military actions create additional stress.

5. Employee Services and Recreation

Originally known as "industrial recreation," this branch of the leisure-service system came into being chiefly in major industries that were beset by labor-management conflict at a time when the union movement in the United States was gaining momentum and was resisted by many company owners. It tended to consist heavily of holiday events, sports leagues, and a limited range of social or special-interest activities designed to build a sense of camaraderie and loyalty among company employees.

Gradually, the range of services expanded to include such elements as extensive sports and hobby activities, company stores and discount buying services, charter travel arrangements, and numerous other program elements designed to help employees in their personal lives and work adjustment—thus helping to improve job productivity, reduce absenteeism, and counter employee turnover. Given the wide range of programs offered, the field became known as "employee services and recreation," with increasing emphasis on fitness and other health-related functions, such as stress management, weight-control, and substance abuse programs, and similar functions that helped reduce insurance costs of companies.

In January 2000, the name of the leading professional organization in this field, the National Employee Services and Recreation Association, was changed to Employee Services Management—signifying the degree to which the other health-related and personnel functions in this field had gained a higher level of priority.

6. Campus Recreation

A sixth major area of leisure-service program specialization consists of recreation activities offered for students and staff on U.S. college and university campuses. Such programs generally fall under two headings: (1) areas of physical recreation, including free play, instruction, intramural and club competition in sports, and outdoor recreation skills and outings; and (2) a wide range of essentially noncurricular campus-life programs, such as dormitory-based social events, cultural and entertainment programs, the coordination of volunteer-service activities, publications, student government, and Greek fraternities and sororities.

The first realm of campus recreation-designed to promote student health and well-being, morale, and satisfaction with campus life—is usually managed by an athletic director and his or her staff or affiliated with a department or school of health, physical education, and recreation.

The second, nonathletic program is often supervised by a dean of student life or office of campus activities, or in some cases coordinated through student- union directors and student-government officers.

While the term "campus recreation" usually applies to programs carried on in colleges and universities, a good deal of community recreation is provided by local school systems. Many school districts sponsor comprehensive adult education and recreation programs that include hobbies, cultural interests, language, instruction and self-help activities and are provided for residents—sometimes in partnerships with municipal recreation and park departments.

7. Private-Membership Organizations

These constitute another area of recreation and leisure service that is directed toward meeting the needs of a special segment of the public, defined either by socioeconomic class, special interest, or residential status.

It includes thousands of private clubs that are often geared to serve wealthy or middle-class individuals and families, such as country clubs, tennis, golf or yacht clubs, businessmen's or women's groups, and similar associations. In the past, many such clubs had restrictive membership policies aimed at excluding minority groups or limiting participation by women, Today, most such policies have been eliminated, although expensive membership and annual fees or the requirement of membership recommendations keep many private clubs exclusive.

Another major area of private-membership recreation is based on residential ownership. Throughout the United States and Canada, thousands of retirement, vacation, and second-home communities offer homeowners or renters swimming pools, fitness centers, tennis courts, and other facilities for play. As later chapters will show, such communities—often described as "leisure villages"—often also schedule adult classes, social events, and other cultural activities and classes.

8. Therapeutic Recreation Service

Therapeutic recreation differs from the preceding seven types of leisure-service organizations in that it does not involve a particular category of sponsor, such as government agencies or for-profit businesses. Instead, therapeutic recreation includes programs that are offered by many different kinds of sponsors, such as hospitals, rehabilitation and after-care centers, public recreation and park departments, nonprofit agencies, college programs, and even commercial recreation businesses that provide outdoor recreation and travel services for persons with disabilities.

As indicated in Chapter 1, therapeutic recreation service is a highly specialized professional field that began as "hospital recreation" and has broadened itself considerably in terms of its scope of service and settings for program delivery. Today, it serves a wide range of individuals of all ages who have both mental and physical disabilities within a continuum of service extending from the use of recreation in the treatment of illness or disease to instruction in leisure skills and participation in community recreation programs.

While therapeutic recreation continues to be offered in clinically oriented treatment centers, its growing emphasis today is in the effort to help persons with disability take part in programs with nondisabled individuals—rather than in separate, segregated activities.

9. Sports Management

This extremely popular area of leisure involvement is similar to therapeutic recreation in that it is *not* offered by a single type of agency, but instead is provided by many kinds of sponsors. Educational institutions, public recreation departments, nonprofit youth-serving organizations, private clubs, employee-service units, and commercial business all offer sports as an integral part of their operations.

So great is the volume of public interest in sport and the level of spending on instruction, participation, and spectator attendance at sports events that it literally constitutes a major industry in itself. Sport encompasses individual and family leisure pursuits for all ages, including individual and dual competition in tennis, golf, volleyball, bowling, and similar activities, as well as team play in such major sports as baseball and softball; field, ice, and floor hockey; basketball, volleyball, and football on several levels; and numerous other athletic events.

There are dozens of different kinds of jobs within the sports spectrum, including coaching and officiating; athletic conditioning and fitness programming; facilities management; the manufacture and sale of sports equipment, clothing, and memorabilia; and sports journalism.

10. Tourism and Hospitality

Although it might be viewed simply as one important aspect of commercial recreation, the tourism and hospitality industry also has strong links to government, sports management, the armed forces, therapeutic recreation service, and other types of leisure-service sponsors that promote travel experiences as an integral part of their own operations.

Tourism, both domestic and international, represents a huge, complex system in its own right—encompassing holiday and vacation travel, trips carried on for cultural and sports attendance purposes, family visits to beach areas and theme parks, and both luxurious and expensive outings and demanding and even dangerous modes of transportation. Increasingly, major cities are relying on tourism to build their revenues and job bases and are building major stadiums and art centers to appeal to visitors. At the same time, sightseeing trips to historic sites and spectacular natural wonders also attract tourism, which represents about two-thirds of all travel (see page 190).

Hospitality in the form of hotels, resorts, restaurants, and shops represents a major element that supports and is closely linked to tourism itself as a major source of employment and economic benefits. While many of the jobs in this field are entry-level positions that pay poorly, they often serve as a threshold to more responsible and financially rewarding career positions.

Functions of Leisure-Service Agencies

The ten categories of leisure-service sponsors that have just been briefly described have as a primary function the direct delivery of recreational opportunities and experiences.

This function may be broken down into two types of tasks:

1. Offering program services with a degree of *organized leadership and/or supervision* within a variety of formats including instruction, free play, competition, special events, sociability and leadership training; and

2. Providing *areas* and *facilities* for essentially undirected participation, such as playgrounds, parks, beaches and pools, biking or hiking trails, and other outdoor resources for informal play.

The chapters that follow show how the different types of leisure-service agencies carry out these primary tasks, as well as related social services designed to meet important community needs. They also show how leisure-service organizations fulfill other functions, including the following: *information-referral, enabling-facilitation,* and *advocacy.*

As outlined by James Murphy and his coauthors, these tasks are assigned especially to public recreation and park departments, which, as government agencies that are held responsible for assisting public recreational opportunity, often play a leading role in coordinating overall community recreational involvement.

Information-Referral

Recognizing that no single organization can possibly meet all leisure needs within the community, public departments may assume leadership in identifying critical community leisure needs and developing lists or directories of existing recreation organizations. Thus they are able to assist community residents in finding programs that meet their special needs.

Public leisure-service agencies, in particular, may encourage planning efforts that develop recommendations to eliminate overlaps in recreation services or to fill gaps in programming for certain age groups or those with special needs. Often, they are instrumental in forming district or neighborhood councils and advisory committees that carry out the information-referral process independently.

Enabling-Facilitation

In a related function, many public departments may assist community residents in developing their own recreation programs or events. These may include making sports fields available for local youth leagues, assisting in carrying out neighborhood cleanup or tree-planting projects, or forming "Golden Age" clubs for senior citizens.

Through this enabling process, the democratic framework of community life is strengthened, as citizens are assisted in taking responsibility for improving their own lives and learning to work together constructively. Public agencies may also help local groups in terms of publicizing their programs and events and helping them obtain available grants to meet social needs.

Advocacy

Public, nonprofit, and other types of leisure-service agencies also may take the lead in promoting public awareness of leisure and recreation as important community concerns. Too often, people are unaware of the potential value of constructive recreation in their lives and thus permit negative forms of play to dominate their free hours or those of their children. In addition to providing services, agencies should strive to document the positive personal, social, and other outcomes of recreational participation and promote public understanding and support for active and creative forms of play.

Beyond this, recreation agencies are often able to serve as spokespersons or catalysts in directing public attention to important community needs. For many years, persons with severe physical or mental disabilities tended to be shunted aside or segregated in American life. Through the efforts of many therapeutic recreation organizations—such as those providing wheelchair sports or those, such as the Special Olympics, which serve individuals with developmental disabilities—the public often gains a fuller understanding of its human needs and capabilities and becomes more willing to welcome them in community leisure settings.

Similarly, recreation and park agencies are often able to mobilize community efforts to support environmental projects and resist varied forms of ecological pollution or decay.

Other Elements in the Leisure-Service System

In addition to the ten major types of agencies that have just been described, there are several other elements within the nation's overall leisure-service system.

Professional Societies or Trade Associations

There are literally thousands of nationally established societies or associations that deal with different aspects of the leisure-service field, without actually sponsoring recreation programs for public involvement. Instead, their functions are to upgrade professional practice in a given area and promote public interest and support for their field of service.

They may sponsor conferences, conduct research, and publish reports or newsletters and journals that contribute both to public understanding and professional practice. They may establish standards of performance or certification systems that identify qualified practitioners on different levels. In major sports organizations, they may set firm rules affecting eligibility of athletes, scholarship awards, team practice and competition schedules, and tournament sponsorships.

In general, professional societies such as the Armed Forces Recreation Society (AFRS) the National Intramural and Recreation Sports Association (NIRSA), or the National Therapeutic Recreation Society (NTRS) have clearly defined areas of responsibility that focus on their specialized program goals. Within the field of public recreation and parks organizations such as the American Park and Recreation Society, the American Academy for Park and Recreation Administration, the National Association of County Park and Recreation Officials, and the National Association of State Park Directors all help government officials in this field to promote their common agendas.

There are hundreds of professional or trade associations within the commercial recreation spectrum, including such groups as the International Association of Amusement Parks and Attractions, the World Water Park Association, the Dude Ranchers Association, the American Spa and Health Resort Association, and the Adventure Travel Society. They often sponsor huge trade shows in which different businesses promote their products and services (see Figure 2-3).

To attract them, and to appeal to visitors and tourists generally, most large cities have convention and visitors bureaus that prepare promotional materials, consult with trade organizations and travel agents both in the United States and abroad, and develop packages

Figure 2-3
Example of major trade show sponsored by the International Association of Amusement Parks and Attractions (IAAPA).

and events in partnerships with public and business groups that stimulate such profitable events-(see Figure 2-4).

Environmental Groups

Groups that promote ecological causes and environmentally sensitive outdoor recreation ventures nationally include Outward Bound, Wilderness Leadership International, the Sierra Club, the National Audubon Society, the National Wildlife Federation, and the National Outdoor Leadership School. Campus recreation is linked to the Association of College Unions International and the National Association for Campus Activities.

Figure 2-4
Example of Convention and Visitor's Bureau: South Charleston, West Virginia. See also page 196.

Numerous associations represent museums, libraries, zoos and aquariums, botanical gardens, and varied population groups such as those of a particular national origin or veterans of a particular war or campaign. Beyond this, there are hundreds of special interest societies representing every conceivable form of play or segment of the population.

Major Annual Events

Another component of the leisure-service system that is not part of the ten major organizations described earlier consists of hundreds of major tournaments, festivals, celebrations, and other events that are sponsored in a single location during the year.

Usually administered by an independent organization, with assistance from municipal government or other groups, such large-scale programs often draw many thousands of spectators or participants and serve as a valuable attraction for the cities in which they are regularly offered.

Several examples include the Indianapolis 500—probably the most famous car-racing event in the country; the All-American Soap Box Derby in Akron, Ohio; the Miss America Contest in Atlantic City, New Jersey; the Mardi Gras celebration at the time of Lent in New Orleans, Louisiana; the Little League World Series in Williamsport, Pennsylvania; and the annual Hershey Track and Field youth competitions.

Professional Preparation Institutions

A final element in the leisure-service system includes the courses and degree-granting programs offered by hundreds of colleges and universities throughout the United States and Canada, which equip young men and women to enter the field of professional recreation, park, and leisure services.

These educational programs, on two-year, four-year, or graduate degree levels, focus either on the broad recreation field with an emphasis on program planning, management, or natural resource functions or on any of the specialized service areas described in this chapter. Their role, in cooperation with the professional societies and trade associations mentioned, is to present the theoretical or philosophical aspects of recreation and leisure, along with guidelines for the effective planning and operation of leisure-service programs.

In addition to their programs for regularly enrolled students, many higher education departments also provide or cosponsor special institutes or workshops for continuing education (see page 240) and offer certification assistance to practitioners working in the field.

Dynamics of the Organized Leisure-Service System

Recognizing that the organized leisure-service system is not a tightly coordinated structure in which all elements play clearly defined roles in cooperation with each other, what are the actual dynamics and interplay of the system's varied parts?

Competition among Subsystems

Clearly, there is vigorous competition among different elements within the overall leisure-service system. For example, within the realm of popular entertainment, when television gained popularity during the 1950s and 1960s, movie attendance dropped sharply. New gambling casinos cut sharply into horse racing, dog racing, and jai alai revenues.

Among such popular leisure pursuits as fitness activities, there is strenuous competition for patrons among health spas and gyms operated by commercial businesses, nonprofit organizations such as the YMCA, and even facilities operated by colleges and universities or employee recreation programs. In the field of outdoor recreation, commercially operated ski centers, packaged hunting guide services, charter boat fishing services, and white-water rafting companies all compete against each other for the leisure consumer dollar.

Often, conflicts occur when it comes to issues of environmental protection. Those seeking to protect the wilderness against economic exploitation and pollution are resisted by alliances of lumber, oil-drilling, or cattle-grazing interests, which often are supported by local residents and political figures because of the jobs they provide.

In areas involving potential moral conflicts, there is growing resistance to the expansion of legalized gambling in many states. Overall, then, leisure must be perceived as an area of organized sponsorship that is marked by competition and conflict on many levels.

Cooperation among Subsystems

However, the leisure-service system is also assisted by an immense amount of cooperation and jointly operated projects carried on by its different component groups.

Typically, state recreation and park departments or agencies concerned with economic development cooperate with commercial recreation sponsors to initiate major joint marketing plans to encourage public participation in activities such as skiing or varied forms of outdoor adventure recreation.

Similarly, state and local leisure-service departments may join with hotels, resorts, and other tourism associations to sponsor holiday celebrations, festivals, sports tournaments, and other cultural events that attract thousands of visitors.

In terms of environmental protection, state park agencies, nonprofit environmental groups, student groups, and other ecologically minded organizations may form alliances to carry out conservation projects, develop "land trusts," protect wetlands, create new biking and hiking trails, or transform waste-dump sites into new resources for outdoor play.

Nonprofit organizations concerned with hunting and shooting sports such as the National Rifle Association and the National Shooting Sports Foundation conduct large-scale hunter safety workshops with schools, scouting organizations, and other groups; in some cases they are backed by funding from federal agencies such as the U.S. Fish and Wildlife Service.

Nonprofit organizations serving people with disabilities often receive funding on a contractual basis from government agencies and form alliances with county or local recreation and park departments, making extensive use of their facilities and special programs.

Impact of Privatization

In many cities today, corporations, foundations, and groups of interested citizens accept responsibility for managing and maintaining urban parks—a leading example being the contract between New York City government and a private group, the Central Park Conservancy, to help the overall operation of this famous public facility.[3]

Similarly, many nonprofit organizations, including church-related groups today receive fiscal support from federal authorities to conduct needed social programs, including youth recreation, on a subcontractual basis. Still, other private and commercial organizations carry out planning studies for government or actually plan, design, build, and manage mayor facilities for public recreational use—a leading example being Skipper Marine Development, which has created numerous huge marinas chiefly throughout the Midwest since the 1980s, in collaboration with government agencies (see Figure 2-5).

The National Recreation and Park Association cooperates with major sports associations or other groups to promote national youth sports programs,[4] while such huge corporations as Adidas, Coca-Cola, Coors, JC Penney, Merrill Lynch, Nike, and Visa make major contributions to help the Women's Sports Foundation sponsor national award events (see Figure 2-6).

As a consequence of all these kinds of interaction, the leisure-service system has become increasingly integrated, with the sharp lines between different kinds of services being blurred in many ways. As a result, the overall field has grown tremendously, and employment in recreation, park, and leisure services has become a significant factor in the nation's economy.

Scope of Employment in Leisure Services

From a career perspective, what are the employment statistics in the overall leisure-service field?

While it is difficult to arrive at exact numbers, the Statistical Abstract of the United States provides broad estimates of employment on a number of levels, some of which lump recreation workers with those in related disciplines.

In a separate report, the *Occupational Outlook Handbook* of the U.S. Department of Labor estimates that there are approximately 38,000 professional recreation therapists today.

Table 2-1
Estimated Employment in Leisure-Related Fields

All government park and recreation agencies (1995)	387,000
Writers, artists, entertainers, and athletes (1997)	2,234,000
Natural resources management (1995)	421,000
Instructors and coaches, sports and physical training (1996)	303,000
Amusement and recreation attendants (1996)	288,000
Social, recreation, and religious workers (1997)	1,357,000

Source: Statistical Abstract of the United States (1998): pp. 331, 417, 420.

Figure 2-5
Example of privatization in the boating industry: Private corporation, SMD Services, in partnership with government marina owners.

PRIVATE PARTNERING FOR COMPETITIVE PARK & RECREATIONAL OPERATIONS

SMD Services specializes in managing recreational operations and facilities in partnership with state, local and federal governments.

Performance contracts are structured to give you the control you need and the results expected.

Our advice, counsel and management, in partnership with you, will produce cost-controlled, operationally successful projects.

BENEFITS TO YOU
MARKET FOCUS   INCREASED REVENUES   LOWER COSTS   IMPROVED EFFICIENCY   PERFORMANCE ACCOUNTABILITY

SERVICES AVAILABLE

OPERATIONS MANAGEMENT
- Overall management & administration
- Management of sites, facilities & departments
- Budget & financial administration
- Enterprise management & marketing
- Regulatory compliance & code enforcement

PRIVATIZATION ASSISTANCE
- Confidential advice on privatization opportunities
- Project feasibility & marketing studies
- RFP preparation
- Contract management & accountability reporting

CONSTRUCTION MANAGEMENT
- Development, renovation & maintenance projects
- Specification writing
- Contract negotiation & administration
- Field supervision
- Onsite construction services
- Design of land & water-based facilities, structures and systems

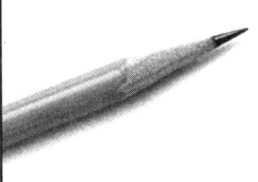

SMD Services
A Management Partner for Public Entities
P.O. Box 249
215 North Point Drive
Winthrop Harbor, Illinois 60096
Phone: 847-872-0292   Fax: 847-872-2072

**Figure 2-6
Example of partnership: NRPA assists
U.S. Tennis Association in national tennis
instruction project.**

While many of the numbers listed by the *Statistical Abstract* refer to job specializations that are in related fields of popular leisure, and while some of the categories overlap, it is obvious that the total number of individuals employed in agencies and businesses amounts to several million people. Many of these individuals have responsibilities that have little to do with specific recreational functions. However, a high percentage of jobs in varied leisure-service agencies involve functions linked to determining recreational goals and objectives, assessing community needs, planning and carrying out programs, designing and constructing leisure facilities, developing marketing plans, and performing other tasks that are at the heart of successful recreation operations. Those planning for careers in leisure services customarily have such future professional roles in mind.

Reasons for Exploring the Total Leisure-Service Field

Before moving on to the chapters that follow in this text, which provide detailed descriptions of the ten major types of recreation, park, and leisure-service organizations, the reader might wish to ask himself or herself, "Why do I need to know about all these different types of leisure-service organizations?"

The reader might continue, "I already know that my special interest is in armed forces recreation or therapeutic recreation or tourism. Why will it be helpful for me to learn about these other fields, if I'm not going to work in them?"

There are several reasons why any individual who is contemplating working in the field of leisure-service management, or who is already enrolled in a college or university curriculum in this field, should be knowledgeable about the total system.

Expand Career Horizons

First, most young men or women who begin study in recreation, parks, and leisure services tend to have had personal experience in only one or two of the specialized subsystems. They may have worked during the summers as a playground assistant or as a health aide in a hospital or rehabilitation center or as an assistant coach in a youth sports league. But typically, they will know very little about the other major branches of the leisure-service field—and their career horizons tend to be limited by their limited past experience.

Therefore, it is helpful for them to gain a fuller picture of the varied elements and job possibilities within the overall system, in terms of knowing which area their own skills and capabilities might lead them to, or which kinds of career choices might offer the greatest potential.

Provide for Career Mobility

Next, one of the important realities of the job world is that individuals frequently make career changes throughout their work life. Different vocational studies have demonstrated that it is common for men and women to make as many as six, eight, or ten significant job changes during the course of a career. Often, such changes may involve a shift from one type of occupation to another.

Typically, in the leisure-service field, it is not at all unusual for an individual to begin work in one type of organization, such as a public recreation and park department, and then advance to a higher-level position in a nonprofit organization or an employee service unit.

Having a solid base of understanding of the entire field will thus prove helpful, not only in terms of making initial career choices, but also at later stages in one's work life.

Develop "Partnership" Capability

Finally, as this chapter has shown, employees in one branch of the leisure-service system frequently must cooperate with those in other types of organizations in joint efforts, partnerships, or other subcontracting arrangements. Again, knowledge of their goals and objectives, policies, and operational strategies is helpful in such situations. Especially for those working in such diversified areas as therapeutic recreation, sports management, and tourism and hospitality, it would be a common occurrence for them to develop links to other specialized services.

The overview of the total field provided throughout this text should prove helpful for any individual considering leisure-service management as a career. Given this understanding, we now move on to an analysis of public recreation, park, and leisure-service organizations.

Suggested Questions for Class Discussion or Essay Examinations

1. What does it mean when we refer to the organized leisure-service system? In your view should spontaneous, unsponsored activities carried on by individuals or groups also be considered part of the leisure service system?
2. The chapter describes elements of both competition and cooperation as examples of interaction among agencies in the leisure-service system. Can you give examples of both kinds of relationships drawn from the text or your own experience? How do they contribute to the overall effectiveness of the system in meeting public leisure needs?
3. Select *any three* of the ten types of leisure-service providers described in the chapter (e.g., public, commercial, and therapeutic recreation). Compare them with each other in terms of their mission or goals, their administrative sponsorship or funding, the populations they serve, and their program emphasis.
4. Beyond the contribution of the ten types of agencies summarized in this chapter, what are the functions of professional societies or trade associations, environmental groups, and higher-education institutions in promoting the leisure-service field?
5. If you are considering entering the leisure-service field, *or* if you have already decided that you intend to prepare yourself to work within a particular sector of the field, why would it still make sense to learn about all types of leisure-service specializations?

Footnotes

[1] Laufer, A. (1975). *Operations Management.* Cincinnati: South-Western Publishing Co. l9.

[2] Murphy, J., Niepoth, E.W., Jamieson, L., and Williams, J. (1991). *Leisure systems: critical concepts and applications.* Champaign, Ill.: Sagamore Publishing Co. 101.

[3] Crompton, J.L. (1997). Partners with business, what's in it for them? *Journal of Park and Recreation Administration.* Winter. 38-60.

[4] Spangler, K.L. (1999). The state of our national programs. *Parks and Recreation.* Oct. 62-66.

Chapter 3

Public Recreation, Park, and Leisure-Service Agencies

Introduction

We now embark on a detailed examination of the ten major types of leisure-service organizations in the United States and Canada today. The first of these involves public, tax-supported agencies, meaning government-sponsored departments that provide recreation, park, and leisure services and, in some cases, other educational, social, or cultural functions.

This chapter presents an overview of such public organizations, including the differing roles of federal, state and local county, special-district, or municipal levels. It describes their administrative structures and strategies, their missions and goals, and presents examples of their facilities, program elements, and services. While most examples are from the United States, two municipal programs in Canada are presented.

The chapter concludes with an overview of employment in public leisure-service agencies, including estimates of total employment in this field, examples of job classifications and descriptions, and summaries of recruitment and hiring practices for persons interested in exploring career opportunities in government agencies.

Government's Role in Recreation and Parks

Of all the different types of leisure-service sponsors described in this text, government agencies represent the one group that is committed to providing a broad spectrum of recreational facilities and programs to meet basic public needs for constructive leisure.

All other types of leisure-service organizations either serve a more specialized group of participants—in terms of their age, socioeconomic status, occupation, or other characteristics—or limit their number through membership requirements or economic constraints. Beyond this, only public departments regard the provision of recreation as a primary responsibility, and place a high priority on protecting the environment.

Government agencies alone maintain a huge network of parks and forest areas, historic monuments and scenic sites, and other important natural resources. In addition, in metropolitan and urban areas, public recreation and park agencies operate extensive, varied facilities for public play, including recreation centers, sports facilities, aquatic areas, and other developed indoor and outdoor resources. On local levels, county and municipal governments offer programs to serve a broad cross section of the public with close-to-home leisure opportunities.

Federal Government Agencies

On the federal level, important recreation-related agencies include the National Park Service in the Department of the Interior; the Forest Service in the Department of Agriculture; the Bureau of Land Management; the Fish and Wildlife Service; the U.S. Army Corps of Engineers; and numerous other bureaus, offices, and agencies with responsibilities linked to environment, commerce, tourism, education, and the needs of special populations.

The specific functions of the federal government in recreation and parks may be listed under the following headings:

Direct Management of Outdoor Recreation Resources, including both recreation- and preservation-related functions and other multiservice uses.

Conservation and Resource Reclamation, including the protection and propagation of wildlife and the setting aside of tracts of land, wetlands, and waterways for conservation purposes.

Open Space and Park Development. Since the 1960s, the federal government has spent billions of dollars under the Land and Water Fund Conservation Act, assisting state and local agencies in acquiring land for conservation and recreation purposes. Through housing and urban development grants, it has also helped municipalities to build and improve local recreation facilities.

Recreation Program Operations. Federal support is also given directly to recreation operations in the armed forces, in veterans' hospitals, and in other institutions.

Assistance to Higher Education. Professional preparation programs designed to prepare practitioners to work with persons with disabilities, the elderly, and other special populations have received federal grants.

Other federal functions with respect to recreation, parks, and leisure services have included sponsoring research and technical assistance with respect to wildlife conservation, urban problems, at-risk youth, and similar needs. Tourism as an economic function has been assisted, and Indian tribes have received assistance in developing recreational and other enterprises on their reservations. Finally, the federal government has established regulations and standards with respect to pollution control, wetland protection, and environmental quality.[1]

Altogether, over 16 trillion visitor-hours were recorded annually at the major federal recreation and park properties in the early 1990s. Visitor-days to national forest sites rose from 233.5 million in 1980 to 341.2 million in 1996. Over 265 million recreation visits to National Park Service attractions were made in 1996, many of them to newly developed recreation areas and seashores in the East, and many of them close to major metropolitan areas.

Problems Facing U.S. Federal Land-Management Agencies

During the 1980s and 1990s, a number of major federal recreation and park agencies faced grave problems linked to funding shortages during a period of fiscal austerity. The National Park Service, in particular, suffered from serious overcrowding and reduced funding for maintenance, supervision of recreation areas, research, and conservation education.[2]

Similar problems faced the U.S. Forest Service, in part because of the growth of lumbering, cattle grazing, and other commercial uses of forest areas. Other huge areas managed by the federal Bureau of Land Management have been threatened by recreational and commercial overuse, and systematic reports have indicated that Environmental Protection Agency regulations have been poorly monitored and enforced.

Measures to Protect the Environment

In response, during the mid- to late 1990s, the federal government took aggressive action to reverse the tide of environmental decay, as well as growing political efforts to open up additional wilderness areas to commercial exploitation.

The National Park Service raised entrance and usage fees substantially to support park operations and sought assistance from major corporations to conduct special projects assisting national monuments and other parks. In Yosemite National Park, the agency initiated new policies to restore the natural environment by limiting car and bus access to the Park's interior and setting new conservation practices in motion.

In 1998, the Forest Service suspended the building of new logging roads in the back country of most of the nation's forests and took action to restore unused, deteriorated logging roads to wilderness status. The federal administration took action to transfer four areas operated by the Bureau of Land Management in Arizona and California, comprising over one million acres of land, and thousands of coastal islands and reefs, to national monument status, which would protect them significantly.[3]

Resistance to Environmental Actions

As an indication of the degree to which recreation, parks, and leisure-service issues are intertwined with economic and political concerns, there has been concerted resistance by ranchers, loggers, businesspeople, and public officials to such environmental initiatives, particularly in the western states. Contending that limiting the use of wilderness areas in their regions is a serious threat to local economics, they argue that wildland-use policies should be made by state and local officials and residents rather than federal government agencies. In many cases, such conflicts have resulted in threats and violent attacks on federal park rangers or installations,[4] and in arson carried out against multimillion-dollar ski centers in Colorado that bordered on wilderness areas.[5]

Federal Role: Problems and Prospects

Despite such problems, it is clear that the federal role with respect to recreation, parks and leisure services will continue to meet major public needs for outdoor recreation, in particular, in the decades ahead.

At the same time, two weaknesses in the federal government's role in leisure services are apparent. First, numerous different agencies in varied branches of the government have at least some connection to recreation, parks, and leisure services. Although there was an effort in the past to coordinate their functions, today they continue to operate without systematic joint planning or assessment of leisure needs and strategies.

A second weakness in the federal government's role is that it lacks continuity in terms of the mission and priorities of the departments concerned with recreation and parks. Inevitably, political expediency takes effect when the appointed directors of the major federal agencies in this field reflect the shifting beliefs of whichever political party happens to be in power at any given time.

State Leisure-Service Agencies

A second important layer of government service related to parks and recreation is carried on through state governments. Each state government in the United States typically operates a network of facilities serving leisure needs.

These include such elements as *wilderness areas*, used for primitive forms of outdoor recreation; *state reserves* or *natural preserves*, which often have unique elements of natural, scientific, scenic, and topographical interest and value; *historical monuments* and *cultural preserves* related to the nation's past; and *recreational areas* and *facilities*, which are often developed for use as campgrounds, downhill or cross-country skiing, backpacking trails, water sites for swimming and boating, and other recreational outlets.

Generally, such resources are administered by state agencies with titles such as "Department of Parks, Recreation, and Conservation," "Department of Economic Development and Tourism," or "Department of Natural Resources." Often such agencies not only operate their own facilities, but also serve as links between the federal government and local agencies. They may assisting directing grant applications for federal aid or in channeling federal assistance to localities.

Direct Program Sponsorship

All state governments maintain hospitals, special schools, or other residential facilities for persons with disabilities. Therapeutic recreation service has been an important professional service within such institutions for several decades, although with deinstitutionalization reducing the populations in such facilities, this need for this function has declined (see page 156).

Professional Preparation.
Many leading state universities house important departments of recreation, parks, and leisure studies, stemming from their earlier sponsorship of physical education majors and, in some cases, resource management or forestry in state land-grant colleges.

Regulation of Local Government Units

Local recreation and park departments are customarily established on the basis of powers given to local governments by state enabling acts, which determine their ability to allocate funds, hire personnel, or acquire and develop property and leisure facilities.

In addition, states develop health and safety standards in camps and other settings for both public, private and commercial sponsors. State employees may inspect camps, swimming pools, resorts, or proprietary owners that provide recreation services, such as nursing homes or other long-term care facilities. In addition, state governments also establish hiring requirements and procedures under civil service codes.

Assistance to Local Governments

State recreation and park, natural resources, or economic development departments may also assist local leisure-service agencies in other ways. Often they provide consultants, schedule conferences, or conduct research and planning studies to promote effective programming throughout local regions.

Other State Functions. Still other state leisure-related responsibilities involve special program areas or social needs. Many states have offices or arts councils that distribute funds to nonprofit arts organizations or performing groups in various areas of cultural and creative activity, in cooperation with the federal National Endowment for the Arts.

Developing New Urban Facilities. Although state parks and other outdoor resources were customarily situated in rural, undeveloped areas far from cities, in many recent cases states have established mayor units in or close to heavily populated urban centers.

As a single example, a new Indiana state park was constructed in Indianapolis: White River State Park, which used state, municipal, private, and commercial funds in the development of an outstanding zoo, family theme park, museums, sports facilities, and other outdoor recreation attractions—all within the city limits.

Legal Basis for State and Local Programs

In the United States, the role of state governments in providing recreation park and leisure services has generally been supported by the Tenth Amendment to the Constitution, which states: "The powers not delegated to the United States [federal government] by the Constitution, nor prohibited by it to the States, are reserved to the States respectively, or to the people."

This amendment, commonly referred to as the "states' rights amendment," is used as the legal basis for states exerting their own authority in such areas as public education, welfare, and health regulations and services.

In turn, the power to establish public, tax-supported recreation and park agencies and other related leisure services is usually granted to local government by constitutional, statutory, or charter provisions approved by state legislatures. Elsewhere, one of the authors of this text has written:

> Although local governing bodies have certain assumed powers in this area under the principle of "police powers, specific legal authority is needed for them to acquire properties, employ personnel, or impose taxes to support recreation. . . .Enabling legislation may range from rather simple authorizations to fully detailed codes that specify such elements as the method of acquiring and developing properties, financing recreation and park programs, and establishing public boards, commissions, and special districts.[6]

Relationships among Different Agencies

Many authorities refer to local, public, tax-supported recreation and park programs as "municipal recreation." This is an oversimplification. Actually, leisure-service programs on this level are often provided not by city agencies alone, but often by a complex of special park districts, county agencies, city governments, townships or boroughs, and even villages and school districts.

In some metropolitan areas, there is considerable overlapping of recreation functions, as in large county recreation and park systems where the county agency provides major parks and outdoor resources such as golf courses, aquatic complexes, stadiums, and nature reserves or major cultural arts programs and events.

On the closer-to-home level, cities, townships, and smaller units of government are likely to operate playgrounds, smaller parks, and recreation centers—including senior centers, youth centers, and facilities for persons with disabilities. They may also sponsor clubs, classes, sports leagues, and arts programs, in cooperation with volunteer citizens' groups and local school districts. Often, city or township agencies conduct such programs *within* the larger park district or county setting.

Park District Operations

Many states have legislative provisions for regional and special park districts, usually in metropolitan areas, which may encompass several separate counties and municipalities.

A leading example of such operations is the East Bay Regional Park Districts in California, which includes two large counties, Contra Costa and Alameda, in the Oakland region. Founded in 1934, the East Bay District has been one of the most progressive and successful park agencies in the United States. With the help of a $53 million bond issue approved in 1973 and a new master plan for the acquisition of new parklands, by the late 1990s, the East Bay Regional Park District was operating fifty parks and twenty regional trails covering 75,000 acres and numerous communities within its two-county jurisdiction (see Figure 3-1).

Figure 3-1
Facilities map of East Bay Park District, showing available recreation activities keyed to park locations.

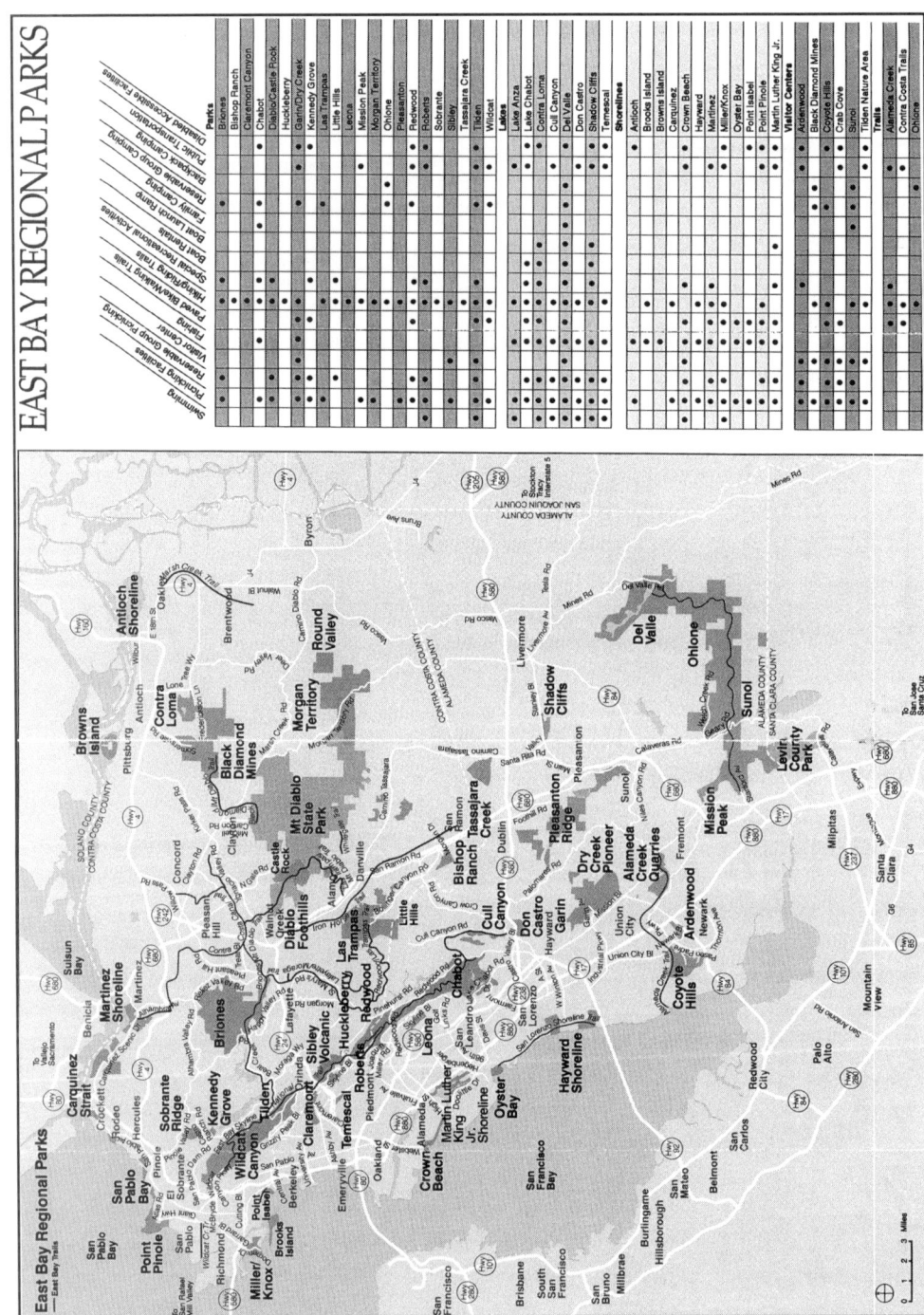

It now offers an immense variety of outdoor recreation experiences to residents of its two counties, including swimming and boating; individual and group picnicking; fishing; hiking and biking trails; family and group camping; backpacking; a visitor center; and special accessible facilities for park users with disabilities. Numerous other special districts around the United States provide similar facilities and services, although usually on a lesser scale.

County Recreation and Park Agencies

The next important example of local, public leisure-service governmental units consists of county departments and commissions. As indicated, these tend to provide large-scale facilities and centralized activities or meet special needs that cannot readily be satisfied by smaller, closer-to-home departments.

Westchester County, New York, Department of Parks, Recreation and Conservation. Situated in a large, wealthy and heavily populated suburban area just north of New York City, this department offers a typical assortment of facilities, such as golf courses, swimming pools, marinas, and camping areas. Beyond that, it places a heavy emphasis on ecologically and historically directed facilities and programs, with nature museums and preserves, wildlife sanctuaries, a working farm, and conservation education activities.

Westchester County sponsors numerous cultural events and expositions in a large county center building and numerous family entertainment programs in its beachfront Playland Park and along the Hudson River. It celebrates Earth Day, a young Farmer's Program, a popular summer music camp, varied ethnic and racial cultural-heritage programs, and nonalcoholic holiday social events. It promotes hiking and biking along county trails, and during early and late summer weekends it closes down a major parkway so families can enjoy biking and in-line skating.

Dade County, Florida, Park and Recreation Department. This Department operates an impressive network of major parks, four miles of sandy ocean beachfront, gardens, historic mansions, camping areas, and five golf courses and three large tennis centers.

As of the early 1990s, Dade County had 8,000 acres of developed park and recreation facilities serving over eighteen million residents and visitors annually. It maintains a famous zoo, Dade County Auditorium, five large marinas, and promotes or assists numerous cultural events and facilities, including several art museums and galleries in the Miami metropolitan area, in cooperation with universities, individual collectors, and other civic groups.

Sarasota County, Florida, Department of Parks and Recreation. Less densely populated than Dade County, this popular outdoor recreation and vacation area along Florida's West Coast offers several miles of beaches along the Gulf of Mexico, along with unique environmental habitats for nature exploration, such as pine flatwoods, hammocks, wet prairies, and swamps—many offering homes for rare endangered species of birds and animals.

The County Parks and Recreation Department sponsors over 120 parks and other sites, totaling 3,000 acres, with varied sports instructional programs and leagues. It conducts over 250 annual and seasonal events, festivals, and celebrations, including an extensive summer camp program for children and a Games for Life (formerly the Sarasota County Senior Games), many in cooperation with other civic groups and associations.

Prince George's County, Maryland, Department of Parks and Recreation. This metropolitan county, which is part of the national capital area, operates an extensive range of athletic facilities, community centers, ice rinks, regional parks, and even the oldest continuing operating airport in the world—home to several flying clubs and flight training programs.

It is also known for an outstanding arts program that offers instruction, exhibit, and performing opportunities to individual artists and performers and county-based dance, theater, music, and visual-arts groups. It offers an extensive network of sports and outreach programs, including instruction, league, and tournament sponsorship, and trips for skiing, rafting, hiking, and biking enthusiasts. It also houses a Special Populations Division, which initiates and coordinates county-wide services for thousands of people in the area with special recreation needs.

Municipal Recreation and Park Programs

What follows next are brief descriptions of several municipal recreation and park programs, with special emphasis placed on their overall range of functions and on innovative leisure-service activities.

Such agencies:

> ... are often perceived as the most obvious representation of the leisure services movement. People living in local communities relate, in a direct and tangible way, to their city's parks, swimming pools, playgrounds, community centers, and other leisure facilities and amenities. The availability of park and recreation services is often viewed as a strong determinant in the decisions made by large corporations to locate their businesses... Leisure amenities, as reflected in park and recreation opportunities, contribute significantly to the livability factor.[7]

Phoenix, Arizona

The Phoenix Parks, Recreation, and Library Department represents an outstanding example of a diversified big-city leisure service agency not only in terms of its facilities—which include typical sports fields, golf courses, and recreation centers—but also in terms of its extensive human-service programs. A recent brochure sums up the programs offered in this community, one of the fastest-growing U.S. cities, a 420-square- mile area with a population of over one million:

> We offer educational, cultural and recreational activities at a variety of facilities throughout the city, including five golf courses, 13 community centers, a main library and 12 branch libraries, 28 swimming pools, and 172 traditional and mountain parks.
>
> Outdoor enthusiasts currently enjoy almost 25,000 acres of desert parks and mountain preserve land within the city limits. The department also boasts marvelous cultural facilities, including the Phoenix Center for the Performing Arts, Shemer Art Center, Tovrea Castle, Heritage and Science Park, and the Pueblo Grande Museum and Cultural Park.
>
> We also have top-notch sports complexes, including the award-winning Maryvale Park and Phoenix Municipal Stadium, spring-training homes to the Milwaukee Brewers and the Oakland A's.

Perhaps the most unique aspect of the Phoenix Parks, Recreation, and Library Department is its commitment to achieving important social goals through recreation and related community services. While these include programs for people with disabilities, the homeless, and other special groups, Phoenix's most impressive project involves a multipronged effort to work positively with at-risk youth in the city. This effort includes a remarkable range of specially funded programs for youth, including camps, sports, river rafting, aquatic, and park ranger activities. Beyond that, it operates a number of police-sponsored centers, a city-streets mobile unit, teen councils and youth centers, and numerous activities and programs dealing with juvenile offenses, including truancy, and teen curfew violations, plus a graffiti cleanup program and, most unusual, "X-Tattoo," a tattoo-removal program to assist youth in removing these body decorations that are often connected with gangs and juvenile crime.

The inclusion of the Phoenix Public Library as one of this department's responsibilities is paralleled in other cities, where varied cultural programs and important human services are linked to recreation and park functions (see Figure 3-2).

Long Beach, California

The Long Beach Department of Parks, Recreation, and Marine, situated in an ideal Southern California coastal location in the Los Angeles Basin, with easy access to the Gulf of Mexico, features many boating activities and services. It operates the world's largest municipally run marina, with 3,800 slips and additional guest mooring facilities, along with a marine stadium, sailing school, and extensive beach and fishing areas.

The Department also offers five golf courses, sixty-nine tennis courts, varied parks and centers, pools, bike trails, and similar facilities. Long Beach sponsors a major cultural center with classes and events in the visual and performing arts, the City's municipal band, sports for all ages, and both youth, adult, and senior social programs. Its senior center activities are notable, including not only dances, parties, and hobby groups, but also such important services as a dental clinic and health department services renter's assistance and housing information; income tax assistance and insurance counseling; a care-giver support group, nutrition and transportation assistance; and several other councils and advisory committees in which elderly persons may play important policy-and decision-making roles.

Finally, because it is in an ethnically and culturally diverse community, the Long Beach Department offers numerous programs designed to promote intercultural understanding, such as Black History Month and varied Latino celebrations and performances.

San Mateo, California

While it operates a typical range of park and sports facilities, the San Mateo, California, Department of Parks and Recreation is particularly outstanding for its network of indoor recreation centers, and its year-round schedule of classes, events, and clubs designed to serve children and youth, adults and seniors.

These include extensive classes and camps, health and fitness activities, concert series, holiday festivals, adventure clubs, pro-beginner tennis and karate instruction groups, crafts, drama, and cooking, with many activities designed for children as young as three or four. Emphasis is placed on promoting family activities, and on teaching parenting and leadership skills. In San Mateo, the Parks and Recreation Department places a high premium on employing highly skilled staff members in such areas as sports and the arts and publicizes them actively in its program brochures (see Figure 3-3)

Figure 3-2
Organization chart of Phoenix Department of Parks, Recreation, and Library.

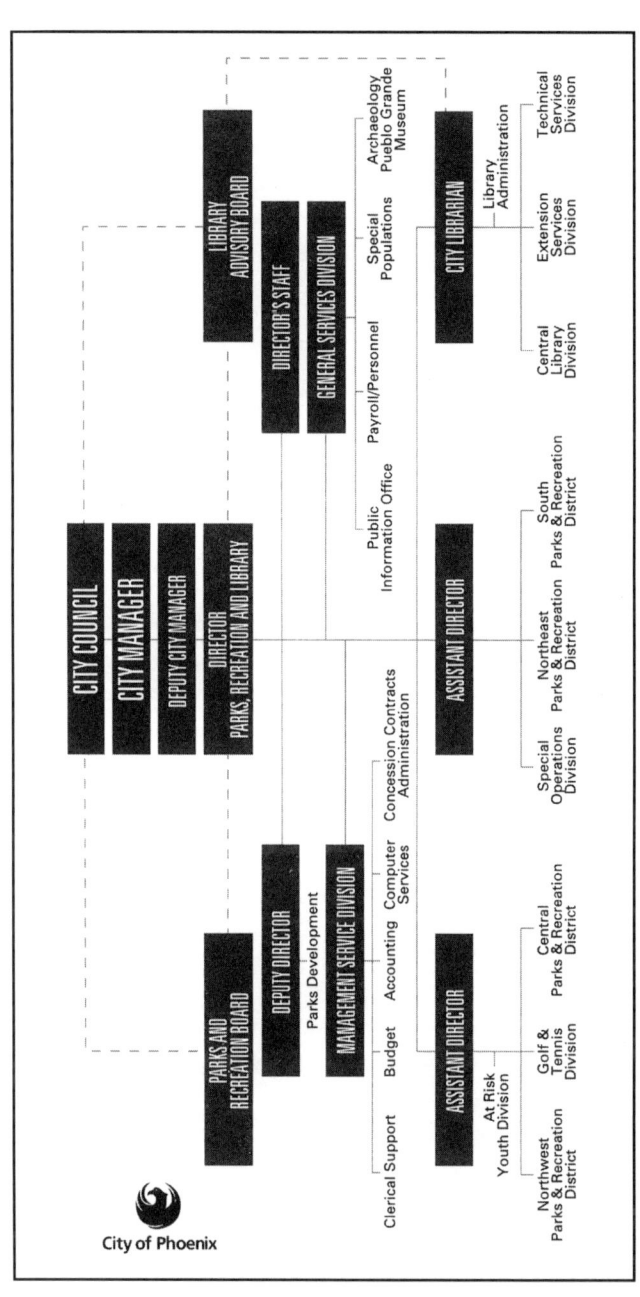

Figure 3-3
Examples of San Mateo's Program in the Arts with its varied dance classes.

Youth Dance

General Information
Dance Office: Beresford Center 377-4772 or 377-4776.
Summer Term: Monday, June 16-Saturday, August 2.
Holidays: Friday, July 4 and Saturday, July 5.
Fall placement letters will be sent out in August.
Fall term begins Monday, September 8.

CREATIVE DANCE

Kinderdance: age 4 (by 6/15) & 5 yrs.
In this class your children will be introduced to the riches of dancing with creative and physical experiences specially designed for 4 and 5 years olds. Girls wear any color leotard; t-shirt and shorts for boys; bare legs, bare feet. All classes are at Beresford, except CD101-151, which is at Lakeshore. While Kerstin Dieterich is on maternity leave, her classes will be taught by either Jenna Cameron or Mae Chesney. No classes 7/4 or 7/5. (7 mtgs for Mon., Tues. and Wed. classes; 6 mtgs for Fri. and Sat.)

Code	Day	Time	Fee	Dates	Location
CD101-111	M	9:15-9:55am	$17/21	6/16-7/28	Beres
CD101-151	Tu	6:15-6:55pm	$17/21	6/17-7/29	Lake
CD101-113	Th	3:10-3:50pm	$17/21	6/19-7/31	Beres
CD101-114	F	3:10-3:50pm	$15/19	6/20-8/1	Beres
CD101-115	Sa	9:10-9:50am	$15/19	6/21-8/2	Beres
CD101-116	Sa	10:00-10:40am	$15/19	6/21-8/2	Beres

Creative Dance: age 5 & 6 yrs.
In this dynamic class children will explore creative and physical self-expression. They will discover new aspects of their bodies, minds, and imagination by learning the basic elements of dance and tools for making their own dances. Girls wear any color leotard; boys: t-shirt and shorts. Both: bare legs, bare feet. While Kerstin Dieterich is on maternity leave, her classes will be taught by either Mae Chesney or Jenna Cameron. All classes at Beresford. (Thursday class, 7 mtgs; Friday and Saturday classes, 6 mtgs.)

Code	Day	Time	Fee	Dates	Location
CD102-114	Th	4:00-4:40pm	$17/21	6/19-7/31	Beres
CD102-112	F	4:00-4:40pm	$15/19	6/20-8/1	Beres
CD102-113	Sa	10:45-11:25am	$15/19	6/21-8/2	Beres

Making Dances: age 7 & up
Develop creativity, self expression and imagination! Students will learn the art and craft of making dances, with the support of classmates and instructors Mae Chesney (first two classes) and Jenna Cameron (last five classes.) Leotard required (any color). Bare feet, ballet shoes or jazz shoes. (7 mtgs)

Code	Day	Time	Fee	Dates	Location
CD323-111	Th	4:45-5:45pm	$25/31	6/19-7/31	Beres

Meet our new instructor, Jenna Cameron, who will be teaching Kinderdance, Creative Dance, and a special class called Making Dances

BALLET

Creative Ballet-Storybook Dances: age 6-8 yrs.
Join us for another fun-filled session of Creative Ballet. The students decide which fairy tales they will base their dances on. Some of the dances will be choreographed, some are based on improvisation. Simple props and costumes from home enhance the dances. Ballet technique will be introduced to give the dancers a foundation for their own creativity. Girls wear leotards, boys wear shorts and shirts. Both: bare feet or ballet shoes. When Kerstin Dieterich begins her maternity leave, the class will be taught by Jeannine Vogt. (7 mtgs)
CD421-111   M   3:10-4:00pm $20/25   6/16-7/28   Beres

Ballet: age 8-12 yrs.
Try our Ballet class taught by our 1996 Snow Queen, Jeannine Vogt! This new class consists of barre, centre floor and across the floor movement. Learn form and technique that will bring out the dancer in you while developing creative expression. Open to new students or those continuing from Creative Ballet. Leotards, tights or bare legs; pink ballet shoes. (7 mtgs)
CD422-112   M   4:00-5:00pm $25/31   6/16-7/28   Beres

Check out our new instructor, Danny G. He will be teaching a Hip Hop class and is also a part of our new summer dance program, "Around the World Adventures."

JAZZ

Hot Summer Jazz: age 9-11 yrs.
Don't miss this special summertime Jazz dance class. Learn Jazz warm-ups, Jazz technique and cool new dances that will give you a foundation for creative expression. You will also learn basic concepts of choreography where the whole class will be responsible for the design of a dance. This will be a fun experience for all those participating. Instructor: Daniel Giray. (7 mtgs.)
CD880-111   W   4:30-5:30pm $25/31   6/18-7/30   Beres

Jazz Intensive: age 11-18 yrs.
Sharpen your jazz dance skills. Learn dance technique and style in this exciting, challenging class. Especially recommended for those planning to audition for the Youth Jazz Performing Troupes in the Fall. Instructor: Christi Costa. (7 mtgs.)
CD882-112   Th   5:00-6:00pm $25/31   6/19-7/31   Beres

LATIN

Youth Ballet Folklorico:
Learn fun and traditional dances of Mexico. Instructor Martin Cruz brings this exciting dance form to beginning through advanced dancers, grades 3-12. Classes held at the King Center, grades 3-6 and San Mateo High School for grades 8-12 yrs.
CD610-141   W   4:00-5:00pm $25/31   6/18-7/30   King
The following programs at SMHS are offered through the Latino Parents Association of the S.M.U.H.S.D. Registration takes place at the first class meeting. For more information call Al Tovar at 952-1485 or 696-259.

Level	Day	Time	Dates	Location
Beginning	T/Th	5:30-6:30pm	6/17-7/29	SMHS
Intermediate	T/Th	5:30-6:30pm	6/17-7/29	SMHS
Advanced	T/Th	5:30-6:30pm	6/17-7/29	SMHS

Summer '97 Activity Guide — Page 19

Kamloops, British Columbia, Canada

The Kamloops Parks, Recreation, and Culture Commission is similar to the San Mateo program in that it offers extensive preschool and elementary-age activity classes and clubs across a wide range of hobbies and leisure skills, extending from science as a play activity to instrumental and choral music, and from creative writing for children to classes in clowning skills. A number of programs are designed to meet the important life needs of children, such as "Safe at Home" or "Streetproofing for Children" workshops, which recognize the dangers that threaten many latchkey children in one-parent families or from homes where both parents work.

Beyond this, the Kamloops Parks, Recreation and Culture Commission places a heavy emphasis on having the public become aware of the importance of leisure and on developing leadership training programs. All preschool program leaders must be officially certified in this field. The department offers several baby-sitting courses for teenagers and it sponsors both youth and adult leadership conferences and workshops. In collaboration with other specialized, nonprofit organizations, it helps to promote or coordinate programs in the arts, boating, heritage activities, aquatics and life-saving, fitness, and sports coaching certification and also hosts numerous major sports tournaments.

North York, Ontario, Canada

The City of North York Parks and Recreation Department is particularly noteworthy because of its outstanding facilities and its strong emphasis on aquatic programming and winter sports that are especially popular in Canada.

In terms of aquatics, the department operates eleven pools that provide carefully graded instructional programs serving groups from infants and toddlers to the full adult age range, making use of a graded sequence of learning stages and performance levels. Its Douglas Snow Aquatic Centre is a comprehensive facility with extensive fitness rooms and equipment, and a busy schedule of activities that include fitness groups, swimming classes, lifeguard and CPR courses, leisure swims, therapy sessions, and the use of whirlpools, saunas, a three-story tube slide, a "Tarzan" rope, and other play-like features.

Similarly, the North York Department maintains three well-designed and -maintained ski slopes and offers extensive skiing and snowboarding classes, clubs, outings, and winter carnival events. Typically, these facilities and programs yield substantial revenues; a five-day skiing camp for seven-year-olds costs $315 to register.

Vail, Colorado

Situated in a wealthy and scenically beautiful Rocky Mountain location, the Vail Recreation District is an outstanding example of public recreation and park agencies that emphasize varied sports and outdoor leisure pursuits.

The district offers major special events and tournaments, such as the Vail Lacrosse Shootout, the country's largest lacrosse tournament; the Vail Invitational Soccer Tournament; and the King of the Mountain Volleyball Tournament. These are supplemented by ongoing classes, camps, leagues, and competitions in such varied sports as wrestling, baseball and softball, flag football, mountain-trail running, ice skating and ice hockey—with many activities serving all age groups and both sexes. The district's Dobson Arena houses numerous special events throughout the year, including major skating festivals, and has been the training site for several National Hockey League teams.

Figure 3-4
Kamloops program brochure showing scenic location and facilities.

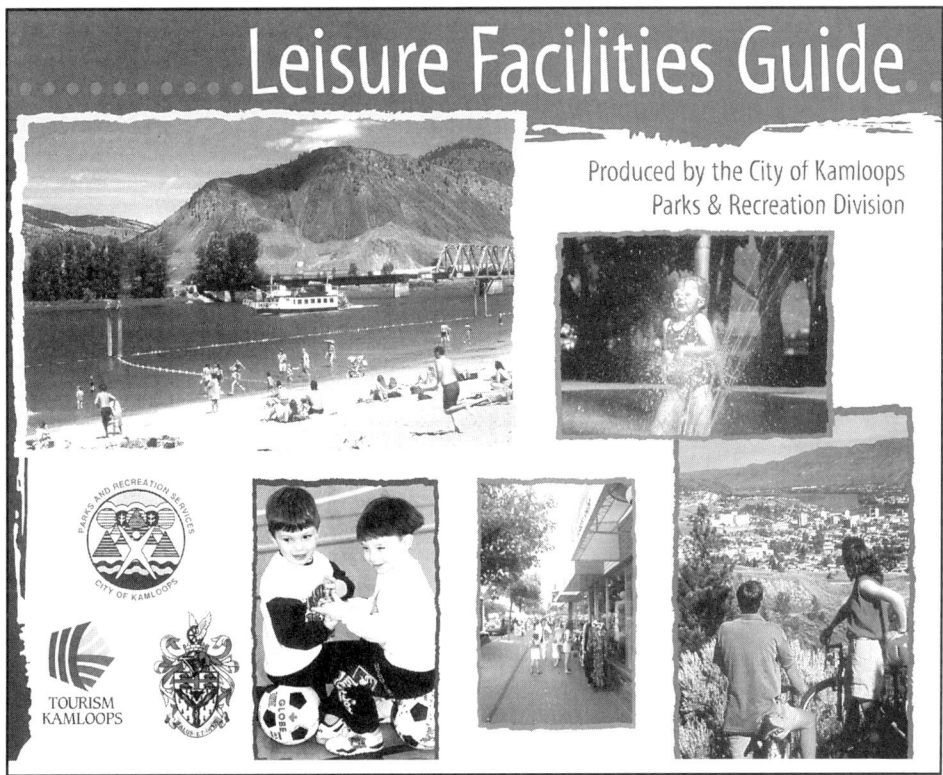

Other featured Vail programs include several camps and pre-camps, as well as a host of nature programs, such as fly-fishing and stream ecology workshops; kayaking courses; hiking; wildflower, bird, and beaver-pond walks; and other conservation and outdoor education activities.

Other Local Programs

Many other innovative programs or trends in social services offered by local recreation and park agencies might be cited, including an extensive, diversified aquatic program in Portland, Oregon; a "Fishing College" sponsored by the Brevard County, Florida, Department of Parks and Recreation, in cooperation with the Coast Guard; in Canada, Vancouver's, support of varied public visual arts projects; impressive new zoo designs and primate areas, as in Philadelphia and New York; and finally, the growing role of public recreation and park departments in Florida, Kansas, and Oklahoma in providing emergency services after catastrophic hurricanes and tornadoes.[8]

Figure 3-5
Examples of adult summer sports leagues in Vail, Colorado.

LEAGUES & DROP-IN

8 ON 8 SOCCER LEAGUE
Come and join us for this fast paced exciting game. Games will be played on a smaller version of a regulation field with eight players per team. A team award and individual champion T-shirt will be granted to the winners of the league. Limited space is available, so early registration is encouraged.
Vail Athletic Field
August 10 - October 5
Mondays
5:20 - 6:20 pm
18 & up
$85/$75 VRD Taxpayer
Register by July 27.

VAIL ATHLETIC FIELD SAND VOLLEYBALL LEAGUE
It's time to get out of the gym and enjoy the mountain summer air on the sand volleyball courts at the Vail Athletic Field. No matter what your skill level is, we have a league for you. Two and four-person leagues will be offered.
Vail Athletic Field
June 15 - September 5
A & BB Monday
C & B Wednesday
5:30 - 6:30 pm
18 & up
$85
$75 VRD Taxpayer
Register by June 3 or until the league fills.

SUMMER 3 ON 3 BASKETBALL LEAGUE
No officials or scorekeepers needed, this "call your own" league is played on a small court and is limited to the first six teams to register. This is the only organized summer basketball in the Vail Valley.
Red Sandstone Gym
Wednesdays, June 19 - August 7
6 - 9 pm
18 & up
$110
$100 VRD Taxpayer
Register by June 12 or until league fills.

SUMMER ADULT SLOW PITCH SOFTBALL LEAGUE
This is a great way for all level players to get some exercise and show their skills! Forty-two men's and 18 women's teams make up several different leagues ranging from recreational to competitive. The end of the season will be completed with a tournament featuring the top two teams from each league. Tournament champions will receive individual champion T-shirts. In addition, league champions will also receive awards. The league always fills in one day, so don't miss the registration deadline!
Ford Park Softball Fields
May 18 - August 14
Monday - Friday
5:30 - 7:45 pm
18 & up
$470
$440 VRD Taxpayer
Register by Tuesday, April 7, 8 am at the Vail Tennis Center at Ford Park.
VRD Taxpayer teams have priority on a first-come first-served basis.

RED SANDSTONE GYM SUMMER OPEN GYM SCHEDULE
Drop in to sharpen your skills with other basketball players at Red Sandstone Gym. Please call the Sports Line at 479-2277 for updated gym schedules.
Red Sandstone Gym
June 2 - August 27
Tuesdays & Thursdays
6 - 9 pm
18 & up
$3 per visit

VAIL ATHLETIC FIELD SAND VOLLEYBALL DROP-IN
The Vail Athletic Field Sand Volleyball Courts are open daily for drop-in and group play. Volleyballs may be rented from the Vail Tennis Center at Ford Park. Reservations for large groups can be made by calling the Sports Office at 479-2280.
Vail Athletic Field
Daily, June 10 - September 6
FREE

Increasingly, the role of public recreation and parks in contributing to individual and community health, both in terms of the direct benefits of active recreation to personal health and as a counterbalance to other forms of negative or self-destructive leisure pursuits is gaining recognition.[9]

New Business-Related Approaches in Government Service

In addition to such changes, many government agencies were encouraged to adopt a new business-like identity during the 1980s and early 1990s. As Chapter 1 pointed out, leisure was increasingly referred to as an "industry," and public and nonprofit leisure-service agencies were urged to adopt entrepreneurial goals and strategies, including sophisticated marketing, promotional, and pricing methods. At a time of cyclic national recessions, with widespread budget cuts, this move was seen as essential.

Marketing Thrust

Expanded revenue sources, partnerships with corporations, innovative fund-raising methods, and new facilities and programs with high profit potential were all part of a drive that would contribute to fiscal self-sufficiency.

This trend continued through the 1990s, with many local governments urged to develop new, more attractive images that used sports, parks, cultural programs, and other tourist attractions to promote a positive, international image. The slogan "reinventing government" became popular, and recreation and park agencies, among others, adopted new, more customer-friendly stances.

Increasingly, new technology made it possible for community residents to have input in government decision-making processes. In San Diego, comments at public hearings were submitted by E-mail; in Boston, residents used the city's Web site to pay parking tickets or complain about potholes; and in Indianapolis, residents received copies of the city's budget through the Internet and sent their own suggestions to the mayor.[10]

"Electronic government" was changing the ways in which residents interacted with county and municipal agencies. In response, public recreation and park departments adopted sophisticated planning and outcome-assessment methods, including strong emphases on customer relations, maximizing revenue-producing facilities and programs, reorganizing their operations, and developing new, creative strategies. Park and recreation departments have accepted a market-pricing philosophy and are forming enterprise funds to permit them to use their revenues for their own purposes rather than turn them back to general municipal funds. More and more, they are using computers for reservations and registrations, monitoring performance throughout their operations, and determining new policies.

Pros and Cons of New Approaches

The entrepreneurial, marketing-based approach that has just been described has had valuable outcomes for many public recreation, park, and leisure-service agencies—particularly for those in well-to-do suburban communities, towns, and cities. In disadvantaged settings, it is less useful, since residents cannot afford to pay significant fees and charges for leisure participation.

Recognizing this, some government leisure-service agencies have developed policies to enable poorer residents to avail themselves of public recreational opportunities.[11] A leading example is in Vancouver, Canada, where the Board of Parks and Recreation has adopted a user-fee policy that favors children and youth, families, groups, and people with disabilities. It uses "strip tickets" for multiple visits, and low priority times for fee discounts. In Vancouver:

> Special programs [are] targeted to groups in communities statistically in need. Each rink and indoor pool will schedule at least four hours of free public sessions each week.
>
> A Leisure Access Card will allow a 50 percent fee reduction in basic Park Board services to persons meeting the assistance eligibility criteria. Further reductions will be available to Leisure Access Card holders for flexipass, swim lessons and ice skate lessons.[12]

Another example may be found in the kinds of partnerships between public and private organizations that are growing throughout the nation. In the Hartford and East Hartford areas of Connecticut, such a partnership group, Riverfront Recapture, has gained funding support to develop a network of small parks along the underutilized and decayed shoreline of the Connecticut River. Beyond its ecological benefits, this project now offers a full calendar of activities, including fishing clinics and tournaments, rowing classes and regattas, and festivals and concerts for the diverse population of the region—including many disadvantaged and minority-group residents in Hartford.[13]

Employment Patterns in Public Recreation

As earlier chapters have shown, governmental recreation, park, and leisure-service agencies employ several hundred thousand year-round workers today—beyond those employed by other types of recreation providers. What kinds of jobs do they have, and what personnel policies control their work and career development?

First, most government jobs exist within civil service structures, which apply at federal, state and local levels. Civil service represents a comprehensive approach to hiring which sought to do away with the "spoils system" in American life, which was a politically driven, patronage-based approach in which jobs were given as rewards for loyalty or direct payments and in which entire workforces might be overthrown when elections bring new officials into power.

Instead, civil service is used to classify and define government jobs, to establish the educational, experience, or skills requirements for them, and to require impartial examinations or other hiring procedures to eliminate political influence. Realistically, this process does not always work, and politics comes directly into play in the appointment of upper-level employees, such as commissioners, division directors or other top management personnel, or seasonal, part-time, specialist or other employees. However, when correctly applied, Civil Service does provide a measure of job security and permanence and helps in the hiring of qualified government personnel.

Classification Systems and Series

In civil service, positions are usually grouped into classes and series to ensure reasonably similar qualifications and salaries across different department lives.

A class refers to a group of positions with roughly comparable qualifications and responsibility levels in different departments. They are usually similar with respect to pay ranges, fringe benefits, promotions, and other personnel matters throughout a federal, state, or municipal civil service system.

A series is a type of vertical classification of employees, usually found within a particular department, with a gradation of skills and qualifications, different levels of salary and status, and prescribed procedures for promotion. Typically, a series of titles within a public recreation and park department might run from "Recreation Trainee" or "Assistant" through several grades of "Recreation Leader", up to "Recreation Supervisor or Director".

Job categories in public leisure-service departments include dozens of different areas, such as playground or recreation center leaders or directors; program specialists, such as arts and crafts, music, or sports program leaders, special population leaders or coordinators, with disabled persons or the elderly; and environmental education and nature specialists. They also include such administrative and managerial roles as resource and facility maintenance, ranging from laborers or gardeners to division directors or planning and engineering specialists; fiscal management and accounting services; and public relations and community relations.

Job Descriptions and Requirements

Customarily, detailed job descriptions are prepared for each such category, either by a governing civil service jurisdiction, such as a federal or state board, or by a municipal civil service personnel office. Job descriptions typically outline the specific responsibilities and functions of a given position and may precisely define the skills required for it.

Example of Duties and Requirements: National Park Service

Federal agencies such as the National Park Service use job descriptions for positions such as park rangers that include detailed statements of responsibilities, training, promotional potential, and necessary qualifications.

For example, duties of park rangers include planning and carrying out conservation functions, conducting programs of public safety (including law enforcement and rescue tasks), directing interpretive programs such as tours and slide shows, planning other recreation programs, and performing administrative, community relations and other functions. To qualify for appointment as a park ranger at Civil Service Grade GS-5 typically requires a combination of educational background and experience in park or conservation work (see page 226). The general picture of employment in the National Park Service is shown in Figure 3-6.

Parks and Recreation Administrator: City of Phoenix

At a higher level of responsibility, the Phoenix, Arizona, Department of Parks, Recreation, and Library outlines the overall responsibilities and essential functions of the position titled "Parks and Recreation Administrator" (see Figure 3-7). In addition to these elements, the job description outlines the necessary skills and knowledge that candidates must have,

Figure 3-6
General information on employment with the National Park Service.

The National Park Service

National Park Service Careers

General Employment Information	Seasonal Employment Information	Volunteer Information
Park Ranger Careers	Administrative Careers	Maintenance, Trade, and Craft Careers
Design and Construction Careers	Park Police Careers	Guard Careers
Other Opportunities	Application and Hiring	Personnel Offices
U.S. Office of Personnel Management On-Line Employment Info..	Office of Personnel Management Job Announcements	Office of Personnel Management Salaries and Wages

Employment

- All positions are filled in accordance with Office of Personnel Management (Civil Service) regulations. Normally, a person seeking an initial appointment to a permanent position must acquire eligibility on an appropriate Office of Personnel Management (OPM) register.
- Although you will be considered without regard to race, color, religion, age, sex, national origin, political affiliation, or other nonmerit factors, you must be a United States citizen. For certain jobs there may be age and physical qualifications. Generally, one must be 18 years old (some positions require age 21).
- The Park Service maintains a headquarters office in Washington, D.C., 7 Regional Offices which are Alaska, National Capitol, Southeast, Midwest, Pacific West, Northeast, and Intermountain, an interpretive design center in Harpers Ferry, WV, and a service center in Denver for park design and construction of facilities.
- Park staffs range from 7 employees in the smallest area to 630 in Yellowstone at peak season.
- Competition for jobs is keen. One must be very well qualified to be seriously considered, especially for permanent full-time positions.
- Equal Employment Opportunity
The National Park Service offers an equal opportunity for all qualified applicants to be selected for jobs at all levels. We take seriously our goal to provide equal consideration regardless of race, religion, color, national origin, sex, physical handicap, age, political affiliation, or any other nonmerit factor.

We encourage all interested and qualified persons to apply for positions with the National Park Service. We heartily believe that our emphasis on employment opportunity yields benefits for the agency, its employees, and its visitors.
Back to Top

Figure 3-7
Job Description, Parks and Recreation Administrator
(Source: City of Phoenix; Job Code 41180, Jan. 2000).

PARKS AND RECREATION ADMINISTRATOR

DISTINGUISHING FEATURES OF THE CLASS:

The fundamental reason this classification exists is to develop, organize and administer the Citywide specialized maintenance and special programming in sports and aquatics activities provided through the Special Operations Division, or a comprehensive park and recreation program in a defined geographic area. Work involves long-range planning for district recreation programs, park development, and park and public facilities maintenance requirements or directing Citywide support services in the areas of Forestry, Horticulture, Specialized and Pool Maintenance, Recreation and Aquatics, centralized inventory and printing services and the Work Alternative Program. Supervision is exercised over Parks Supervisors, Recreation Supervisors and/or Parks Special Operations Supervisors. Assignments are received from an Assistant Director who reviews the work through discussion of results to be achieved.

ESSENTIAL FUNCTIONS:

- Supervises the work of recreation and park maintenance personnel engaged in providing Citywide services and activities;
- Gathers unit production and cost statistics and prepares activity reports;
- Reviews district or division's programs and discusses improvements;
- Evaluates the adequacy of existing district facilities, recommends improvements, and participates in the planning of new recreation facilities, park development, and Citywide programs and activities;
- Establishes priorities for long-range planning purposes;
- Presents ideas regarding parks and recreation activities before departmental management, civic groups, Boards and Commissions and the City Council;
- Plans and prepares budget and budget requests and controls the expenditures allotted;
- Use graphic instructions, such as blueprints, schematic drawings, layouts, or other visual aids;
- Comprehend and make inferences from written material;
- Travel across rough, uneven, or rocky surfaces;
- Work in a variety of weather conditions with exposure to the elements;
- Handles complaints and correspondence which relate to policy;
- Administers the construction, repair and emergency response program for the department on a Citywide basis.
- Demonstrates continuous effort to improve operations, decrease turnaround times, streamline work processes, and work cooperatively and jointly to provide quality seamless customer service.

including a minimum of four years of professional supervisory experience in parks and recreation management and a bachelor's degree in an acceptable field.

Recruitment, Hiring, and Staff Development Processes

After preparing appropriate job descriptions as part of the recruitment process, recreation, park, and leisure-service agencies must publicize position openings to encourage qualified individuals to apply.

This can be done in several ways: advertising in newspapers, newsletters, or through professional publications; publicizing openings at job fairs held at professional meetings; considering college interns who have already had experience in the agency, or other individuals who may have held part-time, volunteer, or seasonal positions; and publicizing job openings on the agency's Web site, or having them listed on Internet job-search data bases.

The hiring process involves a number of steps, including personal interviews; consideration of the individual's application form; follow-up on his or her personal references; examinations (when required); a rating of the applicant's strong and weak points in terms of skills, experience, and personality; and similar elements.

All of these elements go into the review process. Next, applicants are usually placed on an eligibility list, with hiring officers or the personnel department empowered to appoint from the three highest ranked candidates immediately, or when an opening occurs.

Staff Development. As Chapter 11 will show, staff development in public leisure-service agencies includes orientation and in-service training phases, ongoing supervision and counseling, and encouragement to take part in continuing education programs of professional enrichment.

This chapter has presented overall descriptions of the role of public leisure-service organizations, including their functions at three levels of government, innovative programming in a number of agencies, trends in the field, and, finally, personnel practices in government agencies.

Suggested Questions for Class Discussion or Essay Examinations

1. What are the primary recreation-related functions of the federal and state governments, and how do they contrast with each other? On the federal level, what special problems face agencies such as the National Park Service or Forest Service, and what steps are they taking to solve then?
2. The chapter describes several levels of local government agencies involved in recreation, park, and leisure-service operations. Identify and describe at least two of these, and show how they meet different public leisure needs.
3. Many municipal, tax-supported recreation and park organizations do more than simply provide play facilities and programs. What other important kinds of social, environmental, and similar significant responsibilities do such local agencies have? Cite illustrations either from the chapter or from your own experience.
4. Due to financial pressures, as well as an overall change in governmental strategies, many public leisure-service agencies have adopted businesslike, entrepreneurial marketing methods. Explain and give illustrations of this trend, What are its positive effects? Does it also have possible negative outcomes, and how can these be dealt with?
5. Most hiring in public leisure-service agencies is done within civil service structures. Explain the background of this statement and show how it applies in recreation and park employment practices. If there were no civil service controls on governmental hiring, what might some of the possible outcomes be?

Footnotes

[1] For a fuller discussion of the federal role, see Kraus, R. (1997). *Recreation and leisure in modern society.* Menlo Park, Calif.: Addison Wesley Longman, 244-257.

[2] Parks in peril. (1997). *U.S. News and World Report.* July 21, 24.

[3] Janofsky, M. (1999). Amid protests, land-protection plan goes to president. *New York Times.* Dec. 12, A-30.

[4] Ruch, J. (1999). Nature's guardians still face disrespect. *New York Times.* Dec. 22, A-27.

[5] Obmascik, M. (1999). Out of the ashes. *Mountain Sports and Living.* Jan./Feb.. 20.

[6] Kraus, op. cit., 257.

[7] Edginton, C., Jordan, D., DeGraaf, D., and Edginton, S. (1995). *Leisure and life satisfaction: foundational perspectives.* Dubuque, IA.: Brown and Benchmark, 160.

[8] Franklin, S. (1999). Operation recreation relief. *Parks and Recreation.* Oct., 78.

[9] Payne, L., Orsega-Smith, E., Spangler, K., and Godbey, G. (1999). Local parks and recreation for the health of it. *Parks and Recreation.* Oct., 72.

[10] Herszenhorn, D. (1999). For the people . . . governments go on line. *New York Times.* Sept. 30, G-1.

[11] Emmett, J., Havitz, M., and McCarville, R, (1996). Price subsidy policy for socioeconomically disadvantaged participants. *Journal of Park and Recreation Administration.* Spring, 63-80.

[12] *Fees and charges policies* (1997). Vancouver Board of Parks and Recreation Manual.

[13] Marfuggi, J., and Porth, R. (1999). A riverfront runs through it. *Parks and Recreation,* Jan. 48-55.

Chapter 4

Nonprofit Leisure-Service Agencies: The Voluntary Sector

Introduction

A second major category of leisure-service organizations in North American society involves so-called nonprofit or "voluntary" agencies, which serve millions of children, youth, and adults with varied educational, recreational and social-service programs.

These organizations, which are under the control of private citizen boards or other policy-making groups, often rely heavily on volunteer leadership. However, they also employ many thousands of paid, full-time professionals. They are designed to achieve significant personal and social goals for those they serve and for the community at large. While they usually do not refer to themselves as "recreation" organizations, providing sports, cultural and social activities, camping, and similar leisure opportunities are a major part of their operations.

Nonprofit organizations depend on varied sources for financial support: fund-raising drives and voluntary contributions; foundation grants; membership fees and charges for participation; and in some cases, payments for contracted services for federal or state governments. This chapter examines several leading examples of nonprofit leisure-service organizations, and describes their goals, programs, and employment practices.

Scope of Nonprofit Organizations

Nonprofit organizations represent an immense force in contemporary American life, operating within several important spheres of public concern, such as education, religion, environmental action, and charitable and welfare services. It was estimated in 1986 that nonprofit organizations employed 7.2 million people—about one in sixteen working Americans—and that the number would rise to 9.3 million by the mid-1990s.

In February 2000, the *New York Times* reported that the United States had about 770,000 nonprofit organizations, large and small, which took in an estimated $750 billion annually in fees, grants, donations, and investment earning.[1] Of this total number, a sizable segment provides recreation, park, and leisure services, usually as part of a multiservice programming approach.

While many such organizations may sponsor activities or programs that yield substantial revenues, and while they may have annual budgets involving millions of dollars, their purpose is *not* to clear a profit. Instead, they must convincingly demonstrate their charitable nature or their important contribution to community life to obtain nonprofit, tax-exempt status.

Youth-Serving Agencies

There are hundreds of voluntary organizations that serve children and youth and, in some cases, have membership that extend across the full age spectrum. One major segment of such groups is affiliated with religious organizations, although it may welcome members of different faiths. A second segment is totally nondenominational, although in some cases it may use the facilities of individual churches or synagogues.

Often, youth-serving organizations combine a host of social services, such as delinquency-prevention or citizenship training, with social-club programs, sports leagues, camping, and similar activities.

Even those organizations that do not have a formal religious connection, such as the Boy Scouts or Girl Scouts, usually have a strong moral code that they seek to impart to their young members, and which guides all membership and program practices. This function is particularly important today, when so many young people are subjected to a barrage of other stimuli and hedonistic leisure attractions in the popular media of movies, television, rock music, and video games. Experimentation with alcohol, drugs, and sex or involvement with violent and antisocial peer groups threatens the lives of millions of American youth, and it is the mission of the major youth-serving organizations to counter such negative influences.

Environmental learning and vocational development are also part of the agenda of many youth-serving organizations. Another important function of the major nonprofit groups of this type is to encourage youth to take part in healthy, challenging forms of play that will have strong lifetime carryover appeal.

Boys and Girls Clubs of America

With over three million youth served in 2,260 clubs around the United States, the Boys and Girls Clubs of America is the fastest growing youth-serving organization today. Originally consisting of two separate organizations for boys and girls, today the merged club movement holds a U.S. congressional charter and is endorsed by numerous leading civic, veterans, labor, and business associations. Its graduates, men and women whose early formative years included Boys and Girls Club membership, include leading sports, entertainment, political, and business figures.

From its national headquarters in Atlanta, Georgia, the: BGCA movement promotes locally based programs in cities around the country, where boys and girls of all races, religions, and cultures are served in building-centered programs designed to promote healthful life skills, the arts, sports, fitness and recreation, citizenship, and career development. Clubs require no proof of good character, are guidance oriented, and seek especially to serve at-risk youth in disadvantaged communities. While each club is an independent agency, with its own board and staff, the national organization and seven regional offices assist local groups in personnel recruitment and management training, fund-raising and fiscal management, public relations, and building design and construction methods.

With hundreds of its clubs situated in low-income public housing projects and a majority of its members drawn from single-parent and minority families, the Boys and Girls Clubs movement has demonstrated its effectiveness consistently. Operating with 9,500 full-time youth professionals and over 200,000 volunteers, clubs today meet on Native American reservations, in shopping malls, homeless shelters, orphanages, youth detention centers and churches, and on military bases both here and abroad. Recently, a Carnegie Council on Adolescent Development Report concluded:

> An evaluation of Boys and Girls Clubs of America's SMART Moves (substance-abuse prevention) initiative showed substantial differences between housing projects that had Clubs and those that did not. Residential areas with Clubs experience an overall reduction in alcohol and other drug use, drug trafficking, and other drug-related crime. On the national level [the Boy and Girls Clubs movement is a leading example] of theory-based interventions that have shown positive evaluation and replication results.[2]

An important element of the organization consists of Keystone Clubs, teen leadership groups that are designed to help teen club members become productive citizens and leaders through community service projects that improve neighborhood life. Examples of this organization's successful marketing efforts and its ability to obtain grant funds to support its work are shown in Figures 4-1 and 4-2.

Police Athletic League

Operating primarily in poverty areas of large cities, hundreds of Police Athletic League centers today also resist juvenile delinquency and seek to promote good citizenship as a primary thrust. Coordinated by the National Association of Police Athletic Leagues in North Palm Beach, Florida, this movement relies heavily on civilian staff and voluntary funding contributions, along with assistance by officers on special assignment from cooperative municipal police departments. It also uses varied and innovative fund-raising techniques (see Figure 4-3).

Figure 4-1
Example of marketing drive by Boys Clubs of America in 1988 (before its merger with the Girls Clubs organization).

Figure 4-2
Summary of increasing federal support for Boys and Girls Clubs of America during the 1990s
(Source: BGCA Annual Report, 1999)

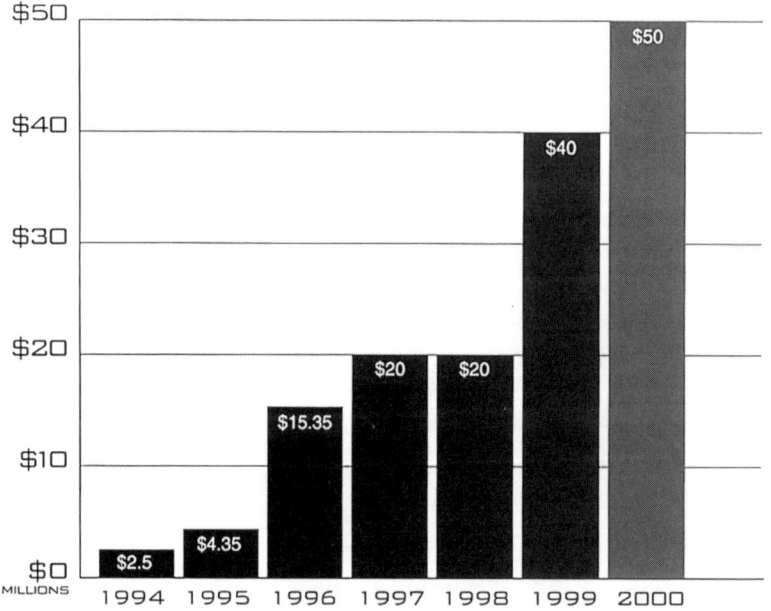

One of PAL's chief purposes has been to promote favorable relationships between youth and the police; and in a number of communities, police play a leading role in funding and staffing its centers. The organization's programs include sports and games, creative arts, drum and bugle corps, summer play streets, adventure camping and wilderness exposure, and varied job-training, counseling, and placement services, including projects serving school-dropout youth. Each year, the Police Athletic League sponsors a number of major tournaments and events, such as an annual conference and training seminar, national boxing championships, and a national PAL baseball "World Series" and youth festival in Niagara Falls, New York.

Boy Scouts of America

In terms of sheer numbers, the Boy Scouts of America reaches more youth and adult members than any comparable organization. With over 4.5 million youth members on five levels, from the youngest Tiger Cubs BSA to Varsity Scouting and Venturing for senior high school students, the organization has over 1.2 million adult members in leadership and staff roles in 138,775 Scout units and Explorer posts.

The Boy Scouting movement is primarily a volunteer organization, although it employs 4,000 paid, professional leaders and executives. Over 40 million people have been involved in scouting since it was incorporated in 1910 and chartered by Congress in 1916.

The primary purpose of Boy Scouting is to develop desirable traits of character and good citizenship. Its program emphasizes mental and physical fitness, vocational and social development, and the enrichment of youth hobbies and prevocational interests, achieved heavily through adventure and camp craft skills and community-service activities.

Once viewed chiefly as a small-town or suburban program designed chiefly for white, middle-class boys, two decades ago Scouting moved vigorously into a new emphasis on serving inner-city, minority-group youth. Today, in addition to its broader program emphases, it sponsors a National Crime Prevention Program in cooperation with national law-enforcement organizations.

Although the Boy Scout movement is intended primarily to serve young boys, many women are involved as scout leaders. High school girls, for example, gain career development skills, along with the boys, in the Learning for Life Exploring program.

Girl Scouts of the United States of America

This is the world's leading organization dedicated solely to serving girls—helping them to build character and develop skills for success in the real world. Today, there are 3.6 million Girl Scouts consisting of 2.7 million girl members and 860,000 adult members. Founded in 1912, Girl Scouts of the USA was chartered by Congress in 1950. Through membership in the World Association of Girl Guides and Girl Scouts, it is part or a worldwide family of 10 million girls and adults in 140 countries.

Through various enriching experiences, such as field trips and camping, sports clinics and team play, community service projects, cultural exchanges, and environmental stewardships, girls are helped to reach their individual potentials, develop positive personal values and learn to contribute to community life.

Girl Scouting serves girls from five to 17 in five age-defined groupings: Daisy, Brownie, Junior, Cadet, and Senior. They participate through more than 226,000 troops and groups

Figure 4-3
Police Athletic League brochure promoting the sale of equipment and promotional accessories.

in the United States and in 81 countries through Girl Scouts Overseas. Through the Girl Scout Promise, and the Girl Scout Law, they commit themselves to religious and patriotic values and to responsible behavior in every aspect of their lives. Girl Scouting provides an excellent example of how modern technology is used in the operation of varied leisure-service organizations. In 1998, for example, the GSUSA used the following technological tools:

Girl Scout Bulletin Board System. Regularly scheduled, real-time [electronic] chats enabled councils to ask questions of GSUSA staff and of their peers in other councils.

Video Teleconferences. Two live nationally broadcast interviews were conducted with the National President and the National Director. Council viewers participated in real time with questions by telephone links.

Software. At national meetings of Girl Scout Council Presidents and Executive Directors, new software systems were used for qualitative information gathering from, and interactive discussions with, over 600 participants.[3]

In addition, Girl Scouting's Information and Referral Center provides assistance to council volunteers and staff, as well as parents and the general public, fielding a growing volume of E-mail inquiries. Like its male counterparts, GSUSA has also responded to the benefits-based management thrust by commissioning a National Outcomes Study by SPEC Associates to determine the positive outcomes of Girl Scouting. It also used the market research firm of Market Dynamics to interview an extensive sample of adult volunteers to gain guidance in its recruitment and program-support efforts.

Over the years, like other youth-serving organizations, Girl Scouting has changed its emphasis from rather broad personal and social goals to more critical challenges—particularly those facing girls and women in today's society. Senior Girl Scouts today do volunteer work in hospitals, museums, child care and environmental programs and often are involved with disabled groups.

Religion-Affiliated Leisure-Service Organizations

As examples of leisure-service nonprofit organizations with religious affiliations or sponsorship, the Young Women's Christian Association and Young Men's Christian Association, like the Catholic Youth Organization or the Young Men's and Young Women's Hebrew Association, serve a broader age range than the youth groups just described. In each case, they involve elements of programming and management practice linked to the major faith that they represent.

Despite this emphasis, the bulk of programming in the YMCA and the YWCA, for example, is similar to activities offered in many public recreation agencies. Past studies have shown that, although these organizations are nominally affiliated with Protestantism, many of their members are Roman Catholic or Jewish. In each case, they sponsor a network of facilities and programs with varied recreation, education, and social-service functions. Although their titles include such words as "young" or "youth," they serve a full range of age groups extending from services for pregnant women and girls (or preschool programs) to senior citizen activities.

Young Women's Christian Association

Like many other nonprofit organizations, the Young Women's Christian Association defines its mission in broad, idealistic terms, such as in the following statement by the national YWCA:

> The YWCA works for the empowerment of women through advocacy on public issues that effect and concern women and the lives they touch. Men can join as associate members with all membership benefits except voting rights. The YWCA's goals encompass the struggle for peace, justice, freedom and dignity for all people and the elimination of racism wherever it exists.

While the Young Women's Christian Association offers a full range of social, cultural, recreational, and sports activities for its members and guests, it focuses heavily on the needs of women and girls today. Many YWCAs sponsor conferences and workshops dealing with domestic violence, job counseling, single-parent roles and day-care options, juvenile justice services, and similar issues. Typically, such programs have titles like "Assertiveness Training for Women," "Career Development," "Personal Finance," "Living Single," "Know Your Body," and "The Divorce Experience." many YWCAs sponsor services for battered women, career planning and employment counseling, and developmental day-care programs.

In addition, many YWCAs, particularly in well-to-do small-town or suburban areas, provide fitness facilities and health-related programs, including seminars, physical fitness assessment, weight-control groups, and similar services.

Young Men's Christian Association

Taken altogether, the YMCA is the largest nonprofit community service organization in the United States, committed to meeting the health and social-service needs of 16.9 million men, women, and children. Through teen clubs, environmental programs, substance- abuse prevention, youth sports, family nights, mentoring and job training, international exchange and other services, it seeks to fulfill the following mission:

> Ys help people develop values and behavior that are consistent with Christian principles. Ys are for people of all faiths, races, abilities, ages and incomes. No one is turned away for inability to pay. YMCA's strength is in the people they bring together.

The YMCA operates under the leadership of a national board, as shown in Figure 4-4. Each individual association is a charitable, independent, not-for-profit organization, qualifying like similar groups under Section 501 (c) (3) of the U.S. Tax Code. YMCAs are required by their national constitution to pay annual dues, to refrain from discrimination, and to support the organization's mission. All other decisions and policies are local choices, including programs offered, staffing, and style of operation.

As an example of how local units exist within the framework of a larger national federation or governing body, a single YMCA, the Peninsula Family YMCA in San Mateo, California, is part of the YMCA of San Francisco, an incorporated nonprofit organization with thirteen branches in a four-county area (see Figure 4-5). Other community YMCAs may be totally separate or independent agencies, but all report participation statistics and financial data to the national board, and all adhere to its policies and make use of its services.

Figure 4-4
Organization chart, National YMCA.

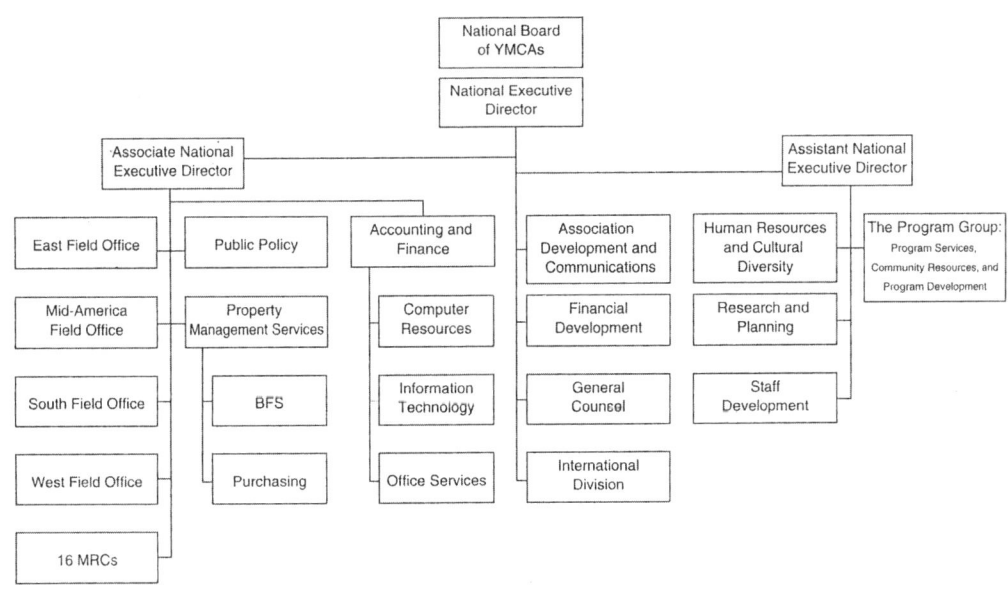

In a report on trends affecting the Young Men's Christian Association at the end of the 20th century, it was noted that Ys collaborated heavily with other community organizations, such as hospitals, local park and recreation agencies, and colleges and schools. Program trends included strong emphases on aquatic, fitness, and camping services, with child care, community development, and family assistance receiving a high level of agency priority. Many Ys serve older adults and members with disabilities, and local units are moving heavily into providing computer-literacy programs, particularly for youth.

As part of its marketing emphasis, the YMCA has developed extensive links with corporate sponsors. For example, in 1998, PepsiCo, Inc., became the first "mission partner" of the YMCA, designating the organization as its charity of choice. In a ten-year commitment to the YMCA PepsiCo will provide an annual gift of $1.6 million to the 2,300 YMCAs in the United States. In terms of their overall budget operation, YMCAs had a total income of $3.1 billion annually in the late 1990s, with the chief sources of revenue payment to take part in Y programs, membership dues, charitable contributions, fees for resident camping, and government contracts and foundation grants.

Finally, it should be recognized that YMCAs represent a major international movement, with programs in more than 120 countries around the world serving more than thirty million people.

Figure 4-5
Program summary of Peninsula Family YMCA activities and services. Despite the name of the organization, the executive director and many leading staff members are women.

PENINSULA FAMILY YMCA
1877 South Grant St., San Mateo 94402 (415) 286-9622

YOUTH & FAMILY PROGRAMS

Child & Family Programs - Holly Cords   294-2614
(Indian Guides, ChildWatch, Birthday Party, Family Events)
Day Camp - Patty Gershaneck   294-2605
(Summer and School Breaks, After School San Bruno)
Swim Lessons/Team - Jill Fleming   294-2609
Youth Sports - Steve Martin   294-2624
(Youth Basketball, Baseball, Karate, Soccer, etc.)
Teens - Justin Moscoso   294-2617
(Teen Leaders, Youth & Government, Teen Activities)

ADULT PROGRAMS

Starting a Fitness Program Sign up for an orientation or assessment, or call Steve, Ben, Becky or Kathy below.
Personal Training - Ben Kwock, RN (Personal Training, Special Medical Needs, Disabilities)   294-2611
Fitness Appointments Hotline (Make/Cancel Appointments, Assessment/Orientation Questions)   294-2682
Aerobics/ Group Fitness - Becky Ruppel   294-2610
Aerobics Schedule Hotline   294-2670
Adult Sports - Steve Martin (Basketball, Volleyball, Triathlon, Biking, Hiking)   294-2624
Adult Swim Programs - Jill Fleming   294-2609
Health Education - Kathy McFarland (Health Classes, Nutrition, Weight Management, Sports Inj.)   294-2638
Active Older Adults - Marie Siddons   294-2622 ext. 414

COUNSELING & YOUTH AT RISK

Project FOCYS Youth & Family Counseling   349-7969
(Professional, Affordable, Sliding-Scale Fee)
Building Futures Mentors - Kimberly Wheeler   294-2619
(Referrals and Adult Volunteer Mentors)
Youth at Risk Program - Dr. Dale Lete   294-2613

ADMINISTRATIVE/ MEMBERSHIP

Executive Director - Beth Salazar   294-2601
Assoc. Exec. Director - Mike Fitzsimmons   294-2602
Membership Director - Mary McNair   294-2603
Membership Bookkeeper - Judy Hartmire   294-2623
Facility Maintenance - Gary Cockrell   294-2607

YMCA Volunteer Hotline   294-2622 ext. 684

Catholic Youth Organization

Operating under the umbrella of the overall Catholic Charities movement, the Catholic Youth Organization was established as a national body in 1951. Today, the National CYO Federation has an office in Washington, D.C., as well as many citywide or diocesan coordinators. While there are many professional CYO leaders, program specialists, and directors, the parish structure is the core of the Catholic Youth Organization, with the parish priest and adult volunteers from church congregations providing the bulk of direct program leadership.

Within a religious context, CYO provides varied retreats, workshops—religious education and service programs that strengthen the character and spiritual values of its members. However, a major part of its youth involvement is in team sports competition in local leagues and against other CYOs, as well as in camping, performing arts, and social programs. Sports, in particular, are highly regarded not only as a means of attracting young people to Catholic Youth Organization membership, but also as a way of promoting desirable moral values and social behavior. The coach is considered an important educator in this sense, and is expected to reinforce the positive influences of home and family, school and church.

Many CYOs operate summer and year-round camps. For example, Camp Christopher in Akron, Ohio, has extensive programs of sports, aquatics, riding, nature study, and self-testing adventure activities, as well as special sessions for disabled campers.

Young Men's and Young Women's Hebrew Association

There are over 250 YM-YWHAs, Jewish Community Centers, and camps serving over one million members throughout the United States and Canada. Unlike the YMCA and YWCA, which are separate organizations, the Jewish Ys combine the sexes in their memberships and programs. Like them, YM-YWHAs do not consider themselves primarily recreation agencies, but instead, community-service organizations with a broad mission statement:

> To meet the leisure-time social, cultural and recreational needs of its membership, embracing both sexes and all age groups.
>
> To stimulate individual growth and personality development by encouraging interest and capacity for group and community participation.
>
> To teach leadership responsibility and democratic process through group participation.
>
> To provide certain limited guidance services, including individual counseling, in preparation for specialized services when indicated.
>
> To encourage citizenship education and responsibility among its members and, as a social welfare agency, to participate in community-wide programs of social betterment.

As this statement suggests, YM-YWHAs and Jewish Community Centers regard themselves as closely linked to the social work movement and often draw their professional and executive personnel from schools of social work. However, they also provide extensive recreational programs, including competitive sports, fitness activities, creative and cultural arts groups, and many other services related to Jewish history, religion, and identity.

Like the YMCA, YWCA, and Catholic Youth Organization, many Jewish Community Centers operate summer, and in some cases, year-round camps. An unusual example is found in Maryland, where the Jewish Community Center of Greater Baltimore manages a well-designed and well-equipped recreation park. (See page 78).

Other Church Groups

Beyond such denomination-wide organizations, many individual sects, churches, and synagogues also sponsor religious-education and recreation-related programs, particularly for young people.

For example, such Protestant sects as Methodists, Baptists, and Lutherans have national youth organizations with a strong spiritual, character-building component, which also stresses social, sports, camping, and other recreational programs. Similarly, individual churches or networks of churches or temples of the same denomination within a city or metropolitan region provide clubs and other leisure programs and leadership-training activities, along with religious education and retreats.

Numerous other nonprofit community organizations—both religious and nonsectarian—sponsor similar services for children and youth. They include such groups as Camp Fire Boys and Girls, the 4-H Club, the Children's Aid Society, and many settlement houses and privately operated recreation centers, particularly in larger cities.

Special-Interest Organizations

Another important group of nonprofit leisure-service organizations includes national associations or program sponsors that are designed to promote public awareness and participation in specific areas of recreational activities. Such organizations may focus on games and sports, hobbies, cultural activities, varied forms of outdoor recreation, and numerous other pastimes.

In addition to directly sponsoring instructional programs, leagues, events and tournaments, and annual award ceremonies and similar programs, special-interest organizations may define classes or levels of involvement, eligibility requirements, and other procedural guidelines for participation. They often develop training programs and certification plans to identify qualified instructors, coaches, or officials in their fields of interest. In addition, they usually carry on research programs that monitor their pastimes and report on statistics of involvement each year.

Sports-Related Organizations

Many nonprofit associations represent a single sport, such as youth baseball, football or soccer, tennis or bowling, and are described in Chapter 9. A number of such organizations have close ties with equipment manufacturers or other companies that comprise their memberships and contribute to their budgets. Despite such forms of support, these special-interest associations are not profit oriented, and they make an important contribution to the nation's wealth of organized recreation and leisure-service programs.

Other special-interest groups in sport and outdoor recreation are totally independent and free of commercial ties, relying fully on their self-generated revenues, which are acquired through membership fees, spectator and television revenues, and similar sources. In some cases, organizations that represent a given field of leisure activity may combine both commercial and nonprofit groups in their memberships.

American Camping Association

This is the largest national body serving the organized camping field, with more than 5,000 members who are camping professionals affiliated with a variety of nonprofit agencies, public authorities, religious and fraternal organizations, and private, commercially operated camps. Camping clearly represents a huge sector of the organized leisure-service movement:

> In 1999, almost nine million young people benefited from a summer camp experience at an estimated 8,500 camps throughout the United States. Approximately 5,500 are resident (overnight) camps, 2,200 are day camps and 750 offer both day and resident programs.
>
> Of the more than 2,200 ACA-accredited camps, approximately 1,430 are dedicated to meeting the special needs of campers with physical, emotional or mental challenges. Approximately 53 percent of ACA camps offer coed programs, 28 percent offer female-only programs and 19 percent offer male-only programs.... According to a 1996 survey of ACA camp directors, parents cite the following as the most important reasons for sending their children to camp: (1) camp helps to build self-confidence and self-esteem (28%); (2) camp is a safe environment (22%); and (3) camp is a place to build social skills and make friends (21%).[4]

With its national headquarters in Martinsville, Indiana, the American Camping Association plays a leading role in inspecting and accrediting all types of summer camps and has established about 300 standards for health, safety, and program quality that are recognized by courts of law and government regulators. ACA accreditation is a voluntary process with a fifty-year history. Beyond this function, the association contributes to the professionalization of the camping field through research, publication, continuing education programs, and acting as a spokesperson and advocate for organized camping.

Other Types of Nonprofit Organizations

Many other national organizations promote specific aspects of the leisure-service field, either by sponsoring national competitions or training programs or by representing a single important area of participation.

All-American Soap Box Derby

One of the most unusual and successful of such organizations is the All-American Soap Box Derby, which is built around a single major annual event held each year in Akron, Ohio.

Operating on three levels, the "Stock," Super Stock," and, "Masters" divisions, the Soap Box Derby involves boys and girls between the ages of nine and 16 in building and racing homemade, nonmotorized cars down a sloping track or street. Originally, the cars were designed and built haphazardly, using orange crates, baby-buggy wheels and other randomly chosen materials. Today, they must be constructed from standardized kits, with the young contestants doing the bulk of the work, although they may be assisted by adults.

Figure 4-6
Details of the JCC Recreation Park, listed on the agency's Web site.

Recreation Park
The Rosenbloom Owings Mills JCC boasts a beautiful Recreation Park complete with six beautiful outdoor pools (large family pool, 6-lane lap pool, 3-4 foot instructional pool and 3 baby pools), four lit tennis courts, a 1 1/2 acre playground, picnic areas, snack bar and a sand volleyball court.

The Recreation Park is open from Memorial Day through Labor Day. Complete use of the Recreation Park is included in the reasonable cost of a full JCC membership.

Sponsored by the Goodyear Tire Company, the Soap Box Derby is a nonprofit organization administered by a National Control Board in Akron, which sets, interprets, and enforces rules and policies in the competition. Local race programs are sponsored by various civic clubs, service organizations, and business firms, leading to local championships in the three divisions that determine who will compete in the All-American World Championship Race in Akron each Year. Today, Soap Box Derby races are held in several foreign countries, and some winners of these events compete in the Akron championship races.

While this may appear to be a relatively simple contest, it involves a complex set of rules and policies and competition stages. For example, local race sponsors must schedule Derby demonstrations, enlisting race entrants and conducting car construction clinics. They must also follow precise procedural guidelines in managing races.

American Sport Fishing Association

As indicated earlier, many nonprofit organizations promote and regulate varied forms of outdoor recreation, from hunting and fishing to sailing, wilderness camping, and riflery and archery. One such organization is the American Sport Fishing Association, a powerful association supported by hundreds of manufacturers of fishing equipment, boat manufacturers, fishing guides and resorts, and fishing advocacy groups.

As an industry trade organization, the American Sport Fishing Association seeks to promote recreational fishing on every level, through sponsoring major tournaments, providing clinics and instruction for professional guides or leaders in the field, holding fishing expositions that attract thousands of enthusiasts in numerous cities, often as part of larger sports shows, and supporting legislation and government action favorable to fishing. Clearly, fishing today represents a highly popular leisure pursuit with major economic benefits-as shown in a mid-1990s research report that calculates the total economic output of fishing as $108.4 billion, with total federal and state sales and excise tax payments of over $5 billion.

In addition, the American Sport Fishing Association spearheads a number of specialized efforts to upgrade public appreciation for recreational fishing. It promotes curriculum-based aquatic education and stewardship, and encourages sport fishing among American youth through its Future Fisherman Foundation.

This program, which sponsors the nationally acclaimed "Hooked on Fishing-Not on Drugs education program, is conducted in cooperation with the U.S. Department of Agriculture, the Fish and Wildlife Service, and the National 4-H Sport Fishing Committee. The association also sponsors a national fishing information service, the 1-800-Ask-Fish program; a fishing tackle loaner program; and the Fish America Foundation, which supports various civic groups in conservation and fishery improvement projects.

National Outdoor Leadership School

Numerous other nonprofit organizations promote environmental education and ecologically friendly uses of the environment. One such organization is the National Outdoor Leadership School (NOLS), established in 1965 in Lander, Wyoming. Since that time, it has taught wilderness skills and leadership to over 30,000 students. Its courses, which focus on different outdoor skills ranging from backpacking, mountaineering, and rock climbing to sea kayaking, sailing, whitewater boating, and skiing, are widely recognized as setting the standard for international outdoor education (see Figure 4-7).

As a private nonprofit school focusing on experiential education, NOLS has nine branch schools located in Alaska, Arizona, Idaho, Western Canada, Washington, Wyoming, Mexico, Kenya, and Chile. It offers over sixty courses in wilderness areas worldwide for students ranging from the teen years to over fifty. In addition to these courses, which often take novices into remote settings for extended periods, it offers advanced instructors courses in five skill areas for experienced outdoor leaders. In addition to formal courses, the National Outdoor Leadership School runs trips for alumni, holds conferences and seminars on wilderness-related topics, conducts research, and produces an extensive body of literature dealing with environmental conservation, wilderness skills, risk management, and leadership.

Overview of the Nonprofit Leisure-Service Field

The nonprofit organizations described in this chapter consist of large, national groups or federations with many thousands, or even millions, of members and program participants.

However, they represent only the tip of the iceberg, with many hundreds of other nonprofit youth-serving or special-interest organizations serving every sector of the recreation, park, and leisure field. As the agencies presented here make clear, although these organizations are nonprofit, in many cases they have impressive budgets and utilize a variety of fund-raising strategies.

Rather than be dependent solely on funds from charitable drives such as Community Chest or United Way campaigns, many volunteer organizations charge substantial fees, sell products identified with their logos, carry on cooperative promotions with major corporations or solicit funding support from them, and obtain helpful grants from government and private foundations.

While little attention is usually paid to such agencies in programs of professional preparation in colleges and universities—and while they are rarely represented at recreation and park conferences—the reality is that such groups employ huge numbers of year-round professional staff members. These men and women work in direct leadership and supervisory roles, as program specialists or administrators in national or regional headquarters or in local councils and service units. As such, these professions should be of interest to all individuals considering careers in the leisure-service field.

Employment Practices in Nonprofit organizations

Unlike hiring practices in public recreation and park agencies, where civil service requirements control most hiring and impose a degree of uniformity on many categories of jobs, employment practices in nonprofit organizations vary widely.

Often, individuals hired for full-time, year-round jobs in such organizations will have come up through the ranks, having begun in an entry-level leadership or clerical position. For more advanced positions, they may be required to have had specialized training or academic degrees in such fields as social work, religious education, and environmental studies. In other cases, business training or a high level of competence in a particular area of program service will be required.

However, many younger persons move into entry-level positions on the basis of having had volunteer leadership experience or long-term membership involvement in a given type of agency. Still others may count on their having done field work or internship assignments in their college course work as experience that is considered valuable. Given these varied expectations, it is helpful to examine hiring and staff development practices in a number of nonprofit organizations.

Young Men's Christian Association

As noted earlier, this organization is the largest nonprofit organization in the United States. It has approximately 36,000 full-time paid employees, with a full-time equivalent of an estimated 25,000 part-time workers.

YMCA employees are hired in many specialized positions on the basis of detailed job descriptions for these professional roles. Staff members attend training programs that cover a variety of topics. (See Figure 4-8, which shows a partial listing of available courses). Since 1989, such nationally coordinated program schools have grown from eleven sites serving 1,700 individuals to twenty-four sites serving close to 6,000 staff members in 1998. Since a new training program was introduced in 1992, over 34,000 certification courses have been offered, and nearly 340,000 certifications have been issued.

Boys and Girls Clubs of America

This steadily growing organization sponsors a unique Junior Staff Development small-group program, funded by American Express, that assists members between the ages of eleven

Figure 4-7
Contents page of National Outdoor Leadership School catalog outlining courses and services.

TABLE OF CONTENTS

A Look At NOLS   3
Meet the people and history behind the leader in wilderness education.

Wilderness Leadership Courses   6
These courses have a sharp focus on wilderness skills education and leadership. Course types:
- Backpacking
- Backpacking and River Travel
- Adventure (for 14-15 year olds)
- Sea Kayaking
- Sailing
- Canoeing
- Natural History

Courses for Educators   24
These courses are specifically designed for current outdoor educators or those wishing to pursue a career in outdoor education. Course types:
- Winter
- Trip Leader
- Backpacking
- Sea Kayaking
- Sailing
- Instructor

Leadership Semesters   32
Semester courses are intensive courses that combine a number of activities for an extended period of up to three months, with an emphasis on skill development and leadership training. Semester locations:
- Australia
- Kenya
- Pacific Northwest
- Southwest
- Alaska
- Mexico
- Patagonia
- The Rockies

Mountaineering Courses   46
These courses are highly skill intensive, with an emphasis on becoming an accomplished mountaineer. Course locations:
- Alaska
- Gannett Peak
- North Cascades
- Wind River Range
- Denali
- Himalaya
- Patagonia
- Waddington Range

Skills Courses   52
These courses focus on learning specific skills in an extended expedition format. Course types:
- Horsepacking
- Rock Climbing
- Whitewater
- Skiing

Safety Is a Priority at NOLS   58
Financial Aid   59
Core Curriculum and College Credit   59
How to Apply   60
Course Dates/Tuition   61
Course Finder   65
Alumni   67

FINDING YOUR WAY AROUND THE NOLS CATALOG
Use the navigation bar on the right hand side of each page. The upper 1/2 of the bar tells you what type of course is on the page. The black section in the middle tells what outdoor skills are taught on the courses on the page (the key to the icons is on page 2) The green section tells you where in the world the courses on that page are offered.
The NOLS Course Finder is in the back of the catalog and will help you find courses by outdoor skill, location, month of the year, length, and age.

SPECIALIZED COURSES

Adult Education
Adult learners are welcome on all NOLS courses. In addition, we offer some courses specifically for those over 25 years of age. The curriculum is the same as it is for any other NOLS course, but offered in a time frame that works for people juggling careers, families and other responsibilities. Look for these courses and symbols on the following pages:

 25 And Over
Wind River Wilderness   8
Alaska Sea Kayaking   13
Brooks Range Backpacking   15
Brooks Range Canoe and Kayak   15
Mexico Sea Kayaking   17
Mexico Backpacking   19
Kenya Wilderness   22

Tanzania Wilderness   23
North Cascades Mountaineering   50
Skiing   56
Whitewater   56

 50 And Over
Alaska Sea Kayaking   13

 Women-only Courses
Women have been welcomed on all NOLS courses since the school's founding in 1965. Additionally, we offer these courses which feature the standard NOLS curriculum in an all-female environment.
Mexico Sea Kayaking   17
Rock Climbing   55

 Alumni-only Courses
Over 300 NOLS alumni return to the school each year to further their wilderness education. Graduates can choose from any of our course offerings. We offer two courses each year which are specifically designed for our alumni.
Gannett Peak Mountaineering   48
Denali Mountaineering   49

Utah's Canyonlands tower above a NOLS course enroute to a new campsite (cover photo by Mark Langston). The school celebrates 35 years of outdoor education this year and this catalog commemorates this landmark. Early day students may remember the red, white and blue patch on this cover.

Figure 4-8
Partial listing of YMCA training programs available in 1997.

1997 Program School Course List *(cont'd)*

Courses listed will definitely be included in the schedule of the Program School listed at the top of the column.

Requests to add courses will only be considered if the request is made to the Program School director at least seven (7) months prior to the school start date.

Refer to each Program School's brochure for the final list of courses available.

Course	Page
Sports	54
Gymnastics Instructor	54
Gymnastics Trainer	54
Youth Sports Director	54
Youth Sports Trainer	55
Youth Volleyball Instructor	55
Youth Volleyball Trainer	55
Youth Racquetball Instructor	55
Youth Racquetball Trainer	56
Triathlon Director	56
Triathlon Trainer	56
Teen Leadership	56
Teen Leadership Director	56
Teen Leadership Trainer	56
Earth Service Corps Director	57
Earth Service Corps Trainer	57
Youth and Comm'y Development	57
Black/Minority Achiever Director	57
Black/Minority Achiever Trainer	58
Youth Achievers Director	58
Youth Achievers Trainer	58
Principles of Youth Work*	59
Principles of Youth Work Trainer*	59
Listening, Feedback, and Pos. Discipline*	60
Listening, Feed., Pos. Discipline Trainer*	60
Character Dev't. and Self-Esteem*	60
Character Dev't. and Self-Esteem Trainer*	60
Safety Issues*	61
Safety Issues Trainer*	61
Case Management*	61
Case Management Trainer*	61
Working with Low-Income Kids*	62
Low-Income Kids Trainer*	62
Under. Your Comm'y and Its Culture*	62
Under. Your Comm'y/Culture Trainer*	62
Conflict Management and Negotiation*	63
Conflict Management Trainer*	63
Under. Teens and Substance Abuse*	63
Under. Teens/Substance Abuse Trainer*	63

Column headers (Program School locations and dates):
Phoenix, AZ • 1/9–15; Mobile, AL • 1/25–31; New York, NY • 2/26–3/5; Des Moines, IA • 4/3–9; Houston, TX • 4/4–10; Denver, CO • 4/18–26; San Francisco, CA • 5/2–8; Tampa, FL • 5/3–9; Columbus, OH • 5/16–22; Springfield, MA • 5/28–6/3; Baltimore, MD • 5/31–6/6; Long Beach, CA • 6/4–10; Tacoma, WA • 7/25–31; West Chester, PA • 8/15–21; Rockford, IL • 9/19–24; Black Mtn., NC • 9/21–26; Rochester, NY • 9/24–30; Nashville, TN • 9/25–10/2; Frmnt Ht. Sprng • 10/4–10; Boston, MA • 10/16–22; Honolulu, HI • 11/7–13

(Youth and Community Development continues on the next page)

* Special scholarships available through Keeping Our Promise Grant. See page 16.

Figure 4-9
Summer camp promotional brochure of Girl Scouts of Southeastern Pennsylvania.

and eighteen in exploring a career in human services—particularly in Boys and Girls Club work.

Through hands-on experiences in the club or community setting, field trips to other service organizations, and one-on-one guidance from club staff, youth prepare for possible future roles as human-service professionals or volunteer leaders in such organizations.

On a broader scale, Boys and Girls Clubs of America spends approximately $9 million a year on leadership training, staff development and support of youth programs through planning and consultation efforts.

While hiring practices vary among different clubs, the general practice has been that individuals employed on a full-time basis in managerial or program leadership roles in Boys and Girls Clubs affiliated with the national organization are eligible for certification as professional staff members—if requirements are met with respect to (1) *education,* involving a degree in an appropriate field from an accredited four-year college; (2) *training and continuing education* with a total of ten credits to be gained in attendance at workshops, conferences, or courses, to be approved by a National Certification board; and (3) *experience,* including at least two years of full-time paid employment in managerial or program positions in an affiliated BGCA agency or on the national staff.

Boy Scouts of America

As mentioned earlier, although Boy Scouting is a volunteer-based organization, 4,000 professional staff members are responsible for working with volunteer committees and community leaders to assist them in organizing and conducting successful Scouting programs.

Different aspects of the professional Scouter's job, as defined in the late 1990s, include (1) *sales,* involving the promotion of Scouting among different community organizations; (2) *finance* in various efforts and campaigns to raise funds to support local councils and troops; (3) *administration* in the total management of assigned districts or service areas; and (4) *public relations,* requiring good communications and interpersonal skills in telling Scouting's story to the public.

Entry-level requirements for Boy Scout positions include a bachelor's degree from an accredited college or university, U.S. citizenship or declared intention to become a citizen, and such personal qualities as willingness and ability to devote long and irregular hours to the organization's objectives. Staff members are also expected to show dedication to serving others and belief in the Scout Oath and Law, as well as adherence to Boy Scouting membership standards. One controversial issue involving Scout hiring practices in the late 1990s concerned the organization's rejection of homosexual staff members in New Jersey and subsequent court decisions overruling and then approving this policy.

Aside from such general requirements, Boy Scouts of America sponsors numerous training programs for volunteer staff members at different levels and in different areas of responsibility.

In *all* youth-serving agencies today, it is essential that leaders subscribe to the basic philosophy of the sponsoring agency in such areas as program goals and values, or issues related to gender roles or intercultural sensitivity. As a single example of the latter point, the Girl Scouts today place heavy emphasis on nurturing racially and ethnically diverse memberships and positive intercultural programs and relationships. (Fig. 4-9 illustrates this point vividly.) Typically, the same Girl Scout organization designs promotional brochures with enrollment messages printed not only in English, but also in Spanish and three Asian languages.

Emphasis on Special Skills

As indicated, in many other areas of nonprofit agency programming, such as sports, aquatics, outdoor recreation, or the arts, emphasis is placed on hiring individuals who have special expertise or certification in a given activity area.

As a single example of organizations that provide such training and expertise, the National Outdoor Leadership School enrolls over 2,800 students and hires over 450 instructors and over 150 full-time and part-time administrators and support staff each year. It has certified over 1,300 instructors since its founding and is actively seeking to diversify its students, instructors, and administrators with a scholarship program for women and members of minorities, in order to equip more individuals for work in outdoor recreation programs. Many other nonprofit organizations conduct similar training courses, institutes, and camps, and many individuals already employed in such fields attend them in order to expand their skills.

Having examined public and nonprofit leisure-service agencies, we now turn in Chapter 5 to the third important element in this field—commercial, profit-seeking recreation businesses.

Suggested Questions for Class Discussion or Essay Examinations

1. How can we call organizations such as the Ys or other youth-serving groups "nonprofit," when they obviously charge significant fees for membership or other program activities? Similarly, does the term "voluntary" mean that such organizations are run totally by volunteers? What role *do* volunteers play in nonprofit leisure-service agencies?
2. Pick any two of the organizations described in detail in the early section of this chapter, such as Boys and Girls Clubs, Boy or Girl Scouts, or any of the Ys. What purposes do they share in common, and in what ways do they differ in terms of program focus, possible funding support, or similar elements?
3. In the past, most nonprofit youth-serving organizations tended to be sharply separated by gender; that is, administrators, leaders, and those served all were of one gender or the other. How has this changed in recent years? Cite examples from the chapter or from your own experience.
4. Many of the nonprofit organizations cited in this chapter deal with outdoor recreation, camping, or environmental concerns. What are some of the positive contributions they make in this area? Based on your own observation, does outdoor recreation always have a favorable impact on the environment?
5. If you were to consider working for a nonprofit organization, what kinds of staff training or continuing education programs might you be able to look forward to within the organization itself?

Footnotes

[1] Johnston, D. (2000). Creating waves in nonprofit sea. *New York Times*, Feb. 2, C-12.
[2] *A matter of time: Risk and opportunity in the nonschool hours.* American Council on Adolescent Development, in Program Brochure, Boys and Girls Clubs of America.
[3] *Annual Report 1998.* New York, N.Y.: Girl Scouts of U.S.A.
[4] *American Camping Association Fact Sheet.* (2000). Martinsville, Ind.

Chapter 5

Commercial Recreation Businesses

Introduction

Profit-oriented recreation businesses provide the greatest variety of leisure opportunities in the United States today, and certainly the highest volume of consumer spending and employment on a year-round, paid basis.

Such entrepreneurial ventures include privately operated campgrounds, resorts, and travel agencies; health and fitness spas; professional sports teams and stadiums; theme parks and water-play parks; skating rinks, bowling centers, and dance studios; residential camps of many types for children and youth; and family play centers.

Beyond such settings and services, manufacturers and retail establishments that satisfy the public's need for sports and outdoor recreation equipment, toys and games, and other products for family recreational use might also be considered forms of profit-oriented leisure businesses. This chapter does not attempt to cover all of these kinds of ventures. Instead, it describes three basic types of recreation businesses, and then analyzes the total field from an employment and careers perspective.

Commercial Recreation Defined

While some writers refer to for-profit leisure-service enterprises as the "market sector" of organized recreation, the most commonly used term for this field is *commercial recreation*. It is easily defined. Bullaro and Edginton write:

> A commercial leisure service organization can be thought of as a business, the primary purpose of which is to serve people while at the same time making a profit. [It] has two basic characteristics. First, it creates and distributes leisure services; second, it has as its primary goal, profit.[1]

The profit motive separates recreation businesses from other types of leisure-service sponsors. Public and voluntary nonprofit agencies may indeed charge for their programs and way even seek to clear a profit on individual activities, but their overall purpose is to contribute to important community, social, and personal needs of participants. Similarly, campus, armed forces, and employee-service recreation programs seek to meet the needs of their members and sponsoring agencies, rather than clear a monetary profit.

However, it would be wrong to assume that commercial recreation sponsors care only about financial gain. Many such businesses, including camps, fitness centers, outdoor recreation ventures, and family play programs may have positive goals and objectives and certainly are interested in maintaining favorable public relations through their efforts and the benefits they provide. But the profit motive is dominant, and must be, to assure their survival in the competitive business world.

Types of Commercial Recreation Businesses

For-profit leisure-service enterprises vary greatly in size and scope. Some are modest mom-and-pop businesses, such as small independent motels, travel agencies, fitness centers, and dance studios. Others are part of large chains that operate within a franchise structure, with individual owners using similar facilities, program formats, and promotional strategies.

Still other recreation businesses, particularly in the fields of popular entertainment, professional sports and travel, and tourism and hospitality, may be units of huge national or even international conglomerates.

Patterns of Ownership and Control

Recreation businesses fall into three categories of ownership and management control: (1) *sole proprietorship*, in which one person owns the enterprise and controls its management; (2) *partnerships*, in which two or more persons own and manage the business, with shared financial responsibilities and powers; and (3) *corporations*, which are legally constituted entities with all the rights and powers of individuals. This last category represents only about one-fifth of all businesses, but about four-fifths of all financial activity. Corporations are typically owned by shareholders (public or private), who elect a board of directors to oversee the management team that actually runs the enterprise.

Of these three alternatives, sole proprietorship is the most common. Although it gives the recreation entrepreneur flexibility and complete decision-making power, as well as *all* the profits—assuming that the venture *is* successful—this approach lacks certain benefits of partnerships. With joint ownership, partners may share not only their financial resources at the outset, but also their technical expertise and managerial skills, their creative talents, and the time and energy needed to build a successful business.

However, for more ambitious or larger operations, the corporation is often the preferred type of structure for recreation businesses. As a legal entity, it has continuity, and the death or retirement of its key members or officers need not terminate it.

An important aspect of leisure-service businesses is that they involve a high degree of risk. Studies have shown that as many as 95 percent of small businesses in varied fields fail within the first few years. They require the entrepreneurial spirit to be successful—that is, the capacity to think and act independently, the willingness to take chances, and the ability to be creative, decisive, and action oriented.

Commercial Recreation in the Leisure-Service System

Although for-profit recreation businesses clearly represent an important component in the overall leisure-service system, the reality is that many commercial operators do not acknowledge their connection with the leisure field or profession. Typically, they do not share the philosophy or goals of public or nonprofit agency heads, and tend to regard themselves simply as businesspeople who are selling products—comparable to automobiles, clothing, or houses.

This attitude is most dramatically illustrated in the attitudes of commercial manufacturers of violent and gory video games, or other entertainment products that are believed to contribute to the antisocial behavior of many young people today.

However, many commercial recreation managers *are* sensitive to such issues and to the impact of their programs on community life. Often, they may work closely with public or nonprofit agencies in planning and delivering their leisure services, even taking part in professional recreation and park conferences or workshops. Therefore, it is inaccurate to charge commercial recreation with being concerned solely with the profit motive, at the cost of contributing in a positive way to society.

In this chapter, three major types of for-profit recreation enterprises are described: (1) outdoor recreation businesses; (2) fitness centers and health spas; and (3) family play centers. A number of other major types of commercial recreation businesses, such as those dealing with sport or travel and tourism, are described in later chapters.

Outdoor Recreation Businesses

Outdoor recreation ventures serve a wide range of popular pursuits carried on in the natural environment, which may be classified under three headings:

Land-based pursuits, such as commercial recreation ventures that support touring, mountain climbing, skiing, spelunking and through equipment rental and sales, guide services, outdoor schools, and the operation of sites for outdoor play.

Water-based activities, including wind-surfing, river rafting, snorkeling and diving, cruising, water skiing, commercial fishing and other aquatic pastimes that require instruction, use of equipment, and planned excursions.

Air-based recreation, such as flying or gliding schools and services, ballooning, parachuting, bungee-jumping, and similar "risk" forms of play.[2]

Such activities may be carried on under carefully controlled conditions, with little personal risk to participants. Others, often described as "adventure recreation" pursuits, may be extremely challenging and dangerous, with a relatively high injury or mortality rate. Obviously, to be carried on successfully, they require highly skilled and responsible leaders or guides.

Of the thousands of outdoor recreation businesses that operate throughout the United States and Canada, many specialize in a single type of activity, such as boating, skiing, sailing, or hunting. Others may offer combinations of activity, such as hunting and fishing, or river rafting and paintball—both to maximize their appeal and to overcome the problem of seasonal change by offering pastimes suited to different times of the year.

Hunting Services

Hunting represents one of the most popular and lucrative—although highly competitive—types of businesses that appeals to a sense of adventure. It is a largely masculine enterprise, although growing numbers of women and girls today are being drawn into hunting. Many hundreds of for-profit enterprises operate hunting guide services or maintain large tracts of land where big game such as deer, elk, bear, and wild fowl may be hunted.

Examples of such hunting businesses (see Figure 5-1) include the following:

Black Bear Lodge in Northern Quebec, adjacent to a wildlife preserve, which offers hunters on a tree stand or in a blind the chance to shoot specimen-sized black bear drawn by "baits"—carcasses placed in nearby settings to attract them.

Mountain View Hunting and Fishing Camps, in New Brunswick, Canada, which offers similar services, including hunting for moose and deer, and packages that include rooms and meals, guides, skinning services, baits, and transportation to and from hunting areas, with licenses available at camp locations.

Continental Ranch in Terrell County, Texas, which packages whitetail deer hunts over a 47,000-acre property, as well as such local game as wild turkey, mountain lions, bobcats, coyotes, and javelina. This hunting service also offers exotic game, including a variety of Asian, Middle Eastern, and African sheep, goats, and antelope. The costs of individual hunts range from a few hundred dollars to several thousand.

Still other commercial hunting companies offer foreign big-game excursions, such as Jeff C. Neal, Inc., in Tulsa, Oklahoma, which sponsors trips to such lands as Turkey, Tanzania, Nepal, and New Caledonia. Angus Brown Safaris in South Africa packages many tours of American hunters who travel in search of a variety of species, such as wildebeest, buffalo, impala, and lions. (See page 203).

While such companies usually sponsor genuine hunts, some American ranch owners offer a number of exotic species—such as big cats which are often purchased from overstocked zoos—and then release them from pens so that they may immediately be slaughtered at point-blank range by trophy-eager, so-called "sportsmen."

Objections to Hunting

Canned hunts of this type are objectionable to most humanitarians and environmental spokespersons. Beyond that, however, many individuals object strenuously to *any* form of hunting, claiming that it represents an inexcusably cruel pastime and epitomizes a macho, gun-worshiping lifestyle that cannot be justified.

In response, speaking for the more than 30 million hunters in the United States, the world's most active hunting organization, Safari Club International (SCI), makes the case that organized hunting helps to keep varied wildlife species in balance and, in fact, through licenses and other fees, has contributed to the survival and recovery of many threatened species (see Figure 5-2).

Figure 5-1
Examples of hunting outfitters in the U.S.

Figure 5-2
Display prepared by Safari Club International to show recovery of wildlife in North America.

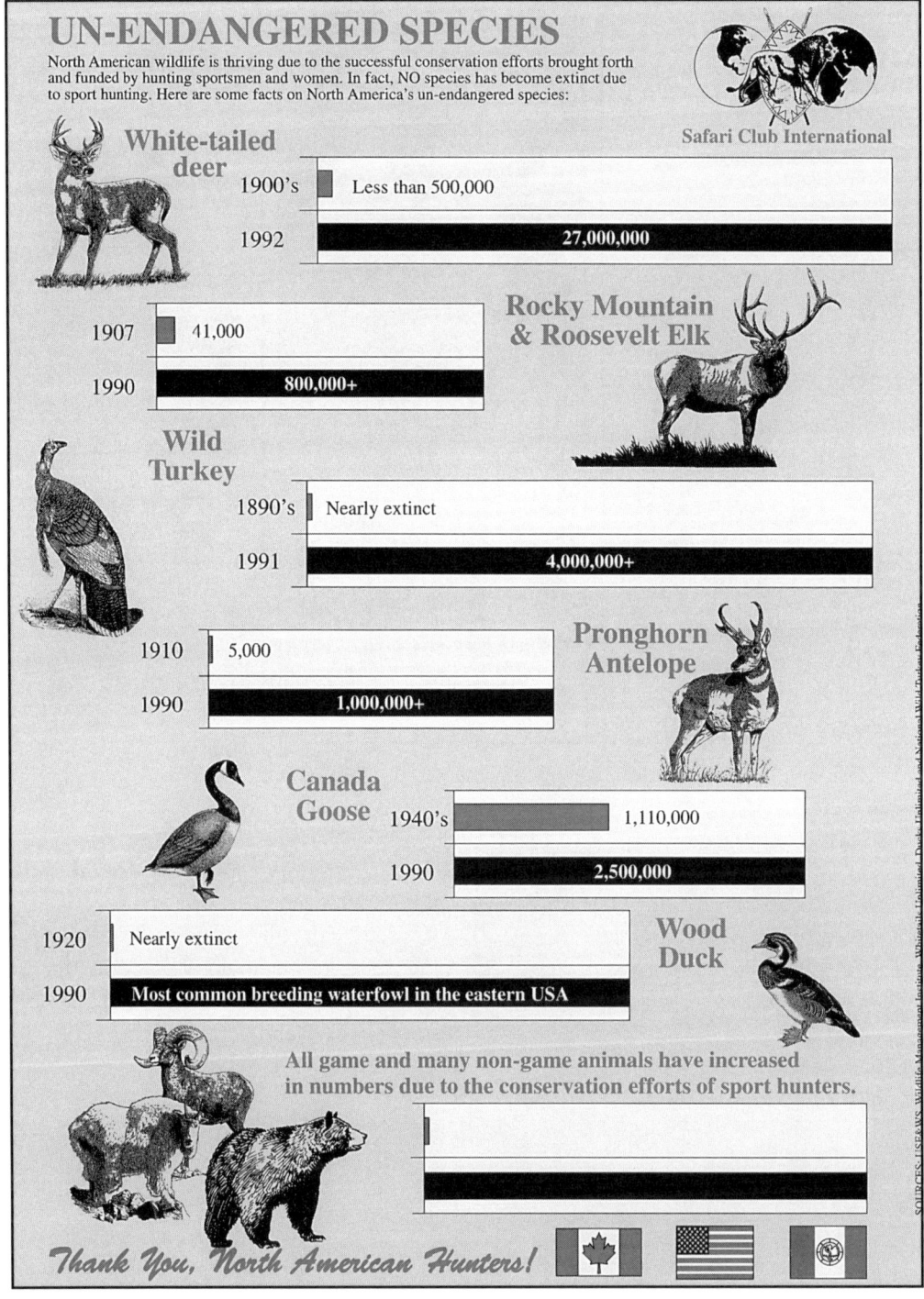

Safari Club International has also led the way in promoting efforts to increase wildlife habitats, feed wildlife herds isolated by severe winter storms, and assist wildlife management and protection programs. Local groups, such as the Delaware Valley Chapter of SCI, have also initiated a Sportsmen Against Hunger program through which Pennsylvania and New Jersey hunters contribute venison harvested from their hunts to feed homeless and needy individuals and families through local charities.

Other Hunting and Shooting Trends

Partly in response to criticism, several trends or governmental actions have either limited hunting practices or substituted other, less deadly forms of gun-based recreation.

A number of American hunters abroad, in countries such as South Africa and Mexico, now hunt big game—rhinos and elephants, jaguars and pumas—not with bullets but with darts that briefly immobilize game. These animals are then captured for breeding purposes, a trend supported by conservationists who seek to support the preservation of large mammals.[3]

A number of other shooting sports have emerged, which do not involve the killing of wildlife. In addition to simple marksmanship contests with teams and leagues in schools and colleges, thousands of individuals have taken up the hobby of "paintball"—a form of mock warfare involving stalking, wilderness tactics, and marksmanship (See page 97).

Other land-based outdoor recreation pursuits include such pastimes as winter sports, organized backpacking, trail rides, and a wide variety of other wilderness-based options.

Skiing

As a leading winter sport, skiing had a sharp and sustained rise in popularity in the years after World War II, with many new ski centers and resorts being established during the period from the 1950s through the 1980s. During the years that followed, with changing demographics that saw many younger skiers marry, raise families, and enter their mid-life period, skiing generally suffered a decline in participation.

In response, many independent ski centers merged or were taken over by larger chains, which could offer more elaborate facilities and services. Increasingly, they began to offer snowboarding, which had become extremely popular among younger winter sports enthusiasts, and also diversified their recreational activities to promote more year-round, rather than seasonal, attendance.

Greater emphasis was placed on attracting families with children through day-care and play programs and ski instruction beginning at an early age. Many ski resorts initiated new marketing strategies, such as the sale of lift-pass tickets to be used by groups of skiers and early-season passes offered at substantial discounts. In the New England states, state recreation and park or economic development agencies took the lead in promoting "value passes," with booklets of coupons designed to be used at any ski center in the state.

Sophisticated electronic-based tickets permit variable pricing according to the time of day, the length of usage by the skier, and even the different lifts that are used. Barbara Lloyd writes:

At Steamboat, Colorado, a late-day ticket costing $30 can be used after 2:15 p.m. until closing at about 4 p.m.; a full-day adult ticket costs about $54 to $56.

At Attitash Bear Peak, New Hampshire, a smart ticket bases skiing time according to which lifts a person uses, and how often. A $119 ticket allots 450 points in a system where each ski lift has a different point value [with a set number of points] deducted electronically from the skier's pass.[4]

Other winter sports offered by commercial concerns include snowmobiling and the increasingly popular snowshoeing. With new, lighter, and more efficient equipment, this sport can be enjoyed in many outdoor settings today. One company, Atlas SnowShoe, well-known for its design innovations, has entered into partnerships with more than 30 ski resorts in Western and Northern states and Canada, where it provides rental snowshoes, maintains trails, and offers guided tours.

Ice Skating

Another popular activity that has traditionally been limited to the winter seasons and northern climates is ice skating, which today can be offered year round and in many regions of the country. Ice rinks can be used for varied pastimes, including free skating, skating lessons, hockey leagues at different age levels, figure skating instruction, speed racing, and, as shown in Figure 5-3, party packages. While a number of rinks are maintained by public authorities, many others are operated by private skating clubs and commercial businesses.

Figure 5-3
Example of privately operated ice rink, offering varied commercial attractions.

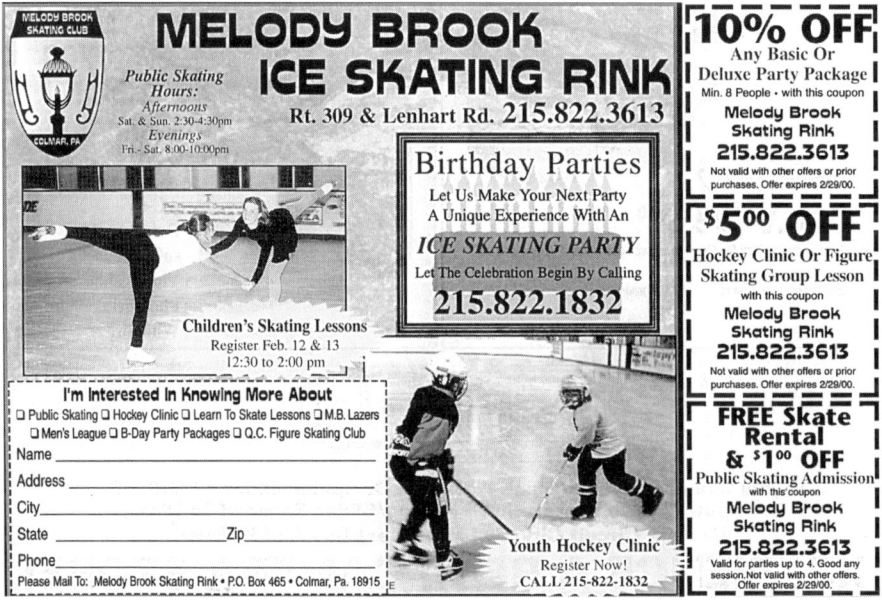

Numerous other land-based outdoor recreation activities are offered as commercial attractions today. Often, local companies combine hunting or fishing with sightseeing, trail rides, photography opportunities, and similar activities. Dude ranches or working farms give city-dwelling families the opportunity to experience the atmosphere and some of the actual life experiences of rural, or Western, living. As a single example of this type of outdoor recreation venture, Winterhawk Outfitters in Silt, Colorado, offers a variety of trail rides on horseback, with overnight tent camping in spectacular settings, fishing, photography, and other sightseeing experiences.

Water-Based Commercial Recreation

One of the most popular forms of aquatic play is swimming, whether on a beach or in a lake or in a public or a private pool. Many entrepreneurs offer other forms of water-based recreation, including boating, fishing, river rafting, wind surfing, and scuba diving.

Boating as a Popular Pastime

Boating represents a vital segment of the outdoor recreation market, with annual retail sales in the early 1990s of over $17 billion. Dwayne Hollins wrote at this time:

> The number of registered boats in the United States and U.S. territories is expected to grow to 14 million by the year 2000. Since more than one-half of the U.S. population lives within 50 miles of navigable waters, it is estimated that more than 73 million people participated [in a recent year] in at least one boating activity-canoeing, houseboating, waterskiing or cruising.[5]

While a great deal of boating is carried on independently, boat owners are served by a host of commercial interests, including manufacturers, retailers, marina operators, repair services, and similar businesses. Boating classes, charter cruises, and other for-profit ventures are also part of this picture. The largest indoor power boat show in America, for example, held at the Atlantic City, New Jersey, Convention Center in February 2000, covered three-quarters of a million square feet of exhibition space and attracted 50,000 visitors to examine a cavalcade of motor yachts, cruisers, sport fishers, trawlers, center consoles, performance boats, and personal watercraft.

So popular is the overall boating field that a number of large corporations have been formed to provide privatized, subcontracted services for governments in the planning, design, construction, and operation of marinas (see page 38).

Commercial Fishing Services

Like hunting, the immensely popular sport of fishing is the basis for thousands of businesses large and small, ranging from tackle shops to party-boat operators in coastal waters and on inland lakes. Numerous resorts throughout Canadian waters, and in the Caribbean and Central America waters as well, take well-to-do sportsmen and sportswomen into ocean territories to fish for tuna, halibut, sailfish, swordfish, shark, and other fighting fish and big-game trophies.

Numerous magazines feature fishing trends and hobbies and publicize major sport shows, tournaments, and services. As in hunting, there is a strong conversation-oriented thrust toward modifying some of the crueler aspects of this sport. Figure 5-4 shows the covers of fishing brochures and magazines, two of which deal with (1) the trend toward "catch-and-release" fishing, in which trophy fish are landed—but then immediately returned alive to the water; and (2) a new legislative thrust to ban shark "finning," the practice of stripping the fins from sharks captured in Pacific waters for sale in the Orient and then returning the fish to the ocean—and certain death.

Such publications make the point that varied forms of recreation do not only have to do with "fun," but also have major economic implications and involve important conservation and humanitarian issues.

Figure 5-4
Examples of fishing magazines and brochures.

White-Water Rafting

A final example of commercial outdoor recreation and adventure pastimes in the water-based area has to do with the immensely popular sponsorship of organized rafting down turbulent streams throughout the United States and Canada.

While much of this is done by private individuals or groups, commercial rafting businesses operate major programs, offering rafting trips, boating and kayaking instruction, schools, and camps. A leading example is found in California, where Whitewater Voyages publicizes its services, including corporate and group rafting packages with luxury coach transportation, lodging, and a variety of boating experiences making use of Web pages and the Internet to reach the adventure-seeking public. (see Figure 5-5).

In the East, a comparable outdoor recreation business is operated by Pocono Whitewater Adventures in Jim Thorpe, Pennsylvania. This successful company offers a wide variety of river-rafting programs from March to November in the historic Lehigh Gorge region, along with numerous other special programs, such as guided hiking trips in the Pocono Mountains, group activities centered on *Skirmish* (the adult version of "Capture the Flag," an adventure sport more widely known as paintball), and biking outings that contribute to funding for the Rails-to-Trails Conservancy (see Figure 5-6).

Fitness Centers and Health Spas

A second major area of commercial recreation ventures consists of fitness centers and health spas. While many of these may be sponsored by nonprofit organizations, such as YMCAs and YWCAs, public recreation and park agencies, and private residential communities, the largest and most successful ones are operated by for-profit companies, such as the Bally Corporation's Holiday Health Spas.

One might question whether attending a fitness center constitutes a legitimate form of leisure activity—or whether it isn't simply a health-related function. The fact is that many such facilities contain a range of equipment and-services, such as exercise-machines, Stairmasters and treadmills, aerobic and weight-management classes, swimming pools and saunas, and refreshment bars or lounges that provide a setting for informal socialization. Often, those who join fitness centers and health spas comment that they find the club setting far preferable to singles bars, as an environment for meeting people.

The motivations for joining fitness centers are several: (1) to maintain cardiovascular health and overall physical wellness; (2) specifically to improve one's physical appearance and body tone, as well as weight control; (3) to relieve stress through regular exercise; and (4) to enjoy the recreational appeal of group-centered exercise. Research has shown that those who gain social or recreational satisfaction are far more likely to continue involvement in fitness routines.

Staffing Patterns

In some cases, for-profit fitness centers will hire activity supervisors who have backgrounds in sport or physical education, particularly if these centers also offer such facilities as indoor tracks, racquetball or squash courts, as well as weight training and the use of equipment such as Nautilus and Universal machines. Many centers will also employ aerobics teachers who have specialized training in areas such as Jazzercise (See page 000).

Figure 5-5
Web page of Whitewater Voyages in California.

Whitewater Voyages — 1-800-488-RAFT

FREE!
- Catalog
- Group Kit
- Screen Saver
- Postcards
- Kern Info

Whitewater Voyages is California's largest, most experienced white water rafting outfitter. Our caring, professional river guides are truly dedicated to making each and every rafting trip the finest possible.

We were the first to conduct raft trips on many of the rivers in this web site, and for many, many years we have guided more people down California rivers than any other rafting outfitter.

With us, you get an incredible selection of California whitewater rivers; state-of-the-art rafting equipment; abundant, healthy, delicious camp cuisine served with panache; smooth shuttles and other trip logistics, caring, skilled, intelligent guides at the top of their profession; and, above all, a supportive atmosphere where you--your needs and enjoyment--are truly cared for!

Whitewater Voyages News

All-Inclusive No-Hassle Corporate and Group Packages A new offering for the 2000 season are these all-inclusive packages. They include luxury coach transport, lodging, camping, river rafting, and all the fun you can stand! A great way to get your group on the water! Read more....

1st Annual Kern River Celebration promises to become one of the best events on the Kern River Valley calendar. Filled with workshops on paddling and guiding, kayaking, nature interpretation, history, and of course, great boating in the Kern, this event will take place May 5, 6, & 7, 2000. It's for everyone who loves boating, loves the Kern River, or would like to learn more about either. We couldn't think of a better way to kick off the Kern River boating season. Details will be available shortly. Check back here..

MYPRIMETIME.COM Interview with Bill McGinnis As a part of their ongoing review of those who have "have lived and worked the individual adventure," myprimetime.com recently interviewed Bill McGinnis, owner and founder of Whitewater Voyages about his philosophies of guideing, working, and living. Read the article here.

2000 SEASON IS HERE! We're anticipating a fantastic season with lot's of whitewater-- and lots of FUN!

Schools and Summer Camps

Whitewater Voyages' schools are known and respected the world over. We are proud that graduates of our whitewater school are working in commercial rafting all over the world, from South America, Europe, Turkey, Central America, New Zealand, Australia, and many other wildly exotic places. And of course, all over North America. Many students come to whitewater school with no interest in becoming commercial guides, but do so for the fun, adventure and learning, and go on to enjoy whitewater rafting as a personal hobby.

But that's not all we offer! Whitewater Summer Camps for Kids and our Youth Leadership Programs are some of the greatest opportunities your children will ever have. There are classes for both Inflatable Kayaks, and Hard-Shell Kayaks, all taught by our qualified instructors with our caring and supportive touch. Read on the areas that interest you:

- Whitewater Guide Schools
- Summer Whitewater Camps for Kids
- Whitewater Youth Leadership Programs
- Inflatable Kayak Classes
- Hard-Shell Kayak Classes

©1999 Whitewater Voyages. 1-800-488-RAFT. All Rights Reserved.
Last Modified 3/5/99

Figure 5-6
Example of biking programs offered by Pocono Whitewater Adventures in Jim Thorpe, Pennsylvania.

However, most commercial fitness centers, as well as programs in employee-service, Ys and other settings, today require that their facility supervisors and leaders are certified by a recognized agency in this field. Essential as a form of legal protection, and also necessary to ensure the quality of their programs, certification may be obtained from varied sources. Several examples of such bodies include the following:

Aerobics and Fitness Association of America (AFAA)
American Academy of Fitness Professionals (AAFP)
American College of Sports Medicine (ASCM)
American Council of Exercise (ACE)
Cooper Institute for Aerobics Research
International Sports Sciences Association (ISSA)
National Sports Performance Association (NSPA)

The credentials and requirements of such certifying bodies vary widely, as identified on Web pages. These pages designate the types of populations personal trainers work with, the knowledge areas tested on examination, the required demonstrations of fitness assessments and exercises, and prerequisites in terms of course work or continuing-education credits to maintain certification.

In addition to providing direct personal training assistance, in many commercial fitness centers staff trainers have a general responsiblity for supervising exercise rooms and acting as salespeople for prospective new club members and handling routine front-desk and office responsibilities.

Many fitness centers began as the nation experienced a surge of interest in personal health during the 1970s and 1980s. When this interest declined in the 1990s, while competition in the field was growing, club managers sought innovative program features that would appeal to a wave of new participants and lend themselves to colorful marketing strategies.

Some commercial gyms, for example, now offer "fitness fantasy" programs, in which participants go through routines as if they were in boot camp, with orders barked at them by tough marine sergeants, and performing typical military physical drills. Other gyms treat class members as if they were fire fighters in training, requiring them to climb ladders, wield sledgehammers, and even "save" 125-pound dummies.

Still others go through training programs geared for professional football players:

> ... [patrons] are put through the same paces NFL players undergo during preseason workouts: ladder drills, shuffles, high knee kicks, plyometric box hopping drills, and medicine ball tosses. Hip-hop music and barking coaches keep bodies pushing.[6]

Other fitness chains have developed small-group exercise programs in which clusters of several members go through a sequence of machine-based and other routines, under close trainer supervision. The International Health, Racquet and Sportsclub Association, a Boston trade organization, estimates that 95 percent of clubs offer some form of personal training service for the approximately 22 million individuals in organized fitness programs today.

Yoga Classes

Yoga, an ancient discipline based on breathing and stretching techniques and linked to traditional Asian philosophical beliefs, has become a popular form of physical exercise and stress reduction for many Americans. In typical classes based on Indian Hatha yoga disciplines, individuals learn specific poses and stretch positions, such as the "tree," the "mountain," and the "triangle." In one special school of yoga, known as the Bikram, or "hot yoga," method, thousands of participants today—including many Hollywood celebrities—enhance their strength, flexibility, and balance in rooms heated to 100 degrees.

Martial Arts

A second, related thrust in exercise programs involves participation in any of a number of Eastern martial arts disciplines, such as different schools of karate, Judo, or tai chi chuan. Many schools and studios teach such skills to children and youth, who enroll both for self-defense values and for the physical training and mental discipline they require.

Jazzercise

This exercise involves a major commercial enterprise, a form of dance-fitness exercise program developed by a single teacher, Judi Missett, in the 1960s that has become the largest such program in the world, with over 1,700 franchised instructors. Today, Jazzercise programs operate in all 50 states and 33 countries, with annual systemwide revenues of over $50 million. Like other popular commercial leisure attractions, Jazzercise offers a number of subsidiary programs, including Jazzertogs, which offers dance-fitness clothing, videos, and other merchandise or accessories; JM Television Productions, CyberStretch, which is a computer safety program used to relieve or prevent repetitive stress injuries; and various Corporate Alliances with nationally known name-brand products and companies that include food, footwear, and credit-card services.

Family Play Centers

As an extension of adult fitness centers, thousands of entrepreneurs in the 1970s and 1980s developed free-play, fitness, and gymnastics centers and studios for young children—in part, as a response to research studies concluding that public, outdoor playgrounds were often poorly maintained or supervised and had a high risk factor.

A number of major chains moved into the "kiddie exercise" field, offering regular workouts for children—in some cases including infants as young as six weeks. Viewed as a sort of Head Start for physical development, such centers and classes introduced children to varied equipment, including hoops, slides, mats, trampolines, and giant balls and used exercises to promote motor skills, balance, and flexibility.

Prompted in part by the concern of American parents over the high failure rate of their children in tests of physical fitness, such new centers thrived, and a number of national chains, such as Playorena, Gymboree, and Discovery Zone, were formed as franchising operations. Some of these chains had hundreds of local studios and thousands of participants overall. Others opened stores selling expensive playsuits, exercise cassettes for children, and indoor exercise equipment.

Over time, public interest in such child-centered exercise businesses declined for a number of chains, which, in response, cut back on their offerings or tried new program features to attract enrollment.

To diversify their appeal and maximize revenues, play centers emerged that included physical activities—but also video games and other computerized game equipment, along with "fun food" services, such as pizzas, hot dogs and hamburgers, and soft drinks. These businesses also evolved into national chains that developed packages for families and party groups that were often placed in shopping malls around the country (see Figure 5-7).

In the upbeat economy of the late 1990s and early 2000s, they thrived. One of the most successful such enterprises has been CEC Entertainment, Inc., formerly known as ShowBiz

Pizza Time, Inc., of Irving, Texas. This company operates a system of 332 Chuck E. Cheese restaurants in 44 states, 277 of which are company operated, 55 of which are franchised.

The Chuck E. Cheese Pizza system has been in operation since 1977, generates annual revenues of over $450 million, and employs over 12,000 people. In addition to its food sales, it differs from other pizza and fast food chains in that it offers video games and rides for all age groups that are particularly popular with children. In addition, it features Studio C, an interactive entertainment experience that simulates a real TV production facility. As children sing and dance on the stage, Chuck E. Cheese "production assistants" operate cameras and a sound-effects console—giving one the illusion of being on a real television. Like other family game centers, CEC Entertainment is a popular site for packaged parties and group special events.

Other Adult Entertainment Ventures

As an extension of such family play centers, many entrepreneurs began to combine the twin appeals of food and games for an adult audience, In cities around the United States, huge restaurants were built that offered casual dining, along with a wealth of video-game arcades and other indoor sports equipment and play settings. Similarly, sports bars featuring food and drink and huge television screens to capture whatever sports events were on at a given time became widely popular.

Throughout the 1990s, various forms of amusement and recreation businesses continued to climb steadily in attendance and revenue throughout the United States, as shown in Table 1-2 (see page 13).

Employment Perspectives in Commercial Recreation

Unlike most public and nonprofit leisure-service organizations, many recreation businesses do not have clearly defined job classification systems or hiring requirements.

With the exception of certification requirements in fitness centers and similar practices in varied areas of outdoor recreation—where organizations such as the National Outdoor Leadership School do provide specialized training—many other for-profit recreation fields do not develop detailed statements of job responsibilities or position descriptions. In some cases, studies have been made of the job functions in a given field. For example, a study of more than 50 ski centers in several states showed that the following functions were important, in the order shown, for ski center managers:

1. General administration and management techniques
2. Control of ticket sales
3. Labor cost control
4. Ability to apply safety rules and understand negligence liability elements; maintaining liability insurance
5. Personnel management
6. Selecting lift equipment and carrying out life preventative maintenance
7. Accounting and auditing capability; financial management
8. Managing ticket and traffic controls

Figure 5-7
Examples of family fun centers.

9. Public relations and marketing skills; developing ski packages
10. Planning and operating ski school activities
11. Managing snow grooming services
12. Operating ground and serial lifts, supervising and carrying out mechanical maintenance

In some cases, personnel managers may define job functions in different areas of responsibility and identify the personal skills or qualities needed to carry them out successfully. Dollywood Theme Park, for example, has done such an analysis, linking work responsibilities in different areas to required employee competences (see page 235).

Often, individuals are hired at relatively low-levels of responsibility, given a brief orientation or assigned to work side by side with a more experienced employee, and then left to learn on the job. For more advanced levels of responsibility, individuals may be given brief training sessions or assisted in taking continuing education courses, as shown in Chapter 11.

Other Aspects of Commercial Recreation

Since the primary emphasis in for-profit recreation businesses is placed on running a successful enterprise, managers place a high priority on employee efficiency and responsibility. Particular emphasis is placed on customer relations, in terms of staff members' appearance and behavior.

Employee Appearance and Behavior

In the early Disney parks, in order to appeal to conventional, "middle American" families, rules were established that governed such elements as hair grooming and coloring of staff members, sideburns and mustaches, cosmetics, perfume, fingernails, jewelry, and accessories. Each employee's "presentism" (management's term for his or her total appearance before the public) was strictly regulated, with rigid taboos controlling behavior with park "guests," use of narcotics or intoxicants, gambling, dishonesty, and similar concerns.

Only in the 1999s did the Disney management decide to permit men to wear mustaches (but no other facial hair) and women to use eye shadow and eye liner. However, even today, some commercial businesses might draw the line at permitting employees to use hair styles such as shaved heads or cornrows, or the use of implanted jewelry such as nose, lip, or tongue rings.

Seasonal and Scheduling Factors

Another personnel-related aspect of many for-profit recreational enterprises is that they are highly seasonal in nature. Most outdoor recreation businesses are governed not only by climatic factors, but also, as in the case of hunting, legal seasons for various types of game. While public and nonprofit leisure-service agencies usually conduct extensive indoor recreation programs, this is not true of many commercial recreation businesses, which must hire large numbers of people during their active seasons and lay them off at other times.

Similarly, many businesses, such as family play centers and fitness centers and health spas, are likely to be busier, during late afternoon and evening hours, or on weekends, when children are not in school or adults are not at work. Therefore, individuals working in such settings must be available for off-hours work, as well as for the possibility of short-notice hiring assignments.

Physical Demands

In many for-profit recreation enterprises, such as those described in this chapter, on-the-job physical demands may be high. Hunting outfitter guides, charter fishing boat operators, and others involved in outdoor recreation, travel and tourism, and theme park programs are all subject to a degree of risk inherent in their job. Crowd control, fire safety, accident prevention, and similar security-related concerns all require that staff members are not only physically capable, but also have sound judgment and the ability to respond positively in emergency situations.

This chapter has discussed a number of the employment aspects of commercial recreation ventures. These aspects will be discussed more fully as Chapter 11, which presents a broad view of the pros and cons of employment in diversified leisure-service agencies and offers constructive guidelines for those entering, this field. The issue of professionalism, which is not heavily emphasized in for-profit recreation employment, will be discussed more fully at that time.

Suggested Questions for Class Discussion or Essay Examinations

1. If the primary purpose of a commercial recreation business is to make a financial profit, does this prevent such ventures from also making a positive contribution to community life? Can you think of some for-profit leisure enterprises that do make such a contribution?
2. In what ways do commercial recreation businesses have an advantage over public or nonprofit agencies in terms of freedom to operate, range of possible programs and services, or funding capability? In what ways are they at a disadvantage? Do you believe that associations representing commercial fitness centers are justified in attempting to have nonprofit organizations such as Ys denied tax exemption because they offer comparable services to those of profit-making centers?
3. Environmentally sensitive individuals and humanitarian groups often attack hunting as cruel and inhumane. In your view, how valid are such charges? What are some of the arguments favoring hunting, which is often an important commercial recreation activity?
4. Can you give examples of how new technology has contributed to various forms of for-profit recreation enterprises in such fields as outdoor recreation, winter sports, and popular entertainment? In the area of electronic play and communication, what are the positive and negative aspects of such products and services as video games and the Internet?
5. The factor of seasonal and climate change affects many activities, such as skiing or attendance at water parks. How have some entrepreneurs compensated for this problem by diversifying their offerings to create more year-round appeal?

Footnotes

[1] Bullaro, J., and Edginton, C. (1986). *Commercial leisure services: Managing for profit, service, and personal satisfaction.* New York: MacMillan, 17.

[2] Edginton, C., Jordan, D., DeGraaf, D., and Edginton, S. (1995). *Leisure and life satisfaction: Foundational perspectives.* Dubuque, IA.: Brown and Benchmark, 224.

[3] Boroughs, D. (1999). Hunters shoot hut don't kill. *U.S. News and World Report.* Nov. 15, 45.

[4] Lloyd, B. (1999). Buying lift tickets without speed bumps. *New York Times.* Dec. 2, D-5.

[5] Hollins, D. (1992). Marinas are big business in Texas. *Parks and Recreation.* November, 42.

[6] Marcus, M. (1999). Beyond sit-ups. *U.S. News and World Report.* Feb. 8, 57.

Chapter 6

Armed Forces and Employee-Service Programs

Having reviewed three types of leisure-service organizations that serve a broad cross section of the population, we now examine two kinds of sponsors that meet more specialized needs.

Military recreation is provided by the Morale, Welfare and Recreation (MWR) service of the U.S. Department of Defense, within the four major armed forces units: Navy, Army, Air Force, and Marine Corps. Its purpose is to promote the morale, fitness, and overall well-being of members of the military and their dependents, which the military deems integral to the success of the entire national defense effort.

Recreation and related services are sponsored by thousands of corporations throughout the United States for similar reasons. By promoting the health, fitness, and morale of employees, they seek to maintain a positive climate in the work environment; reduce illness, absenteeism, and employee turnover; build constructive staff relationships; and promote company productivity.

This chapter deals with both types of specialized leisure-service operations, describing their background, organization and scope, and program elements and current trends in their operations.

Recreation in the Armed Forces

For several decades, the U.S. Department of Defense has maintained an impressive and diversified program of recreation and related services for uniformed personnel and dependents, civilian employees, retired military personnel and their dependents, and the surviving spouses of individuals who died while on active duty.

Operating on a large scale, in the 1980s this program, directed by both military personnel and civilian staff members employed by the Department of Defense, served about nine million individuals. Provided on almost all 923 military installations in the United States and 363 bases in 29 foreign countries, the Morale, Welfare and Recreation program at this time had a total budget of about $3 billion, much of it from nonappropriated (self-generated) funds. It employed 215,000 people, including 8,700 uniformed personnel, 8,900 civilian employees on tax-appropriated salaries, and a much larger number of employees—almost 200,000—on nonappropriated payrolls.[1]

While these numbers have declined significantly because of budget cuts and base and personnel downsizing during the 1990s, armed forces recreation continues to be a huge, highly professionalized leisure-service enterprise.

Goal of Military Recreation

With its historical roots dating from World War I, when Special Services Divisions were formed to provide social and recreational programs that would sustain high morale, reduce homesickness and boredom, and curb AWOL (absent without official leave) and venereal disease rates, today military recreation is mandated to carry out the following functions:

1. Maintain a high level of esprit de corps, promote job efficiency, contribute to military effectiveness, assist in recruitment and retention of military personnel by making service an attractive career, and aid armed service personnel in their transition from civilian to military life.
2. Promote and maintain the physical, emotional, and social wellbeing of military members; their families; and other eligible members of the armed forces.
3. Encourage constructive use of off-duty leisure time with opportunities for developing new talents and skills that not only contribute to the military and civilian community, but also serve as counter-attractions to negative or self-destructive uses of leisure time.
4. Provide community support programs and services for military families, especially when service members are involved in armed conflict or stationed in remote settings.

In discussing the role of recreation in the armed forces, the following sections of this chapter will deal with the organization and administration of the Morale, Welfare and Recreation Program in the Department of Defense, as well as current trends in its funding and staffing, program services, and employment and Staff development practices. Primary emphasis will be placed on one service branch-the U.S. Navy.

Organization of Armed Forces Recreation

First, it should be understood that the Defense Department is a highly complex system, with many branches that are typically designated by titles shortened to acronyms for convenience, as shown in the following official passage that describes the management of Morale, Welfare and Recreation in the Navy and Marine Corps, and also in Figure 6-1.

Figure 6-1
Chart showing complex structure of U.S. Navy MWR, including levels of authority and regional divisions.

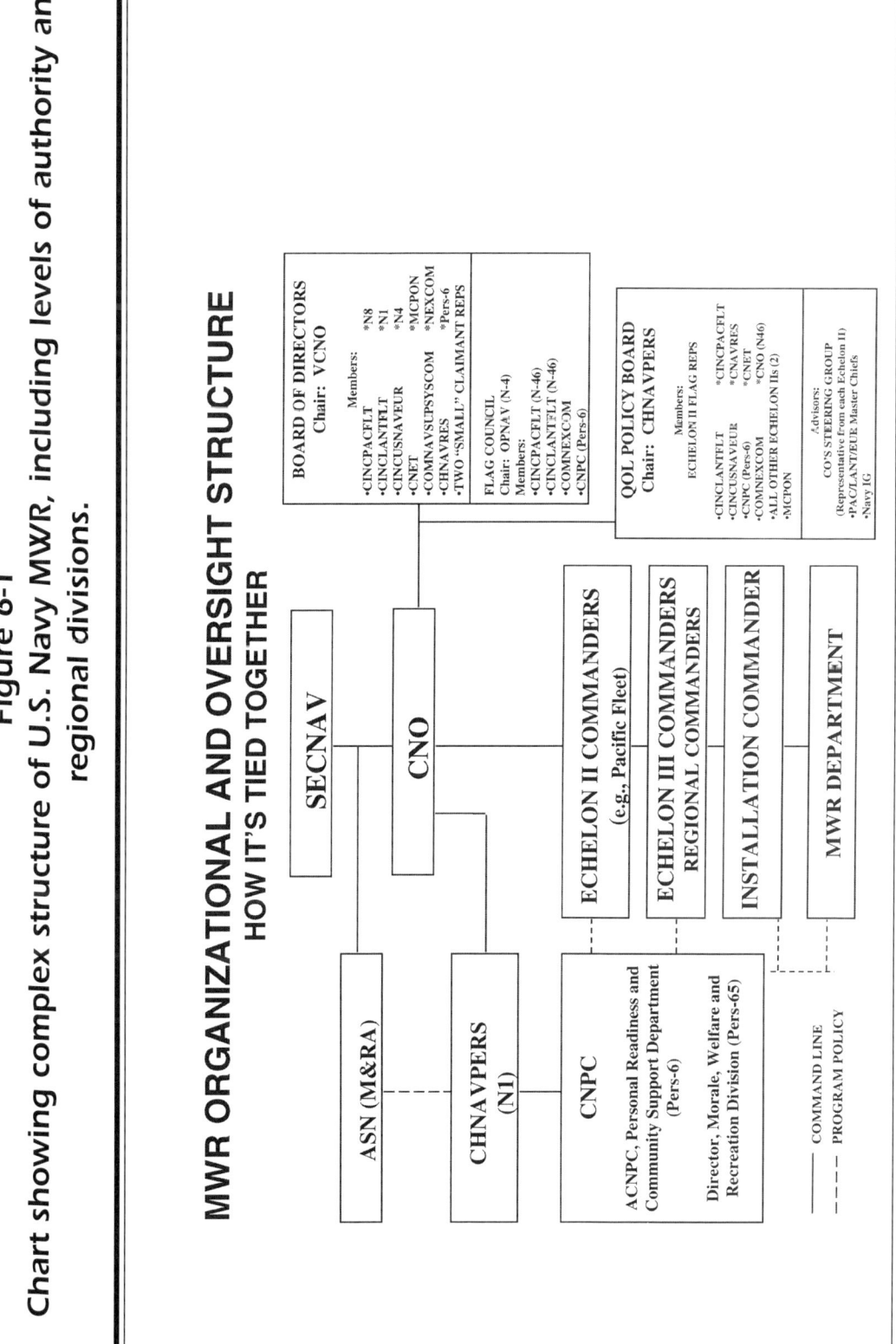

... the Assistant Secretary of the Navy (Manpower and Reserve Affairs) provides broad policy guidance on MWR programs while the Assistant Secretary of the Navy (Financial Management) has responsibility for financial policy provisions applicable to MWR activities.

The Chief of Naval Operations (CNO) and the Commandant of the Marine Corps (CMC) are responsible for detailed policy and coordination of MWR within their respective services. Further, within the Navy, the Chief of Naval Personnel (CHNAVPERS) acts as an agent for the CNO and the commander, Naval Supply Supply Systems Command has been assigned technical management responsibility for the Navy Exchange System (including temporary lodging facilities). Within the Marine Corps, MWR program responsibility has been assigned to the Morale Welfare and Recreation Support Activity (CMCMW).[2]

Funding of MWR Programs

MWR programs are supported by a combination of nonappropriated funds (NAF) and appropriated funds (APF). NAF revenues generated by MWR business activities, such as restaurants, clubs, golfing, and bowling, are used to support over 50 different activities, ranging from fitness centers to libraries, child development programs, sports, outdoor recreation, hobbies, and other pursuits. Based on the Department of Defense Authorization Acts of fiscal years 1987 and 1988, these activities are structured into the following three categories, with fund allocations authorized accordingly:

Category A Activities most directly support mission requirements and include activities such as sports, fitness, libraries and movies aboard ship [in Navy MWR programs]. By DOD policy, these activities are authorized to receive the highest level of APF support to finance their operating costs-up to 100 percent of expenses.

Category B contains community support activities such as youth, child development and recreational skill development programs (e.g., personal computer instruction programs, auto repair skills and instruction). These activities are given appropriated support at approximately 65 percent of total expenses.

Category C encompasses business activities or profit generators such as food and beverage services, large bowling centers, golf courses, marinas, etc. With the exception of overseas and remote bases, APF support for Category C activities is limited to indirect expenses such as fire protection and security, equating to about five percent of expenses ... over and above these limited APF support entitlements, Category C activities are expected to be self-sufficient (i.e., revenues sufficient to cover operating costs).[3]

The financial balance between Navy MWR-appropriated and self generated funds in a recent year is shown in Figure 6-2, which presents the budgeted or planned breakdown, and the actual figures for fiscal year 1999. NEX dividends refers to revenues from Navy Exchange profits.

Figure 6-2
Financial report, U.S. Navy MWR, fiscal year 1999.

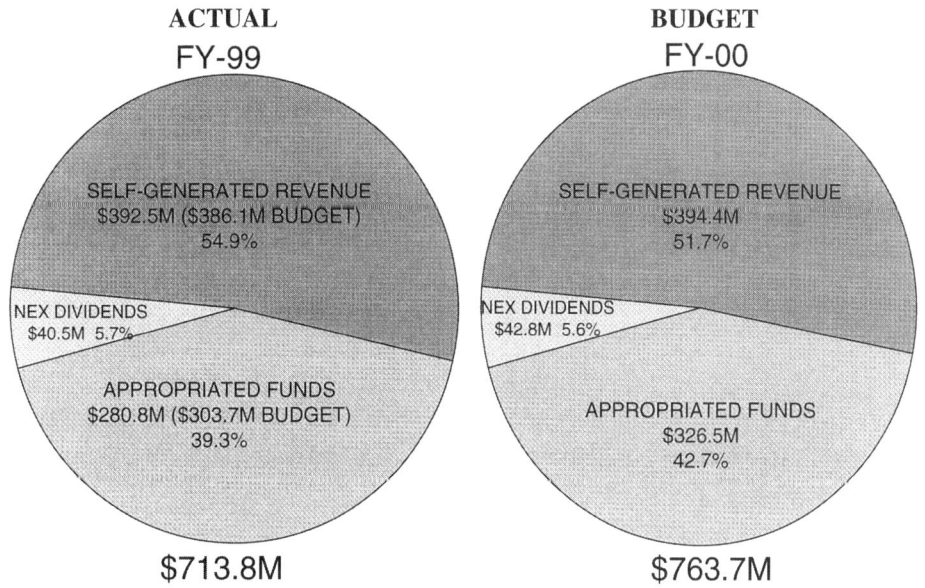

MWR Program Elements

A number of key program elements in the Navy MWR operation are shown in Figure 6-3. Several of these, such as the "Afloat Recreation Programs," or the "Fleet Recreation Center Program," are unique to the Navy and would not be found in other branches of the armed forces. Other important program elements include a marina services program, Navy clubs, a motion picture service, outdoor recreation facilities and equipment rental, a single-sailor recreation program, and other special events, parties, and community contact services.

Program Activities in the Overall MWR Operation

Throughout the military, MWR programs typically cover a broad range of physical, social, cultural, and entertainment pursuits. For example, the U.S. Air Force offers activities under the following headings: (1) sports; (2) motion pictures; (3) service clubs and entertainment, including parties and special events, dramatic and musical activities; (4) crafts

Figure 6-3
Major U.S. Navy MWR program activities and services.

NAVY MWR

RECREATION

Afloat Recreation Programs: Sports, tours ashore, leisure reading, ticket rebates, board games and underway athletics.

Aquatic Programs: Swimming pools, beaches, lakes, open swimming, lap swimming, swimming lessons, pool parties and other special events.

Auto Craft Skills Center Program: Facilities that allow Sailors to work on their vehicles and acquire automotive skills.

Bowling Program: Sailors can bowl just for fun or in a league, and make new friends during "cosmic" bowling.

Fleet Recreation Center Program: Recreation information, entertainment, ticket and local tour services, special events e.g., picnics, carnivals, holiday celebrations, passive activities (e.g., reading, board games, cards), recreation rooms, fitness and exercise areas, laundry facilities, and food concessions.

Golf Program: Course play, driving ranges, cart rentals, class and personal lessons, snack bars, and pro shops.

Information, Tickets and Tours (ITT) Program: Local recreation information (on and off base), entertainment tickets and local tour services.

Leisure Travel Program: A full range of travel services such as airline reservations, car rental, lodging, tours and other travel services.

How To Do Business With Navy MWR

and hobbies; (5) family activities, particularly for children and youth; (6) special-interest groups, such as aero, automotive, motorcycle, and powerboating clubs, and hiking, skydiving and rod and gun clubs; (7) rest centers and recreation areas (8)open messes; and (9)libraries.

Special efforts are made throughout the armed services to compensate for the stress and boredom of military life and to overcome problems of drug and alcohol abuse that have traditionally been a problem of many servicemen and servicewomen. The past pattern of assuming that drinking at bars and clubs is a normal way to spend one's leisure time has begun to give way to the view that this form of socializing may lead to a limited and often self-destructive lifestyle. Today, greater emphasis is placed on encouraging nonalcoholic social programs and a fuller range of active leisure pursuits

Innovative MWR Programs

Throughout the military, different service units and bases have initiated innovative and successful programs within a number of different recreational areas.

In the Air Force, for example, sports programming has typically included six major elements: (1) instruction in basic sports Skills; (2) a self-directed phase of informal participation in sports under minimum supervision or direction; (3) an intramural program, in which personnel assigned to a particular base compete with others at the same base; (4) an extramural program, which includes competition with teams from different Air Force bases or with teams from neighboring communities; (5) a varsity program, which involves high-level competition with players selected for their advanced skills, who compete on a broader national or international scale; and (6) a program for women in the Air Force.

A unique addition to MWR sports programming has been "Start Smart," a project of the National Alliance for Youth Sports. In this program, which was initiated at the Marine Corps Air Station at Cherry Point, North Carolina, and has since been adopted at over 50 other bases, throughout the United States and in England, Germany, Turkey, Japan, and Korea, children as young as three years are drawn into motor skills and beginning sports activities, while their parents participate along with them.[4]

Fitness

Health and fitness are important elements in military recreation. To improve fitness levels of personnel, the Air Force has installed Health and Wellness Centers (HAWC) these centers are well equipped and are staffed with leaders qualified to provide the following services: fitness and health risk assessments, exercise programming and weight counseling, stress management and smoking cessation assistance, and similar activities.

On some military bases, fitness is promoted through well-publicized and challenging special events. At the Marine Corps Base at Camp Lejeune, North Carolina, the Lejeune Grand Prix Series features a number of competitive events that involve hundreds of service personnel in a European Cross-Country race over natural terrain; a Tour d'Pain, a grueling endurance cycling race; a Masters Swim Meet: a Davy Jones Open Ocean Swim; a Toughman Triathlon, and other types of races.

The Marine Corps Base at Quantico, Virginia, initiated "Semper Fit," a modern, full-service fitness program staffed by certified exercise physiologists with a variety of activities emphasizing a healthy lifestyle. Operating in a pre-World War II hangar, this project has evolved into a historic program for physical fitness, mental health, and wellness.[5] Numerous other bases have developed similar programs.

Outdoor Recreation

Depending on their surroundings, some military units have developed varied outdoor recreation and adventure-type programs. Fort Carson, Colorado, has sponsored a ski program featuring an annual Ski Expo, with over 150 vendors and representatives of ski areas and average attendance of more than 5,000 skiing enthusiasts. Responding to widespread interest in mountain climbing and rock climbing, this Army base has constructed a 17,400-square-foot outdoor recreation center that features a 32-foot-high indoor climbing wall with the look and feel of natural rock, and climbing routes geared to different skill levels.

Many other bases, such as Tyndall Air Force Base in Florida, offer a variety of adventure pursuits, such as rafting, canoeing, scuba diving in Bonita Bay, and other outdoor pastimes. To facilitate such leisure involvements, some bases have established campgrounds or other living facilities at nearby locations that lend themselves to outdoor recreation. For example, the MWR unit at the Marine Corps Air Ground Combat Center in Twentynine Palms, California, has opened eight vacation cottages on Lake Havasu, three hours away from its base—and an ideal setting for water skiing, jet skiing, fishing, and other lake activities.[6]

Family- and Youth-Centered Programs

Today, major emphasis In MWR operations is given to meeting the needs of the families of military personnel. It is recognized that family life in the armed forces imposes a number of significant strains, particularly when families are separated, assigned to remote bases, or under the pressures of conflict and international confrontation. Many of the problems found in civilian life, such as substance abuse or intrafamily physical violence, may be more severe among military families.

Problems of Military Youth

The Office of Family Policy of the U.S. Defense Department has identified important concerns of youth, such as

- Increases in parental deployment absences that intensify other risk factors
- Growing reports of youth violence and gang activity around and on military bases
- Lack of positive activities during after-school hours
- Nationwide increase in at-risk youth problems, which in turn affects military youth
- Geographical separation of families due to teens in high schools, and problems associated with the transfer of military high school youth.[7]

Community and Family Support Programs

To overcome such problems, as well as meet broader family needs, the Department of Defense initiated an ambitious Community and Family Support Program in the late 1990s, with specific goals and objectives to be achieved by 2005. This program has several important components:

1. *Child Development Program:* designed to meet the need for full-day, part-day, respite, volunteer, and hourly child care, using highly professional, inexpensive services and well-equipped and well-staffed centers and learning programs.

2. *Family Advocacy Program:* addresses prevention, identification, and treatment/rehabilitation of child abuse and neglect, and other family-related problems in Department of

Defense installations by offering counseling, offender-accountability measures, and other services to protect family members.

3. Family Center Programs: facilities and programs intended to provide other educational and preventive services and to assist armed forces members with problems of transfer, relocation, and redeployment and eventual transition to civilian life. Crisis assistance, employment aid, personal financial management, and other services are provided within this structure.

4. Youth Program. Morale, Welfare and Recreation programs are particularly active in this area, promoting the health fitness, social adjustment, and good citizenship of youth in armed forces families with comprehensive educational and recreational services in such areas as sports, outdoor recreation, libraries, special interest activities, and youth clubs (see Figure 6-4).

Figure 6-4
Brochure advertising for community and family support program.

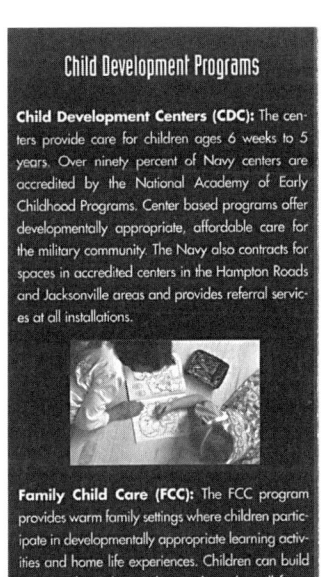

Newer MWR Management Strategies

To deal with challenges stemming from downsizing and reductions in force, and to justify its mission-related role, the Morale, Welfare and Recreation program in the Department of Defense has made intensive use of consultant teams, planning conferences, and sophisticated evaluation studies to upgrade its total operation. Borrowing from both business-related and governmental strategic planning methods, MWR has highlighted such priorities as the following:

Innovation and Reinvention: approaches that emphasize a fresh examination of the organization's role, responsibilities, opportunities, and policies and developing new and more promising priorities and functions.

Regionalization: the development of 10 major regions within the United States and abroad, to meet various needs specific to these regions and to reduce costs and eliminate redundancies.

Strategic Sourcing and Privatization: a drive toward promoting partnerships with community organizations and businesses in joint efforts and to develop commercial sponsorships to support or enrich varied programs and services.

Performance-Based Controls: extended use of benchmarking (comparative analysis with other agencies), cost analysis, and benefits based measurements of outcomes to guide fund allocations and assist ongoing planning.

Public Affairs Strategies: Projects to enhance public understanding and support for MWR, through Congressional Newsletter, MWR Times, information directories, Web pages, and other media outlets.

Employment and Career Development

Civilian employment in armed forces MWR programs includes a huge range of positions and job titles. In Navy recreational services alone, there are approximately 50 such job categories on nonappropriated fund salaries, under such headings as:

Club Management: Consolidated Club Manager; Assistant Club Manager; Executive Chef; Food and Beverage Manager

Child Care: Child Development Center Manager; Family Home CareCoordinator

Supervisory Recreation Specialist: Athletics; Community Activities; Entertainment; Information; Tickets and Tours; Leisure Skills Development; Outdoor Recreation; Physical Fitness; Arts and Crafts Support Programs; Marina Manager; Computer Operator; Personnel Management Specialist; Purchasing Agent; Supervisory Accounting Technician

Uncertified Specialized Manager: Aero Club Manager; Bowling Center Manager; Golf Course Manager; Recreational Programs Manager

For each such position, there is a detailed job description that includes including such elements as its pay plan and civil service grade, major duties, knowledge required for the position, supervisory controls, guidelines for performance, level of complexity and physical demands, personal contacts, and work environment. Naval manuals provide guidelines for applying for positions, and a regularly issued Job Opportunity Bulletin provides notification of current job openings, along with information on their locations, salary levels, hiring schedule or time frame, and specific work functions. Issued by the Bureau of Naval Personnel in Millington, Tennessee, this bulletin is the best current source for civilian employees seeking job transfers or upgrading.

Internship Opportunities

Particularly for college students seeking to explore the possibility of a career in military recreation, the Navy MWR Division offers a range of internship opportunities, in both the continental United States and a variety of overseas locations (see Figure 6-5).

Figure 6-5
Details of Navy college student internship program.

Job Training Programs

Like other categories of specialized leisure-service agencies, armed forces recreation provides an extensive range of on-the-job training programs. Currently, there is a strong emphasis on "train the trainers" education, which is an attempt to strengthen supervisory competence in the field. For example, the MWR Training Branch began field implementation of a new thrust in this area in 1999 and averaged 40 courses a month under 125 facilitators and 51 coordinators, with a total of over 3,500 field personnel trained in the first year of operations.

Training for senior managers includes a heavy emphasis on financial management and achieving a high level of "customer" service and satisfaction; other positions have similar specialized goals. The overall training programs sponsored by the Bureau of Naval Personnel offer direct-leadership courses in many areas of MWR operations and are described as follows:

> Open enrollment courses are offered tuition free to employees of Navy military MWR activities, although there may be activity fees to help defray the cost of each instructor's travel or the cost of training rooms or equipment ... Courses offered through the Army or Air Force have full or partial tuition charges.
>
> [The MWR Training Program] offers as many courses in as many different areas of the world as can be arranged with current resources. [Its] intent is to minimize student travel and per diem costs, making training accessible to as many qualified students as possible.... [Host sites for training must] provide a liaison officer, training site, and other logistical requirements.[8]

An overview of MWR training programs, as they were offered in 1999, is provided in Figure 6-6. In addition to such continuing education programs, each year a number of training workshops and conferences are sponsored by the Armed Forces Recreation Society, including sessions at meetings of the National Recreation and Park Association.

Figure 6-6
Visual presentation of the scope of Navy MWR Personnel Training (1999).

Our Mission
- Develop and deliver a comprehensive support program for fleet and shore-based commands having Navy MWR activities
  - through training programs
  - using performance management techniques
- Methods
  - Centralized Training Development
  - Train-the-Trainer
  - Decentralized Delivery

Our Students
- Navy MWR Employees World-wide
  - NAF, GS and Active Duty
- Command Internal Review
- Civilian MWR Employees *
- CBQ Employees *
- Marine Corps MWR Employees *

◆ * for a fee

Program Scope
(Not Including Customer Service Training Efforts)

- 2,300 + Navy and Marine students per year
- 200+ classes / workshops per year (ours and others)
- 180 NPC courses (ours only)
- 100+ classes conducted on request
- 100+ classes conducted by field course managers
- 100 Field Course Managers

Midlevel Manager Training
- MWR Manager *
- MAnagement Skills TRaining (MASTR) *
- Advanced Program Mgr Workshop
- Customer Service
  - Achieving *
  - Motivating *
- Cost Control for Clubs *
- Fleet Recreation Management * (w/651)
- Quick Service Training (w/655)
- CARE Training (w/655)
- F&B Management Course (joint services)

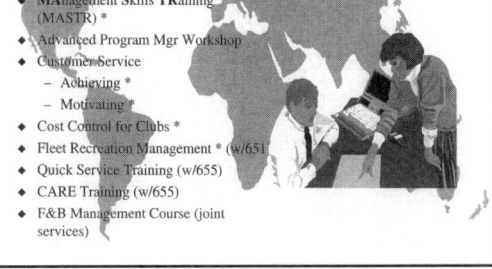

Employee Services and Recreation

Employee services had its roots in the early 20th century, when growing unionization and conflict between management and workers created widespread tension in America's workforce. At this time, a number of companies began to introduce varied recreational programs, including sports leagues, special-interest clubs, holiday celebrations, and similar leisure activities. Their purpose, in what came to be called "industrial recreation," was essentially to create a more favorable social climate and provide employee benefits and positive experiences that would lead to a positive work climate and greater on-the-job efficiency.

At this time, employee recreation, which came to be viewed as part of personnel administration, varied in administrative sponsorship patterns. Some companies took complete responsibility for organized recreation programs providing facilities and leadership, sometimes with an advisory council of employees. Others provided facilities and a degree of financial support, with employees taking responsibility for planning and conducting programs. Some corporations built large gymnasiums, meeting rooms, and recreation centers; activity programs included varied sports, classes, and clubs in hobby interests and areas of personal development, family activities, parties, picnics, and a wide range of other pastimes.

Example of Recreation Facilities

An example of the outstanding facilities developed by some companies is the Project Employees' Recreation Association (PERA) of the Salt River Project in Tempe, Arizona, which developed five major recreation complexes at company units and generating stations during the 1970s and 1980s (see Figure 6-7).[9]

Figure 6-7
Extensive facilities operated by the PERA Club in Arizona.

PERA Club Facilities

Valley PERA Club		Coronado Generating Station	Fitness Center
83-Acre Park	Snack Bar	PERA	Big Screen Television
Lighted Softball Field	10-Acre Grassed Park	144-Acre Park	Warehouse
Recreation Offices	Tent (60' x 140') w/ seating for 600	Employee General Store	Banquet Facility
Two-Story Clubhouse	Basketball Court	Sand Volleyball Courts	Aerobics Room
Employee General Store	Archery Range	Divisional Office	Meeting Room
General Store Warehouse & Office Building	Fitness Trail	Prairie Schooner Cocktail Lounge	Kitchen
Swilling's Cocktail Lounge	Jogging Track (2.5 mile)	Shuffleboard	Horseshoe Pits
Administration Annex	Executive Meeting Center	Billiard Table	Patio, Ramada and BBQ Area
Big Screen Televisions	Maintenance Facilities	Big Screen Color Television	**Roosevelt PERA**
Billiard Table	Camping Gear Storage	Racquetball Courts	Houses (8)
Fitness Center Building	Paint Storage Building	Horseshoe Pits	Kitchen/Meeting Facilities
Dance Hall	Wood Shop	Banquet Hall	Recreation Hall
Assembly Hall	Covered Maintenance Storage	Kitchen Facilities	Maintenance Shop
Lighted Swimming Pool	Deep Pit Bar-B-Que	Picnic Ramadas	Wood Shop
Locker Rooms	Administration Building	Bar-B-Que Grills	Sports Court
Shaded Pool Areas	Haunted House Facility	Shooting Ranges	Horseshoe Pits
Shaded Game Area	Grassed Picnic Area	Jogging Track	Bicycle Rentals
Lighted & Covered Ping Pong Area	Recreation Warehouse	Softball Field	Swimming Cove
Lighted Tennis Courts (4)	Remote Park Restroom Complex	Maintenance Facility	Caretaker's Home
Lighted Playground		Fitness Center	Divisional Offices
BBQ Grills	**Stewart Mountain PERA**		Employee General Store
Kitchen Facilities	Houses (3)		
Big Horn Terrace Meeting Room	Grass Park	**Navajo Generating Station**	
Lighted Picnic Ramadas (5)	Remote Restrooms	PERA	
Shuffleboard Area	Trails Leading to River	17-Acre Park	
Game Equipment Checkout		Divisional Office	
		Employee General Store	

Diversification of Services

Through the post-World War II period, the range of employee services in manufacturing concerns, insurance and banking companies, airlines, health care systems, and other corporate organizations expanded greatly. Increasingly, leadership in the field was provided by the National Employee Services and Recreation Association (NESRA).

Health Care and Fitness Programs. As an example of expanded programming in this area, Smith Kline Beecham, a major pharmaceutical corporation, sponsored a Life Management Center in the 1980s and l990s that provided personalized exercise services to all company employees in its Wellness Rx Facility:

> The Facility is open 13 hours a day, Monday through Friday. It is staffed at all times with degreed exercise physiologists who assess employees' initial levels of fitness, discuss their goals, [and] then develop individualized exercise programs. These programs are regularly checked and updated. Formal re-evaluations and reviews are scheduled every six months... Regular exercising at the Wellness Rx Facility has helped many of our members improve their health. For example, several members with hypertension lowered their blood pressure so much that their doctors have lowered the dosage on their medication.[10]

Similarly, Borg-Warner Automotive, a manufacturing company in Bellwood, Illinois, sponsors a Wellness Center which has over 4,000 square feet of cardiovascular and strength training equipment, a flexibility station, lockers, an aerobics and dance room, a fitness testing room, and a blood pressure station. Along with such physically oriented services, the Center's concept of wellness takes into account preventive maintenance and rehabilitation and injury prevention and is linked to Borg-Warner's other Occupational Health, Safety and Environmental Health services in promoting total employee well-being.[11]

Many companies introduced other programs designed to help employees meet significant health needs: stress management groups, substance-abuse services, weight-loss and other wellness functions. Such programs were demonstrated through research to have a measurable impact on employee performance, reducing absenteeism and illness and helping to limit job turnover. In a number of large concerns, medical insurance costs were significantly reduced, and it was concluded that employee morale and loyalty to management goals had been strengthened.

The chairman and CEO of Texas Instruments Inc., in Dallas, Texas, expressed the view of many company executives:

> We see employee services and recreation as one part of a total package that includes competitive salaries, benefits and health promotion services and activities. All of these are designed to let our people know we value them, and we view them as key contributors to our company's success.... We've tried to design our ES & R programs to address the total well-being of our employees and their families by providing them with programs that can enhance their physical, mental and emotional health.[12]

Community Role of Companies

During this period, a growing number of companies also became more active in assisting communities in solving their social and environmental problems. As earlier chapters showed, partnerships were formed in many cities to promote environmental causes, work with at-risk youth, and focus on health concerns within community life. Companies sponsored festivals promoting understanding, major sports tournaments, projects advocating gender equity, and marathons and other sports events and facilities.

An outstanding example is the Chase Corporate Challenge, sponsored by The Chase Manhattan Bank, which began in 1977 with 200 runners from 50 companies racing through New York City's Central Park. Today, the Corporate Challenge Series is the world's largest participatory road racing program, with 19 races in 16 cities that attract more than 190,000 participants from over 6,000 companies, including events in Germany and England (see Figure 6-8).

Figure 6-8
Scenes from a recent Chase Corporate Challenge event.

In many corporations, such community-directed functions are the responsibility of employee-service and recreation managers. Typically, the employee services manager for the M. D. Anderson Cancer Center at the University of Texas in Houston, Texas, assumes responsibility for recruiting

> employees for community events such as the Houston/Tenneco Marathon and the University of Texas Health Science Center Sportathon. We sponsor health fairs and guest lectures during the Texas Medical Center Wellness Week. We promote cultural events in Houston throughout the workplace with the Council for the Visual and Performing Arts.
>
> We maintain seasonal special events, such as our Employee Christmas Dinner, Christmas decorating contest, National Hospital Week, Savings Bond drive, United Way, etc . . . We handle discount programs for employees dealing with sporting and cultural events and various coupon books. We maintain our institutional bulletin board which publicizes our programs and those from other departments. We are also in charge of the monthly Outstanding Employee Award program.[13]

Shifting of Program Emphasis

During the 1990s, the program emphasis in many employee services and recreation units shifted heavily in the direction of such programs. In 1997, Patrick Stinson, executive director of NESRA, identified 10 important elements that fit under the employee services "umbrella." These were (1) recreation activities; (2) employee stores; (3) United Way; (4) discount buying services; (5) dependent care functions; (6) health promotions; (7) service awards; (8) blood drives; (9) company travel arrangements; and (10) special events.[14]

Continuing Emphasis on Recreation

Many employee services units continued to promote recreation as a primary responsibility during this period. For example, a large printing concern in Strasburg, Virginia, Judd's Incorporated, centralized its employee services functions in 1993, so it could provide varied health-related and safety programs for all its employees. However, Judd's also gave heavy emphasis to recreation activities that served employees working on 28 different shifts. Its Committee for Activity, Recreation and Entertainment (CARE) became incorporated as a nonprofit organization in 1996 in order to promote an extensive sports program:

> In addition to sponsoring a Little League Baseball team, a Men's Intramural Basketball team, a Judd's Golf outing, and a Men's Independent Softball team, the committee sponsors a Summer and Winter Challenge Cup. This is a competition between area companies.... Each team has company shirts, a fight song and a banner for Opening ceremonies. The Winter Challenge Cup consists of Basketball, Volleyball and Bowling. Companies send teams that comply with minimum and/ or maximum gender requirements (men and women). There is also a Masters category for persons over the age of 40.[15]

Judd's CARE organization also sponsors bus trips to entertainment events, an annual seafood feast, a company picnic, a Christmas/Awards banquet, a book fair, an annual tube float, and a family events calendar.

Changing Employee-Services Identity

Despite the continuing emphasis on recreation in many companies, it was apparent by century's end that the field of employee services, which had begun with a primary focus on recreation during the "industrial recreation" era, was now far more diversified.

In the 1980s and 1990s, with a growing emphasis on customer satisfaction, quality-driven products, benchmarking, and benefits based management emphasizing concrete outcomes of programs, there was pressure to provide those services that would contribute most directly to company efficiency and profitability. At this time, the structure of many workforces changed radically, with many companies downsizing after mergers or corporate buyout. With smaller staffs and more telecommuting employees, part-time or special-project workers, and with more diverse staffs in terms of gender and ethnicity, corporations became increasingly sensitive to changing employee needs.

New Title for the Field

Given this background, the dominant professional organization in the field, the National Employee Services and Recreation Association (NESRA), changed its official title in January 2000 to the Employee Services Management Association (ESM). At the same time, it issued a statement of the key elements in employee services that was similar to Patrick Stinson's earlier breakdown (see Figure 6-9). In this new, official statement, while recreation remained one of the 10 most important components of employee services management, it was no longer a featured element, but merely parallel in importance with the rest of the field.

Professionalism in Employee Services

Relatively few college or university leisure-studies departments offer specialized options in employee services, and there are few individual courses in the field. The main source of professional development therefore is the Employee Services Management Association. This organization today is a leading force in the field, carrying out research, conducting conferences and workshops, consulting with individual firms and program managers, and stimulating new advances in the field. Through the years, it has

> led progressive companies through opening employee stores, promoting wellness programs and creating solutions to dependent care issues; plus orchestrating dynamic special events, coordinating group travel and managing sports leagues.
>
> Today, ESM Association members motivate employees to participate in community service projects at their workplaces, collectively donating $371,780,000 and 490,000 pints of blood to United Way just last year. ESM Association members

Figure 6-9
January 2000 statement of Employee Services Management Association.

THE TEN COMPONENTS
OF A WELL-ROUNDED EMPLOYEE SERVICES PROGRAM

- Employee Stores
- Community Services
- Convenience Services
- Dependent Care
- Recreation Programs
- Recognition Programs
- Special Events
- Travel Services
- Voluntary Benefits
- Wellness

Employee Services Management (ESM) Association is the only association providing resources for a whole gamut of employee programs that encourage employees to live balanced lives while positively affecting an employer's bottom line. A well-rounded employee services program includes all of these components. In some instances, an employee services manager oversees all components from one department. In other cases, companies have many of these programs in place, but they are implemented by a range of employees in various departments.

Employee services are here to stay. While the specific offerings may change with time, employee services will always exist to encourage employees to live balanced lives as they help the company achieve its goals. Valued employees are more likely to be productive and loyal to the company.

ESM Association promotes the following programs as the key ingredients to a successful employee services program.

EMPLOYEE STORES
Employee stores are physical retail establishments or on-line buying sites that allow employees to purchase a variety of items to save employees time and money. The top selling items in employee stores are logo clothes/items, T-shirts, discount tickets, sundries, and greeting cards. Each employee services manager spends about $71,170 annually on store merchandise/inventory.

COMMUNITY SERVICES
Employee services managers organize employee efforts to feed the hungry, clothe the needy, educate the less fortunate and shelter those without a home. These programs help unite employees of all levels and reinforce a positive statement about their employers, who are providing outlets for them to make a difference in their communities.

Figure 6-9 cont.

CONVENIENCE SERVICES

On-site services such as dry cleaning, discount ticket sales, resource and referral services, car services, and more, attract and retain qualified employees in today's tight labor market. On-line Employer Sponsored Value Plans (ESVPs) bring products, services and savings to employees' fingertips. These programs make it convenient for employees to run errands and buy gifts during lunch and still return to work on time. Employers benefit from the outcome of these services through lower absenteeism rates.

RECREATION PROGRAMS

Sports leagues and special interest clubs allow employees to express themselves as individuals. Through involvement in these activities, employees develop a broader range of skills, learn to be leaders and enjoy coming to work.

SPECIAL EVENTS

Holiday parties, company picnics, company celebrations—all of these are special events employee services providers plan to further direct company goals and unite employees.

VOLUNTARY BENEFITS

Employees turn to employee services providers to help them search for the best values on voluntary, portable insurance policies, services and warranties. ESM Association's Employee Preferred is the official provider of insurance at a value price. Insurance policies include automobile, home, long-term care/personal care, serious illness, group life insurance, prepaid legal, and home office; services include benefits consulting and Internet banking; and warranties include automobile and home service agreements.

DEPENDENT CARE

Employee services managers provide employees with solutions to the demands of eldercare, childcare and even petcare. Whether they are managing on-site facilities, a consortium back-up center, summer day camps, lunchtime education programs, or outsourcing research and referrals, employee services providers help employees address dependent care issues.

RECOGNITION PROGRAMS

Employers of Choice quickly reward employees for solid contributions to the company's goals. ESM Association members spend $41,800,000 collectively on employee recognition programs each year. Association findings show more and more employee services providers taking on the role of main purchasing agent for all of their companies' recognition programs.

TRAVEL SERVICES

From planning group trips to providing discount information packets for specific destinations, employee services managers help employees get away from it all with travel services.

WELLNESS

ESM Association members focus on health promotion by offering lunchtime seminars, fitness incentive programs, personal development opportunities, on-site fitness centers, ropes courses, experiential training, and more. These programs encourage healthy lifestyles and help reduce medical claims, in turn, saving employers money.

To compete for the best employees, employers must implement employee services programs. In existence since 1941, (formerly National Employee Services and Recreation Association, NESRA), ESM Association is your one-stop resource for how-to information, suppliers and services for employee programs. Look to ESM Association for articles on the latest trends in employee services, immediate access to pioneers in the field and model programs that can save you time and money. Begin your membership in ESM Association today. You'll be on the road to helping your company become an Employer of Choice and stay that way.

ESM Association, 2211 York Rd., Suite 207, Oak Brook, IL 60523-2371, Phone: 630.368.1280, FAX: 630.368.1286, E-mail: esmahq@esmassn.org, URL: http://www.esmassn.org

develop outlets for companies to recognize employees in a manner that boosts productivity, positively affect the the company's bottom line. Members frequently call Association Headquarters to receive personal attention to their daily challenges . . .[16]

Today, approximately 2,300 companies are members of the Employee Services Management Association. A new membership category for individual professionals in the field has been established, effective in 2001. To certify individual professionals, a revised process based on experience and a comprehensive examination, with accompanying requirements for continuing education credits (CEUs) is also being put in place.

To cultivate professionalism, the ESM Association has developed a Center of Innovative Education in the field, which provides state-of-the-art conferences, local chapter meetings and workshops, and new Work/Life in Motion event. It also cooperates with other organizations, such as the Wellness Councils of America, the National Tour Association, The Motivation Show, and the Incentive Marketing Association, to develop collaborative projects. It has over 40 chapters in over five major regions in the United States, and it is steadily growing in membership.

Suggested Questions for Class Discussion or Essay Examinations

1. Obviously, the chief purpose of the armed forces is to defend the nation. This purpose would seem to be remote from the task of sponsoring recreation programs. Why, then, does the Department of Defense maintain an extensive Morale, Welfare and Recreation (MWR) system, complete with hundreds of facilities and thousands of professional leaders and managers?
2. What are some of the key elements in armed forces recreation programs? Which of these, described in this chapter, seem to be geared especially for Navy service personnel? Why are family needs and youth programs especially important, and what programs are provided in this area?
3. Explain the difference between appropriated (APF) and nonappropriated (NAF) funding support, and show how fiscal support of different MWR activities is apportioned according to their relevance to important Navy needs.
4. As in the armed forces area, what are the important purposes of employee services and recreation in terms of the needs of companies and other institutions maintaining such programs? What criteria can be used to determine whether employee services are achieving their stated goals?
5. This chapter identifies 10 key elements in employee services management today (see page 124). In your view, which of these involve clearly recreational kinds of services, and which do not? Why has fitness programming become a particularly important service provided by most companies today?

Footnotes

[1] Korb, L.J. (1982). *Morale, welfare and recreation program overview.* Washington, D.C.: U.S. Department of Defense, 3.

[2] *Program management handbook.* (1995). Millington, Tenn.: Bureau of Naval Personnel, 5-17.

[3] *Get on board: MWR division.* (1999). Millington, Tenn.: Bureau of Naval Personnel, 5-6.

[4] Start smart: Popular on military bases worldwide. (1998). *Parks and Recreation.* December, 27.

[5] Dorazio, C. (1999). Getting semper fit. *Parks and Recreation.* December, 62-64.

[6] Merkel, D. (1999). An oasis in the desert. *Parks and Recreation.* December, 56.

[7] *Strategic youth action plan.* (1998). Arlington, Va.: Defense Department Office of Family Policy, 5

[8] *MWR training program.* (1998). Millington, Tenn., Bureau of naval Personnel, 3.

[9] Ellis, K. (1997). Pera club. *Employee Services Management.* August, 15.

[10] Kurzeja, L. (1995). SmithKline Beecham wellness r/x facility. *Employee Services Management.* May-June, 16.

[11] Begley, K. (1999). Wellness drives B-W automotive. *Employee Services Management.* November-December, 30.

[12] NESRA's employer of the year. (1991), *Employee Services Management.* May-June, 17.

[13] Member success profile. (1991). *Employee Services Management.* September, 13.

[14] Stinson, P. (1997). The employee services umbrella. *Employee Services Management.* April, 11.

[15] Fleming, T. (l997). Judd's incorporated. *Employee Services Management.* August, 8-9.

[16] The only resource you need. (2000). Oak Brook, Il.: *ESM Association.* January, 2-3.

Chapter 7

Campus and Private-Membership Recreation

Introduction

A major sector of recreation programming designed to meet the needs of older teenagers and young adults is provided by campus recreational sports units and student union organizations in colleges and universities. In addition, many school districts also sponsor diversified leisure programs for both youth and adults, in some cases in partnership with local public recreation and park agencies.

A second focus of this chapter concerns the sports, fitness, aquatic, and social programs offered by private-membership groups, such as country clubs, yacht clubs, and golf clubs, for their members. Similar leisure offerings are often available in varied types of residential settings, such as retirement villages, condominiums, and apartment complexes or vacation and second-home communities, where recreation facilities and programs are provided for residents and their guests.

Overview of Campus Recreation

Thousands of colleges and universities throughout the United States offer organized programs of leisure activities for their students and, in many cases, faculty and staff members as well.

Such programs consist heavily of sports activities ranging from instructional classes and free play to intramurals and large-scale tournaments. These activities, along with outdoor recreation pursuits, are usually sponsored or administered by either a department of collegiate athletics or campus officials linked to departments or schools of health, physical education, and recreation.

Many other leisure activities are of a broader cultural or social nature; they involve clubs, social events, concerts, performing arts events, film series, lectures and forums, dances and festivals. These programs are often provided within a college union structure operating under the direction of a dean of student life or similar administrator, and with student committees helping to set policy.

Goals of Campus Recreation

Such programs are encouraged by college and university administrators for a number of reasons: (1) they assist in the orientation of new students and their adjustment to campus life; (2) they contribute to the academic growth of students in subject-field areas; (3) they serve as a means of maintaining a healthy degree of control over students' lives; (4) they enhance the image, appeal, and recruitment and retention success of higher-education institutions; and (5) they offer a positive means of improving the quality of life of the students on campus, and of promoting their well-rounded development.

Student Orientation and Adjustment

Many students entering a college campus for the first time—either after high school graduation or upon transferring from a community college—have difficulty adjusting to their new environment. Loneliness and insecurity are common, and many younger students do poorly in their work, are beset by personal problems, and actually leave campuses within the first few weeks or months after enrollment.

Varied student orientation programs can help to overcome such problems, helping students learn about the institution's structure, policies, services, and opportunities. Social events, workshops and entertainment programs provide the opportunity for students to relax and have a chance to make friends quickly.

Contributing to Academic Growth

Many clubs and other service programs expose students to more advanced or specialized opportunities within their fields of curricular interest.

Typically, music or drama majors may join performing groups on campus, and art students or journalism majors may gain immediate valuable experience on the campus newspaper or literary magazine.

Political science majors may join political clubs of their choice, run for campus office, and serve on governance committees and study groups. Those in the physical or social sciences are also likely to find noncurricular groups that help them extend their classroom experiences. In the most obvious examples of curricular enrichment, majors in physical education, recreation, and dance have the opportunity to compete on appropriate levels of play, assume leadership roles, and gain valuable performing and production experience.

Needed Control Over Campus Life

In the distant past, most colleges and universities maintained—or attempted to maintain—strict control over the lives of students in such areas as drinking, sexual behavior, gambling, observing dormitory curfews and similar concerns linked to health and safety.

Then, in the 1960s and 1970s, many institutions responded to student demands for greater freedom and autonomy by introducing much less structured degree requirements, and by eliminating restrictive rules governing student behavior.

However, by the early 1990s, college administrators realized that the newfound freedom of students had gone too far. Severe problems had arisen in such areas as drinking and drug-taking, violence, hazing and other forms of destructive behavior. *The Chronicle of Higher Education* reported:

> Drug arrests rose by 7 percent and alcohol arrests by more than 3 percent on college campuses in 1997, the sixth consecutive year of increases, according to a [national] survey... In 1996 alcohol arrests increased by 10 percent and drug arrests by [5] percent.[1]

Decades after American college students defiantly rejected curfews, dress codes, and dormitory house mothers, a new revolution got under way in undergraduate life. Ethan Bronner writes:

> Reflecting a range of societal changes—consumerism, litigiousness, a shift in generational relations and increased fears about campus drinking—colleges are offering and students are often demanding greater supervision of their lives.[2]

He points out examples of this extended supervision. For example, Pennsylvania State University has opened an alcohol free, adult-supervised student center with entertainment on weekend nights. Dartmouth College ended single-sex fraternities, which had served as the basis for the 1978 movie *Animal House*, and Princeton ended a 25-year tradition known as "Nude Olympics," in which sophomores ran naked at midnight after the first snowfall. Increasing numbers of other colleges began to ban or limit drinking, particularly in fraternity houses, and to punish offenders of hazing policies.[3]

At the same time, along with stronger enforcement of control policies, it was recognized that constructive recreation and social programs needed to be provided for students as counter-attractions.

Enhancing Institutional Image

Clearly, maintaining a vibrant and impressive institutional image is part of the purpose of offering diversified campus recreational and cultural programs.

While many colleges and universities rely on their successful sports teams to achieve this goal, or on their high academic rating, other positive elements include having active programs in the performing arts, thriving student clubs and activities, trips and outings, and many campus groups that represent different factions or student interests. These elements contribute both to the external image of colleges and to the recruitment of capable, highly motivated students.

Contributing to Student Development

Finally, the cocurricular program of student activities yields important benefits, not only with respect to curricular enrichment, but also with its potential effect on the student's character and personality development

As individuals discover their talents, undertake challenging tasks, assume meaningful campus responsibility, and enjoy positive social relationships with other students and faculty members, they grow in meaningful ways.

Recreational Sports Programs

During the last three decades of the 20th century, many colleges and universities expanded their programs of club and intramural sports, often offering extensive skills classes and opportunity for practice and competition on many levels. Increasingly, instead of being limited to facilities designed primarily for physical education use or for varsity athletics, institutions have built new sports facilities, aquatic and fitness centers, and field houses to serve such needs.

In the late 1990s, Lewis, Jones, Lamke, and Dunn pointed out that recreational sports programs had their roots in college and university athletic departments, when administrators realized that the bulk of students could not, or would not, participate in intercollegiate athletics but had a strong desire to take part in sports. Today, they write, recreational sports programs are offered in every type of college and university setting:

> This area is growing because of the age range of the population it serves, the ability to provide adequate on-site facilities for comprehensive programming in a variety of sports activities, and the opportunity to conduct programs for different levels of ability and interest.[4]

Examples of Recreational Sports

The Recreational Sports Division of Virginia Commonwealth University in Richmond sponsors a huge range of activities on several campus locations. These include a major fitness program, with such elements as varied dance skills, kick boxing and other martial arts, yoga, interval challenge exercise, and water-fitness activities; intramural sports and sports clubs in basketball, outdoor soccer, softball, volleyball, floor hockey, badminton, and racquetball; an outdoor adventure program with ski trips, kayaking instruction, wall climbing, winter camping, mountain biking, and white-water rafting.

The recreational sports program at Virginia Commonwealth University is relatively inexpensive, and is supervised by an extensive staff of coaches, instructors, and other managers. (An example of just one sector of the overall program is shown in Figure 7-1.)

While some colleges and universities have less extensive recreational sports offerings, most provide a good selection of individual, dual, and team sports and outdoor recreation activities. Typical programs at the University of Northern Colorado at Greeley and Southern Illinois University at Carbondale, are shown in Figure 7-2 and Figure 7-3.

Figure 7-1
One element of recreational sport and fitness programs at Virginia Commonwealth University.

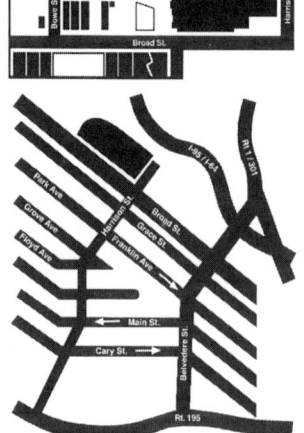

College Union Programs

Another important element in campus-based leisure-service programs consists of the broad range of student clubs and special interest groups, publications, cultural activities, social and entertainment events, and other student services that are usually under the direction of a dean of student life or similar college or university administrator. Such groups often include religious organizations, ethnic associations, gay clubs, computer clubs, and many other student groups linked to different academic fields of interest, and different branches of national organizations.

Figure 7-2
Club programs at the University of Northern Colorado.

ATHLETICS and RECREATIONAL SERVICES

... the power to succeed

INSTRUCTIONAL PROGRAMS MARTIAL ARTS

AIKIDO I
Introduction to the martial art of Aikido fitness and self-defense techniques. (8 weeks)
IN 1302.100
Instructors: Hilary Dawson & Perry Plewes
Date: January 24 - March 22
Time: 7:30 - 8:55 pm
Days: Mondays & Wednesdays
Location: McKinnon Apparatus Gym
Members: $40.50 + GST = $43.33
Non-Mem: $50.65 + GST = $54.20
No classes February 21 and 23

AIKIDO II
Building on Level I with more advanced techniques. (8 weeks)
IN 1302.101
Instructors: Hilary Dawson & Perry Plewes
Date: January 24 - March 22
Time: 7:30 - 9:25 pm
Days: Mondays & Wednesdays
Location: McKinnon Apparatus Gym
Members: $40.50 + GST = $43.33
Non-Mem: $50.65 + GST – $54.20
No classes February 21 and 23

KENDO
Introduction to this physically demanding Japanese martial art, based on the use of the Samurai Sword tradition. (8 weeks)
IN 1303.100
Instructor: Ted Davis
Date: January 25 - March 23
Time: 6:00 pm - 7:25 pm
Days: Tuesdays & Thursdays
Location: McKinnon Apparatus Gym
Members: $38.50 + GST = $41.20
Non-Mem: $48.15 + GST = $51.52
No classes February 22 and 24

SHOTOKAN KARATE
Shotokan Karate is a traditional form of unarmed combat which originated in Japan as a form of self-defense. Classes focus on developing the various thrusting, kicking, and blocking methods, karate stances and lunge techniques, as well as offering instruction on hand-hold reversals and general self-defense. (8 weeks)
IN 1306.100
Instructor: Paul Molinari
Date: January 25 - March 23
Time: 7:30 pm - 8:55 pm
Days: Tuesdays & Thursdays
Location: McKinnon Apparatus Gym
Members: $38.50 + GST = $41.20
Non-Mem: $48.15 + GST = $51.52
No classes February 22 and 24

TAE KWON DO
Tae Kwon Do is a 2000 year old blend of mental and physical disciplines that will help to promote personal well being as well as security. Master In-Gu Hwang will introduce you to both the traditional style from Korea and the modern Olympic style.
IN 1323.100
Instructors: Master In-Gu Hwang
Date: January 28 - March 24
Time: 6:00 pm - 7:30 pm
Days: Fridays
Location: McKinnon Apparatus Gym
Members: $40.50 + GST = $43.33
Non-Mem: $50.65 + GST = $54.20
No class February 24

WADO KAI KARATE
Beginners will learn to perform the basic calisthenics, kicks, blocks, punches and kata of this karate style which emphasizes speed and dynamic, explosive techniques. (8 weeks)
IN 1305.100
Instructor: Michael Alberti
Date: January 24 - March 22
Time: 8:00 pm - 9:25 pm
Days: Mondays & Wednesdays
Location: McKinnon Apparatus Gym
Members: $38.50 + GST = $41.20
Non-Mem: $48.15 + GST = $51.52
No classes February 21 and 23

WOMEN'S KARATE
This course provides the traditional training and self-defense skills in an environment specific to women. (8 weeks)
IN 1304.100
Instructors: Leslie Bowers & Kathy Singleton-Bowers
Date: January 25 - March 25
Time: Tuesdays, 8:00 pm - 9:25 pm
Saturdays, 1:00 pm - 2:25 pm
Days: Tuesdays & Saturdays
Location: Tuesdays, McKinnon Dance Studio
Saturdays, Gordon Head Dance Studio
Members: $29.50 + GST = $31.56
Non-Mem: $36.75 + GST = $39.32
No classes February 22 and 26

Fit Tip
*"Energy follows thought.
You actually become what you think."*
Lynne Namka

Figure 7-3
Southern Illinois University offers an even greater range of physical recreation activities, including cricket, rodeo, triathlon, and "ultimate" frisbee.

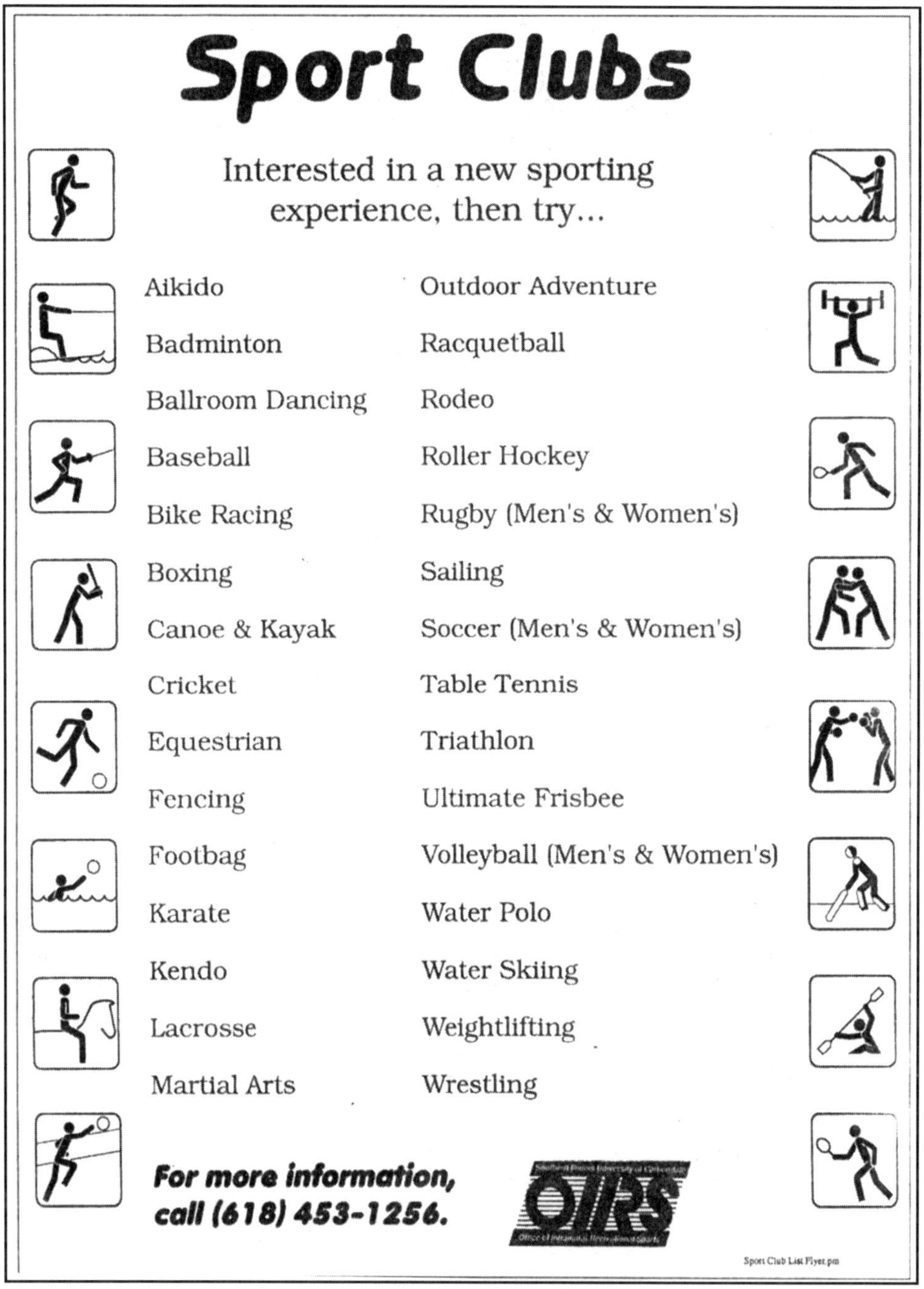

Sport Clubs
Interested in a new sporting experience, then try...
Aikido
Badminton
Ballroom Dancing
Baseball
Bike Racing
Boxing
Canoe & Kayak
Cricket
Equestrian
Fencing
Footbag
Karate
Kendo
Lacrosse
Martial Arts
Outdoor Adventure
Racquetball
Rodeo
Roller Hockey
Rugby (Men's & Women's)
Sailing
Soccer (Men's & Women's)
Table Tennis
Triathlon
Ultimate Frisbee
Volleyball (Men's & Women's)
Water Polo
Water Skiing
Weightlifting
Wrestling
For more information, call (618) 453-1256.
OIRS
Sport Club List Flyer.pm

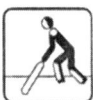

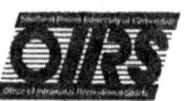

Funding for the support of such services is often provided by a campus-wide activities fee, or by the institutional allocation of other funds to support overhead expenses and maintain key staff personnel. Certain activities, such as concerts, trips, and dances, will typically be supported by fees on a self-supporting basis. Often, these programs are housed in a college union building, or student activity center, with satellite programs in dormitories and other campus settings.

In most colleges and universities, student advisory groups or officers play a role—often in conjunction with faculty or administrative representatives—for planning and determining policy for student services. For example, at San Diego State University in California, the

> Associated Students Organization sponsors a remarkable range of films, concerns, recreational and athletic programs, legal services, and other activities. This multi-million-dollar corporation, funded by annual student fees, operates the Aztec Center, the college's student union building. In addition, it runs a highly successful travel service, intramurals and sports clubs, special events, leisure skills classes, lectures, movies, concerts, an open-air theater, a large aquatics center, a campus radio station, a child-care center, a black students council, a general store, a campus information booth, and many other services and activities. Within this spectrum, the bulk of the leisure activities on the San Diego campus are operated directly by the Recreation Activities Board, a unit within the overall Asssciated Students Organization.[5]

In other settings, such as Concordia University in Montreal, Canada, the student union program is seen as an important vehicle for promoting student growth as responsible citizens and taking responsibility for varied university functions—including such social issues as "animal rights" and even international and United Nations concerns (Figure 7-4).

Staffing Patterns

As several of the programs previously described indicate, many campus recreation activities require substantial leadership, in terms of instructors, coaches, supervisors, and coordinators.

Particularly in sports programs, leadership is often provided by skilled graduate students who may have such responsibilities as part of graduate assistantship grants. Within the general student services programs, faculty members often serve as advisors to special-interest groups.

Full-Time Staff Members

Many campus recreation programs are managed by full-time, professional directors who continue in these roles—in some cases linked with academic appointments—within athletic departments or other higher-education administrative divisions. While their professional identification is not as clearly defined as it is in other areas of recreation, park, and leisure services, usually they are active members of such professional societies as the National Intramural and Recreational Sports Association (NIRSA) and the Association of College Unions International.

Lewis and his co-authors point out that campus recreation often has a strong tie with the overall field of recreation and leisure services in that many college students gain direct experience in recreation programming and management through their undergraduate participation in it. They learn to deal with budgets, participant problems, facility manage-

Figure 7-4
Brochure of Concordia University Student Union program.

ment and scheduling, and working with campus constituency groups and advisory committees and boards:

> Student employees, often assigned a great deal of responsibility, learn how to deal with the challenges of providing recreation services and programs to a large, diverse, and demanding population. Those experiences better enable them to pursue a job in the "real world" within the profession of parks and recreation."[6]

School-Sponsored Recreation

While the term "campus recreation" is usually applied to college and university settings, the linkage between recreation and educational systems may also be seen on the elementary and secondary school levels.

Through the 20th century, many school districts sponsored extensive programs of after-school clubs, sports, and performing groups—in part to extend the school's formal educational program and in part to carry out the mandate of educating for leisure that many administrators had accepted in the early years of the century.

New School Pressures on Children

However, in the final decades of the century, it was apparent that many school districts were being pressured to make children work longer and harder at academic studies. In response to public demands that children perform at higher levels on standardized tests, and political pressures to fund privatized, alternative, or "charter" schools, if fundamental skills are not taught more effectively, many school systems lengthened class schedules and required children to attend summer sessions to make up for poor work. Other states and school districts have lengthened the school year and adopted year-round school schedules.

In addition, many schools have lengthened their school day. In *The New York Times*, Jodi Wilgoren writes that the "revolution" begins at 3 p.m. as, every afternoon in thousands of schools across America, students are staying after the final bell.

> The explosion in after-school programs—federal financing alone has ballooned to $454 million this year from $1 million in 1997—represents nothing less than a reimagining of the school day for the first time in generations, as educators and policy-makers seek to respond to the realities of working families and what may be missing from the classroom.[7]

There is growing concern that the pressure to improve performance on standardized tests has resulted in children being confined to long hours of sterile classroom drills, and has also squeezed out enrichment programs in music, art, and even science. Math and reading performance expectations are being pushed down to the youngest learners, and in numerous school districts, recess, formerly a time for relaxed play, has been eliminated.[8]

With pressure to learn computer skills and other languages, physical education requirements have been cut back heavily during the 1990s in many schools.

Counter-Pressures: Awareness of Children's Needs

At the same time, many educators, psychologists, and parents feel that the unrelenting emphasis on lengthy drills and test-centered learning is harmful—and that creative learning experiences and other enrichment activities are being neglected.

The wave of youthful violence in school after school during the 1990s, culminating in the tragic Columbine school massacre in Littleton, Colorado, in 1999 has made many parents increasingly concerned about the social climate in American high schools. There is growing realization that many schools are divided into cliques of "jocks," "preps," "stoners," "freaks," and even "trench coat Mafia." Beyond this, parents and educators alike recognize that to prevent youthful hostility and violence in the schools, it is not enough to have security guards and metal detectors at the doors. Instead, the social climate of the schools and the whole issue of character development and the teaching of positive social and moral values need to be explored and strengthened.

With "early intervention" having become a catchword among educators, there is a new emphasis on watching for signs of troubled students and responding promptly to threats or overt clashes among groups. The status-obsessed, ranking-conscious, and competitive nature of many school environments needs to be rethought—leaving strong implications for the potential role of student clubs, interest groups, government, and recreational sports for all students.

Trends in Adult Education and Recreation

Thus far, many school administrators have put far more emphasis on providing adult education and recreation programs than on offering comparable after-school activities for children. In school after school across the country, evening and weekend classes have become increasingly successful, as they offer a range of courses dealing with every type of pastime, adult learning challenge, and necessary practical skills.

Figure 7-5 shows one page of a much fuller schedule of noncredit classes offered at the Hatboro-Horsham Adult Evening School in Pennsylvania. In addition to the courses listed here, other popular offerings include "accounting fundamentals," "aerobics," "aikido," "Indian cooking," "Mid-Eastern Dance," "ballet," "tap dance," "dog obedience," "firearm safety and personal protection," "floral designs" "folk/rock guitar," home buyers' workshop," "Italian for beginners," "knitting," "meditation," "financial investing," and dozens of other leisure-oriented subjects.

Such courses are typically taught by experts in the specific areas covered who may or may not be certified teachers and who are usually hired based on the assumption that class enrollments will either meet a given level or be canceled.

In addition to public school systems, many community colleges are also offering such courses as part of adult continuing education programs, either with or without credit. Increasingly, such education-based classes are representing an important sector of adult leisure-time opportunities in America today. With the growing number of elderly persons who are seeking meaningful leisure experiences, college-and school-centered programs of this type promise to become even more popular in the years ahead.

Private-Membership Organizations

A seventh important category of organized leisure-service programming is provided by private-membership groups that customarily serve only their own members and their guests. There are several basic types of such membership groups:

(1) country clubs, yacht clubs, tennis clubs, and hunting and fishing clubs that often own their own buildings and properties; (2) fraternal and service organizations that offer similar hospitality services; and (3) retirement communities, vacation and second-home developments, and condominium units.

Such organizations are typically structured in one of two ways:

(1) as *membership associations* formed by groups of private individuals who establish their own policies and rules and maintain control through elected boards and officers; and (2) as

Figure 7-5
Schedule of courses offered by Hatboro-Horsham Adult Evening School in Pennsylvania (January 2000).

HATBORO-HORSHAM ADULT EVENING SCHOOL

REGISTER IN PERSON FEBRUARY 1 & 2 7:00-8:30 P.M. AT KEITH VALLEY MIDDLE SCHOOL, 227 MEETINGHOUSE ROAD, HORSHAM, PA
BRING CHECK OR MONEY ORDER ONLY

7. ALGEBRA, Basic, Part I   Wed. 6:30-8 p.m. $35
The course will cover basic operations, integers, linear equations, simple number and coin problems, factoring and solving of quadratic equations, the course may go further depending on the class. Improve your scores on placement tests. A textbook will be used and cost will be extra. Bring notebook and pencil to each class.
RUTH CLARK, Math Teacher

8. THE ART OF BALLOON SCULPTING   Tues. 7-9 p.m. $20
(Beginners)   5 weeks – Starts Feb. 8
This course is designed for beginners with the desire to learn the art of balloon sculpting. Focus will range from one balloon sculpture to multi balloon sculptures. Material fee $15 includes balloons and air pump.
JOE ST. MARIE, Instructor

9. THE ART OF BALLOON SCULPTING   Tues. 7-9 p.m. $20
(Advanced)   5 weeks – Starts Mar. 14
This course is designed for the more advanced student. Active class participation.
JOE ST. MARIE, Instructor

10. THE ART OF CLOWNING   Wed. 7-9 p.m. $35
Bring out the clown that is inside of you! Learn how to develop a clown character from what to do, to the makeup, and costume. Leave your worries at home – have fun!
PATRICIA CORSON, Instructor

11. ART (DRAWING)   Wed. 7-8:30 p.m. $35
For the beginning or advanced student. Learn to draw in a variety of media. This course includes: composition, perspective, color and figure sketching. Bring charcoal pencil and charcoal pad (12 x 18") on first night.
MIRIAM SEDERGRAN, Instructor

12. ART (OIL PAINTING)   Tues. 7-8:30 p.m. $35
Essentials of oil painting. You will learn perspective, color mixing and composition. Individual instruction for the beginner or advanced student. Bring your own materials - canvas - oil paints.
G. W. CATERER, Instructor

13. DRAWING (PORTRAIT)   Wed. 8:30-10 p.m. $35
Learn proportions and face structure necessary to draw a successful portrait. For the beginning or advanced student. Bring your choice of media: Charcoal pencil and charcoal pad, pastels and pastel pad, or pencil and sketch pad on first night.
MIRIAM SEDERGRAN, Instructor

14. ART (Acrylic Painting)   Tues. 8:30-10 p.m. $35
For the beginning or advanced student. Course includes understanding color, value, composition, weekly still life set-ups. Individual help. Bring paints & brushes on 1st night.
MICHAEL KUYPER, Instructor

15. ASTRONOMY   Wed. 7-8:15 p.m. $30
8 weeks – Starts Feb. 9
Learn about the wondrous universe out there: the planets and their satellites, comets, stars, the zodiac, and other wonders of outer space. Study strange things like "Black Holes" and "Gravitational Lenses." You will learn how to recognize constellations and learn the difference between a star and a planet. Discuss the expanding universe concept, the "Big Bang" theory, and the various types of telescopes. Bring a notebook.
DOM RAIMONDO, Instructor. Dom Raimondo is a former member of the Royal Canadian Astronomical Society and a present member of "The Planetary Society" U.S.A.

16. INTRODUCTION TO BIRDING   Sat. 8:30 a.m. $35
This course will consist of a series of leisurely Saturday morning bird walks at several local birding "hot spots." Beginners, as well as more advanced birders are welcome to come out for some fresh air, exercise, friendly conversation, a good bird watching. Begin with the winter species and move right into the fabulous spring migration. Shake those winter blahs! First session will be held on Tuesday evening February 15 at 7:00 p.m.; subsequent sessions meet on alternating Saturdays, at 8:30 a.m. at designated sites, the final session will be held in mid-May.
CHARLOTTE PERRY, Instructor

17. SATURDAY BIRDING   Sat. 8:00 a.m. $25
Feb. 26, Mar. 25, Apr. 29, May 13
For beginners and advanced students four Saturdays to local "Hot Spots" with popular instructor John King. Come out and enjoy the birds and walks. Schedule available at sign-up or call: 215-646-1768 and it will be mailed out to you.
JOHN KING, Instructor

18. BASIC BOATING   Wed. 7:30 p.m. $20
This course is conducted by members of the Pennsway Power Squadron. The schedule of instruction includes: handling under normal and adverse conditions; seamanship and common emergencies; "rules of the road"; aid to navigation; compass and chart familiarization; running lights and equipment; boat trailering; river boating; and mariners compass and piloting. A certificate is issued upon completing this course and a written examination. Cost of supplies is $26.00.
PENNSWAY POWER SQUADRON

19. BASIC MATH   Tues. 8:30-10 p.m. $35
Fractions, adding and subtracting fractions, division, word problems, percentage and decimals. Improve your ability to place higher on tests.
This course will help give you skills or improve skills in business or day to day living.
KENNETH YOWELL, Instructor

20. BRIDGE, Beginners   Tues. 7:15-9:15 p.m. $35
Standard American Goren Point Count will be used in this course. All bidding procedures, play of cards, conduct and ethics will be covered. This course is for beginners. Class time will be divided between lecture and actual play.
CHARLOTTE PERRY, Silver Life Master, Qualified Club Director, Instructor

21. BRIDGE II   Wed. 7:15-9:15 p.m. $35
This course is for those who have had beginners bridge or have not played in years. We will review the basics: Stayman, Jacoby transfers, Jacoby 2 NT, New suit signals, as well as other conventions. One hour lecture and one hour play of the hand.
CHARLOTTE PERRY, Silver Life Master, Qualified Club Director, Instructor

22. CAKE DECORATING   10 weeks – Wed. 7-9 p.m. $35
Learn to make beautiful cakes at home. Ten lessons devoted to basic cake preparation, basic borders, drop flowers, the rose, basketweave, character pans, figure piping and much more. Student supplies extra.
AUDREY READ, Instructor

COMPUTERS

23. COMPUTERS FOR THE NOVICE   Wed. 7-9 p.m. $35
5 weeks – Starts Feb. 9
Want to know about computers? We start with finding the "on" button, using the mouse, finding and getting into basic programs and saving your work. This is a basic beginner class and will prepare you for more advanced classes.
KATHLEEN RUGGIERI, Instructor

24. INTRODUCTION TO   Tues. 7-8:25 p.m. $50
PERSONAL COMPUTERS   5 weeks – Starts Feb. 8
Learn the capabilities, terminology, operations and applications of the IBM PC microcomputer. Instruction includes an introduction to computer theory and terminology, Windows, MS Word processing, and the Excel spreadsheet program. Each class includes a teacher-supervised laboratory period where students will run their own machine. Microsoft Office. Material fee, included in registration.
THEODORE ROTH, Instructor

25. NEW COMPUTER USER WITH   Wed. 8:35-10 p.m. $50
INTRO TO THE INTERNET   5 weeks – Starts Feb. 9
This is the course if you have a new computer with which you are not yet familiar. We will start with which device to turn on first and how to hook them up. Then learn about the hardware and applications that come with your computer...Windows, Paint Brush, and Write will be explained and used. We will demonstrate the internet with emphasis on how to use and download files to graphics. No prior P.C. required.
Class will be in a Lab with computers which students will use every night. Lab fee included in cost.
THEODORE ROTH, Instructor

26. NEW COMPUTER USER WITH   Tues. 8:35-10 p.m. $50
INTRO TO THE INTERNET   5 weeks – Starts Mar. 14
Same course as previous.
THEODORE ROTH, Instructor

27. WINDOWS   Wed. 7-8:25 p.m. $50
5 weeks – Starts Feb. 9
Look at how Windows finds and runs your programs. What is the control panel all about? Use those programs that came with Windows. Learn the advantages of the Windows environment with less hassle.
Windows files that have "INI", "DLL" and "SYS" extensions will be covered. File management is covered using Explorer. Missing icons and lost files will be traced. You will print and copy to disk crucial information.
This is a workshop atmosphere, with lots of hands on experience on our new computers. Some limited P.C. experience helpful. Material fee included in registration.
THEODORE ROTH, Instructor

28. WINDOWS   Tues. 7-8:25 p.m. $50
5 weeks – Starts Mar. 14
Same course as above.
THEODORE ROTH, Instructor

29. OFFICE   Tues. 8:25-10 p.m. $50
5 weeks – Starts Feb. 8
A survey of Microsoft's suite for business. We will look at Word, build a spreadsheet in Excel, setup a database in Access and time permitting, integrate them. We will use the sort and query capabilities of both Excel and Access. We will create a macro to increase your productivity. Knowledge of Windows is required, more computer experience will be helpful. Material fee included in registration.
THEODORE ROTH, Instructor

30. OFFICE   Wed. 7-8:30 p.m. $50
Same course as above.   5 weeks – Starts Mar. 15
THEODORE ROTH, Instructor

31. CRUISE THE INTERNET   Wed. 8:35-10 p.m. $50
5 weeks – Starts Mar. 15
Browser, Home pages and Search Engine will be covered. Will start with how to get access to the Web, using various providers including AOL. Discuss the two main brousers: Netscape and Internet explorer. We will use a protal to locate people, search for information, get maps and routes, weather. We will down load files, text and graphics and look at where the down loaded files will go; (For example, to disk or print.) The course is hands on and interactive using cable "That is fast" as our access. Some knowledge of Windows required. Lab fee included in registration.
THEODORE ROTH, Instructor

commercially owned bodies that also operate with closed membership lists, and often use selective screening procedures.

Country Clubs

This major segment of private-membership leisure-service organizations has represented an important type of recreation sponsor through the years. Such clubs may specialize in golf, tennis, yachting, or similar forms of play, and often maintain elaborate facilities as well as buildings that house social events, restaurants and similar accommodations.

In general, country club fees are substantial, and while screening policies that barred individuals of racial or religious minority group background have generally been overthrown by lawsuits and state legislation, their membership rolls tend to be composed of the most prestigious and well-to-do families in the community. One exception remains, in that many golf clubs in particular have persisted in denying women full membership rights and in limiting their participation in terms of available hours for play. Recognizing that golf clubs, as well as other social or business associations, are places where executives and leading professionals often discuss business matters and plans, this slight has represented a serious handicap for many women.

Recently, a number of court decisions have overturned such policies, as in Massachusetts, where

> . . . women members of the Haverhill Golf and County Club in Massachusetts have won a stunning jury verdict of $1.9 million in damages for being systematically denied full memberships and equal access to the golf course in prime playing time. The award, and the prospect that the court might now take control of the club, is sure to make clubs around the country review their policies.[9]

Overall, such private-membership clubs provide a variety of sports or outdoor recreation leisure opportunities for all ages, as well as regular social events through the year. In some cases, business clubs in larger cities, which relied on companies paying extensive memberships fees for their executives, have suffered from rulings by tax authorities that no longer permitted the companies to claim such expenses as tax write-offs. As a result, many of the most prestigious business and luncheon clubs, which have traditionally been places where the power structures in politics, business, and the professions met regularly, have experienced serious declines in membership.

Residence-Based Memberships

A rapidly growing form of private membership organizations that offers extensive leisure-service programs consists of various "leisure villages," retirement communities, second-home or vacation developments, apartment condominium associations, and other types of real estate development.

In such settings, which have been popping up rapidly in recent years, organized recreation has represented with an important sales lure and a highlight of daily life. Typically, such developments provide swimming pools, tennis courts, fitness centers, and often a network of clubs, special-interest groups, and social programs throughout the year.

More than 18,000 residents, for example, of the Leisure World retirement community in Laguna Hills, California—a development that recently transformed itself into California's newest city—have enjoyed pools, tennis courts, riding stables, and an assortment of recreational programs.

Sun City, Arizona Similarly, the immense and diversified settlement founded by developer Del Webb in the desert not far from Phoenix, Arizona, became the nation's largest retirement community, with 46,000 residents. From the beginning, Sun City

> ... was like a giant year-round camp. Golf courses snaked behind back yards and scores of hobby clubs sprang up for activities like square dancing and lawn bowling. "If you can't find something to do in Sun City "early residents liked to boast, "you're probably already dead."[10]

Today, residents are served by over 140 chartered clubs offering varied leisure pursuits and hobbies, and by seven multimillion-dollar recreation censors that offer everything from swimming and weight training in elaborate fitness centers to photo labs, sewing, ceramics and art classes (see Figures 7-6 and 7-7). In the expanded developments of Sun City West and Sun City Grand, the leisure lifestyle continues to offer a major sales attraction. Growing numbers of Sun City residents today also enjoy roller blading, hiking, rock climbing, and even in some cases training to run marathons or biathlons. An ambitious few take part in "heli-hiking—where they are dropped by helicopter in remote corners of the Canadian Rockies—which is startling evidence that many "elderly" people today have overthrown the knitting-and-shuffleboard stereotype of past generations.

In the retirement community of Pelican Cove in Sarasota, Florida, residents enjoy not only the standard recreational and social programs typical of such developments, but also Pelican Cove University. This informal, noncredit educational institution offers a wide range of sophisticated courses in literature and popular culture, politics, economics, and investment strategy—staffed by members of the community themselves who were formerly professors, lawyers and doctors or successful artists and critics (see Figure 7-8).

Other Residential Structures

Particularly in larger cities, other residential developments serve a broader range of people from different socioeconomic classes and ethnic and racial groups.

In the mid-1970s, for example, a huge apartment development known as Starrett City was built in Brooklyn, New York, to serve middle-income families of varied ethnic and racial backgrounds—about half of them of African-American, Hispanic, or Asian origins. Now known as Starrett at Spring Creek, the development provides a large clubhouse with meeting rooms and space for hobby and dance classes, as well as extensive pool and tennis activities and classes and social programs through the year.

On the outskirts of many cities, housing developments today often are managed by community associations that take responsibility for street cleaning and grounds maintenance, security, and the operation of varied leisure facilities. In 1970, there were about 10,000 such associations throughout the United States. But, writes Diana Schemo:

Figure 7-6
Brochure featuring Sun City recreation activities.

DEDICATED TO THE VERY BEST IN ACTIVE ADULT LIVING.

Artist rendering of the Sonoran Plaza.

What characterizes the Sun City lifestyle most are the residents and the multitude of special interest clubs and organizations which are formed as the community grows and evolves. Clubs which are commonly found at a Sun City include:

- Aerobics
- Art
- Ballroom Dancing
- Bicycling
- Billiards
- Bocci
- Bridge
- Calligraphy
- Canasta
- Ceramics
- Computers
- Golf
- Hiking
- Inline Skating
- Leathercraft
- Needlework
- Sewing
- Synchronized Swimming
- Tennis
- Woodworking

Figure 7-7
Examples of social events, tours, and other programs for Sun City West residents, used in promoting home sales.

Grand Events Calendar

Richard DeFay
Sales Associate

Remember, you're always invited and we hope to see you soon.

July 19
Major League Baseball
Arizona Diamondbacks vs. St. Louis Cardinals

The motorcoach leaves Sonoran Plaza at 5:15 p.m.

$32 per person covers game ticket and transportation.

Every Weekend through August
Ice Cream Home Tour

Grab a spoon and cool off any Saturday or Sunday between 8:00 a.m. and 5:00 p.m. at Café in the Park located in the model home center. Tour Sun City Grand's 23 model homes ranging in size from 1,100 to 2,965 square feet.

Coming in August
Summer Concert Series

Bring your blankets and lawn chairs to enjoy a diverse medley of local jazz, classical, and pop musicians under the stars in the outdoor amphitheater.
Call 623-546-7458 for details.

August 18
Major League Baseball
Arizona Diamondbacks vs. Chicago Cubs

The motorcoach leaves Sonoran Plaza at 5:15 p.m.

$32 per person covers game ticket and transportation.

August 25
Casual Dance

Slip on your dancing shoes and grab a partner for an evening of music and summer romance at the Sonoran Plaza Ballroom. Call 623-546-7458 for details.

September 1
Labor Day Weekend Barbecue

Kick off your Labor Day weekend with a pool side barbecue. While you're there check out the new outdoor lap pool.

Cocktails at 5:00 p.m., dinner served at 6:00 p.m.

Price: $12. Call 623-546-7458 for details.

By 1990 there were 130,000 associations housing 32 million Americans in arrangements as varied as co-op apartment buildings, condominiums and walled neighborhoods of free-standing houses. All these arrangements share a reliance on homeowner boards to provide services and govern residents. By 2000 [the estimate is that] the associations will number 225,000.[11]

Vacation Homes and Time-Shares

A final example of private-membership organizations that offer leisure facilities and programs is the establishment of vacation home developments or time-share arrangements, which have become increasingly popular in recent years.

The post–World War II baby boom, with millions of couples reaching the age and financial capability that made it possible for them to afford vacation homes, led to a steady climb in the number of such developments—particularly in the Southern or Southwestern states, where "snowbirds" stay during the winter months and return to the North in the spring.

Time-shares, which typically involve the purchase of a condo-type apartment for two to four weeks use each year, have gained increasing popularity and often are located in resort communities—including many complexes in skiing and winter sports areas. Originally, time-share buyers were locked into spending vacations in the same place year after year. But, writes Edwin McDowell:

> ... now many buyers split their week into two-, three- or four-day pieces. They can carry over unused days into another year. They can trade land-based time shares for a vacation on cruise ships .... [Often, owners trade their shares with others. One couple] swapped for weeks in Switzerland, Florida, California and New Orleans.[12]

Leisure opportunities provide such complexes with much of their appeal. At many ski resorts from New England to Colorado, instead of shutting down after the winter months, managers are adding summer camps for children and activities for adults. Smugglers' Notch, for example, has almost 50 summer programs for children three to 17, and 40 more for families and adults—with many of the participants owning time-shares.

Staffing Patterns in Private-Membership Clubs

Of all the types of leisure-service organizations described in this text, private-membership groups have the least professionalized staffing arrangements and identity.

Many of their recreational facilities and programs are administered by club or community managers, who are also responsible for other maintenance and security functions. Often the planning of recreational schedules and events is taken care of by residents who volunteer their time. While clubs may employ many paid leaders, such as golf and tennis professionals, fitness specialists and ski instructors, usually they identify chiefly with their area of special expertise, rather than with the broader leisure-service field.

In some private-membership settings, there *may* be extensive recreation staffs. For example, at the Lake Naomi Club, a 3,000-acre second home community country club nestled in the Pocono Mountains of Northeast Pennsylvania, organized programs are offered in such recreational activities as tennis; aquatics; sailing; golf; fitness; "kids' camp"; teen, preteen, and family events; and other pastimes. A leadership staff of approximately 28

Figure 7-8
Partial listing of courses offered by Pelican Cove residents.

1998 Pelican Cove University Schedule

Instructor	course	time place
	MONDAY	
Herb Rosenthal	Computer Forum begins 1/12/98	9:00-10:15 Pelican Pavilion
Judy Martin	Meditation: every other week begins 1/12/98-	10-11am Harbor Club
Givens Thornton	Understanding Human Behavior- every other week --begins 2/2/98	10-11am Harbor Club
Herb Weisenger	Shakespeare in progress: Julius Caesar; Antony & Cleopatra	10:30-12:00 Pelican Pavilion
Ann Funaro	Italian- begins 1/5/98	2-4:15 Wilbanks (up)
Maurice Shapiro	Current Events-begins 1/5/98	8:00pm Harbor Club
	TUESDAY	
Sara Sutley	Spanish- in progress next class	10:00-11:30am Wilbanks
Roger Goodman	Poetry- begins 1/13/98	11:00-12:30- Harbor Club
Eric Winters	Etymology next class 1/13/98	11:30-12:30 Wilbanks (down)
Barry Cohen	Homer's Odyssey- begins 1/13/98	1:00-2:30 pm- Harbor Club
Evelyn Pitcher	Children's Lit begins 1/20/98	2:30-4:00 pm-Wilbanks (up)
	WEDNESDAY	
Chan Sweetser	Financial, Tax & Estate Planning: 1/14, 2/18, 3/18	9:00-10:30am Pelican Pavilion
Bernice Rosen	Looking at Dance- begins 1/7/98	10:30-12:00 Harbor Club
Miriam Weiss	Great Books- begins 1/7/98 every other week	1:30-3:00pm Wilbanks (up)
	THURSDAY	
Vivian Cristol	Creative Writing- resumes 1/8/98 every other week	10:30-12:00 Wilbanks (down)
Jim Schoener	Legal Problems resumes 1/8/98	10:00-11:30 Harbor Club
Dan Klugherz	Documentary Films- begins- 1/29/98	1:30-3:00- Harbor Club
	FRIDAY	
Frank Schaal	Handwriting Analysis- begins 1/9/98	10:00-11:30am-Harbor Club

individuals directs these activities, and the Lake Naomi Club regularly employs college interns in its summer programs.

Particularly for club or condominium managers in settings where food services and living accommodations are offered, the field that they are closest to is the hospitality industry—with their responsibilities similar to those found in many tourism enterprises. A number of the staffing responsibilities, professional associations, and operational guidelines in this area of leisure services are described in Chapter 10.

Suggested Questions for Class Discussion and Essay Examinations

1. What is the underlying rationale for the provision of recreation services on American college and university campuses today? How has the philosophy of campus governance and supervision of students' lives changed since the l960s? Why?
2. What are some of the main elements today in campus sports, outdoor recreation, social and cultural activities? How does participation in such programs contribute to the academic goals of the institution or to the overall quality of campus life?
3. As a specialized field of leisure-service management, how closely linked is campus recreation to the overall field of recreation, parks, and leisure services? Describe the functions of the National Intramural and Recreational Sports Association (NIRSA) in this area.
4. This chapter identifies several types of private-membership recreation sponsors. Describe two of these, indicating those who are served, the nature of the programs, and the potential of this field as an area of employment for recreation professionals.
5. Although most private-membership organizations used to be heavily segregated, in racial and religious terms, today many of the discriminatory barriers to membership have been removed. However, how does the nature of most such organizations continue to be exclusive, based on the way they are established and financed?

Footnotes

[1] Drug and alcohol arrests increase at colleges. (l999). *New York Times.* May 23, 26.
[2] Bronner, E. (1999). In a revolution of rules, campuses go full circle. *New York Times,* Mar. 3, A-1, 15.
[3] Walsh-Sarnecki, P. (1999). *A dry spell at Michigan State.* Knight-Ridder Newspapers. Apr. 11, 10.
[4] Lewis, J., Jones, R., Lamke, G., and Dunn, J.M. (1998). Recreational sports: Making the grade on   college campuses. *Parks and Recreation.* December, 73.
[5] *Annual Report.* (1985). Associated Students' Organization of San Diego State University, Calif.
[6] Lewis, et al., op. cit.
[7] Wilgoren, J. (2000). The bell rings but the students stay, and stay. *New York Times.* Jan. 24, A-1.
[8] Johnson, D. (1998). Many schools putting an end to children's play. *New York Times,* Apr. 7, A-1.
[9] Equality on the golf course. (1999). *New York Times* editorial. Dec. 29, A-25.

[10] Shapiro, J. (1999), No sunset for sun city. *U.S. News and World Report.* June 28, 78.
[11] Schemo, D. (1994), Community associations thrive. *New York Times.* May 3, B-6.
[12] McDowell, E. (2000). A few weeks to call your own. *New York Times.* Jan. 29, C-1.

Chapter 8

Therapeutic Recreation Service

Introduction

Therapeutic recreation represents a specialized area of organized leisure services that is not provided by a single type of sponsoring agency. Instead, it is offered by many different kinds of organizations that serve persons with disabilities: public, nonprofit, commercial, and others.

Beginning with a discussion of the development of therapeutic recreation and its earlier models and philosophy, this chapter continues by focusing on two dominant approaches in the field today: (1) the *clinical*, or *treatment-oriented*, model; and (2) the *special recreation*, community-based approach. In each case, it describes the basic steps involved in service delivery and gives examples of different programs in action.

Early Development of Therapeutic Recreation

Although centuries ago there were a number of examples of the use of sport and other forms of play in the treatment of ill persons, it was not until the early 1900s that activity therapy and recreation began to become more fully recognized as useful forms of adjunctive treatment in American hospitals and rehabilitation centers.

Under the auspices of the Red Cross in hospital wards and convalescent centers, and in military and Veterans Administration hospitals during and after the two World Wars, more and more recreation services were increasingly provided. At first viewed as diversional and intended merely to maintain patient morale, they gradually evolved into more purposeful programs and came to be viewed as part of a "continuum of care," designed to help individuals recover from illness or other trauma and return successfully to community life.

Legislation Assisting Persons with Disabilities

After World War II, in the late 1940s and 1950s, this movement steadily gained momentum. Several federal laws strengthened the drive toward providing rehabilitation for disabled persons and giving them the right to expect special educational services and other necessary assistance.

For example, the Rehabilitation Act of 1973 (P. 93-112) contained Section 504, often referred to as the "Nondiscrimination Clause," which prohibited discrimination against disabled persons in any programs or services receiving federal support.

In November 1975, the U.S. Congress enacted Public Law 94-142, the Education for All Handicapped Children Act, which supported the expansion of such services for disabled persons as physical and occupational therapy and recreation, which were identified as important "related services."

Beginning in 1978, Congress began to allocate substantial funds for demonstration projects assisting social and recreational programs for disabled adults by implementing recommendations made under the 1973 act. Then, in 1990, Congress passed the Americans with Disabilities Act, which gave disabled persons the same civil rights and protection against discrimination that other minorities had received during the 1960s and 1970s. More than any other legislation, this law had a profound effect on educational institutions, businesses, and organizations providing public recreation opportunities by requiring them to meet the needs of disabled persons more fully.

Early Models of Therapeutic Recreation Service

While recreation services had become widely accepted by the 1950s in a wide range of institutions—particularly psychiatric hospitals, special schools or residential centers for mentally retarded individuals, and nursing homes—they did not have a clearly stated and widely adopted philosophy or statement of purpose.

Some, particularly those in long-form care or "custodial" institutions, limited their programs to relatively superficial entertainment or hobby interests. Others used recreation as a specific tool to achieve significant treatment goals, often with the encouragement of medical authorities. The models of service that were identified at this time ranged from "custodial" approaches, which saw recreation chiefly as a means of keeping long-term patients or residents contented, to "medical-clinical," or "education-and-training" models, which had more serious goals and objectives.

NTRS Leisurability Model

In an effort to resolve these differing approaches, the National Therapeutic Recreation Society carried out a lengthy study process and, in 1981, officially approved a model of therapeutic recreation service that had been suggested by Scout Gunn and Carol Peterson.[1] Known as the "Leisurability Model," this approach had essentially three components:

1. A *rehabilitation* or *treatment component* in which recreation is clearly used as therapy,
2. A process of *leisure education* involving counseling and other learning experiences designed to promote positive leisure attitudes and skills,
3. *Facilitation of actual participation* through provision of appropriate recreational activities for enjoyment and other personal benefits.

Example of Philosophical Statement

While the leisurability model has generally been accepted within the therapeutic recreation field, different institutions or groups of practitioners may offer somewhat different statements of their philosophy and program goals. For example, in the mid-1980s, the staff manual of the Piersol Rehabilitation Center at Philadelphia's University of Pennsylvania Hospital defined the Center's philosophy in the following statement:

> The purpose of the Therapeutic Recreation program is to provide recreational activities and experiences which are modified to meet an individual's physical, emotional, mental and/or social limitations and abilities. Activities are aimed at promoting the functional independence of the individual and aiding in his/her total rehabilitation process.
>
> Recreational activities are directed toward maintaining and/or improving the physical and mental health of the patient. The overall goals of the Therapeutic Recreation program are: (1) to facilitate favorable adjustment to treatment and to the hospital environment; (2) to stimulate socialization and interaction; (3) to promote optimal psychomotor, cognitive and affective functioning through adapted activities; (4) to provide leisure education; (5) to encourage a constructive, meaningful and independent leisure lifestyle; and (6) to prepare the patient for participation in community recreation programs, upon discharge.[2]

In addition to these goals, the Piersol statement emphasizes the need to focus on specific psychomotor, cognitive, and other skills or deficits of patients, and to assist them in maintaining positive community contacts and awareness. The therapeutic recreation staff works in conjunction with the overall rehabilitation team—including occupational and physical therapists—involves family and friends where possible, and provides a transitional program for discharged patients through regularly scheduled "Alumni Club" meetings.

Therapeutic Recreation Today: Two Emphases

By the 1990s, the therapeutic recreation field embraced an extremely wide range of services, patient or client populations, and settings. The field was defined in February 1994 by the National Therapeutic Recreation Society's Board of Directors in the following terms:

> Practiced in clinical, residential, and community settings, the profession of therapeutic recreation uses treatment, education, and recreation services to help people with illnesses, disabilities, and other conditions to develop and use their leisure in ways that enhance their health, independence, and well-being.

The settings served expanded tremendously and included many different-kinds of institutions and organizations, such as the following:

- Hospitals under varied sponsorship (Veterans Administration, military, public health, state, county, municipal, voluntary, and proprietary) that deal with a variety of patient populations (general, chronic disease, psychiatric, pediatric, and others).
- Schools or residential centers for those with specific physical disability (including the blind, deaf, orthopedically disabled, or neurologically involved) or those with mental deficiencies or retardation.
- Penal institutions for adult criminals, or custodial institutions or special schools, reformatories, remand centers, or camps for youth who are socially maladjusted or committed because of delinquent acts.
- After-care centers for discharged mental patients or those who are not hospitalized, but are receiving day clinic services; institutions serving drug addicts under treatment; or other centers serving those who require continuing special services in the form of counseling, training, psychotherapy, and sheltered or guided social experiences.
- Nursing homes, extended-care or health-related facilities, chiefly for geriatric patients who either require intensive nursing and medical care or who are unable to live independently in the community.

Considering the availability of such a wide variety of programs with different objectives and resources, it is apparent that the field has centered essentially on two major types of therapeutic recreation at century's end. These are: (1) *clinical,* or *treatment-centered, therapeutic recreation,* which takes a highly purposeful approach, using such elements as patient/client assessment, the development of treatment plans or protocols, and careful evaluation and documentation of outcomes; and (2) *special recreation,* which is carried on with the full awareness of the individual participant's needs and capabilities, and with modification of activities where appropriate, usually in community settings—but without formal treatment plans or highly individualized program services.

The Clinical Approach

This model of service tends to be the primary focus of professional societies in this field; higher education curricula in therapeutic recreation service; and most textbooks, journals, and other sources of research on the subject.

Essentially, this model is linked to the earlier medical model of service, except that it need not be based on the diagnoses or recommendations of medical authorities, but rather may draw its foundational principles and methods from other treatment areas. It seeks to be as solidly grounded as possible in scientific terms, comparable to other treatment disciplines, and convincing in terms of patient or client outcomes, in order to justify acceptance as a service compensated under third-party insurance reimbursement plans.

Patient/Client Assessment

Patient/client assessment represents the first important step in the clinical model of service, and it provides the basis for understanding a patient's or client's needs and for developing a sound treatment plan.

At an early point, Kinney explained the purpose of assessment as a tool in therapeutic recreation:

Clinical assessment of clients by therapeutic recreators has become an essential ingredient of program planning in the most effective treatment centers. Not only is assessment the baseline upon which activities are planned, but many treatment teams are finding that the information provided by recreation assessment is useful in related areas of life functioning as well.[3]

In the past, assessment often began by having individuals fill out an interest inventory or activity preference checklist or by reviewing their past recreation experiences—through an interview process, if necessary. In some settings, the approach was to observe the patient or client in social situations or actual recreation programs to determine his or her level of interaction, social skills, and other relevant information.

Gradually, assessment methods became more sophisticated. Now, depending on the patient's or client's type of disability—and recognizing that physical illnesses or disabilities may also be accompanied by emotional disturbance or social limitations—a range of other areas might be explored, such as affective, cognitive, psychomotor, medical, educational, or past vocational and a vocational experience.

Analysis of Physical Capability. If the purpose of the assessment is to determine an individual's capability within varied spheres of daily-life activity—along with elements of cognition and communication—an assessment form (such as that shown in Fig. 8-1) might be applied at any or all of three points in the treatment process (on admission, on discharge, and as a follow-up procedure).

Development of Treatment Plan

Based on information gathered through such procedures, as well as input from medical or social service staff members, a review of the patient's or client's history and input from family, friends, and other sources, a treatment plan is developed. This plan might include a set of goals for treatment that incorporates both general goals that are applicable to most individuals with disabilities and specific goals aimed at meeting the needs of the particular individual.

Specific goals focus on the individual's areas of need in terms of his or her emotional, social, cognitive, and psychomotor strengths and weaknesses. They in turn are translated into recommendations for individual, small-group, or large-group involvement and also for a sequence of exposure to various kinds of positive growth experiences.

Realistically, the actual content of the treatment plan would be dependent on the available resources of the clinical setting (i.e., the numbers and types of staff members and patients or clients, the facilities available, and the constraints of the program's schedule).

Figure 8-2 illustrates a fairly typical plan for a patient in a mental health care setting. It outlines the general plan for treatment, but does not give specific details of activities or the evaluation criteria or progress reporting method.

Use of Protocols. Treatment plans for individual patients or clients that provide fuller details are often referred to as *protocols*. These usually contain specific information dealing with (1) goals and objectives of group involvement or prescribed activities; (2) the basis for selecting activities in terms of patient/client characteristics and needs; (3) specific program content, including the nature of group experience, activity modification, or frequency; (4) a method of monitoring and evaluating treatment outcomes; and (5) a plan for program continuation or follow-up as required.

Whenever possible, patients or clients should be meaningfully involved in developing the treatment plan or protocol through interest surveys and shared planning discussions.

Figure 8-1
Rating form measuring functional independence. (Source: Research Foundation, State University of New York.)

LEVELS		
	7 Complete Independence (Timely, Safely) 6 Modified Independence (Device)	NO HELPER

	Modified Dependence
	    5 Supervision
	    4 Minimal Assist (Subject = 75%+)
	    3 Moderate Assist (Subject = 50%+)
	Complete Dependence
	    2 Maximal Assist (Subject = 25%+)
	    1 Total Assist (Subject = 0%+)
		HELPER

	ADMIT	DISCHG	FOL-UP
Self Care			
A. Feeding			
B. Grooming			
C. Bathing			
D. Dressing—Upper Body			
E. Dressing—Lower Body			
F. Toileting			
Sphincter Control			
G. Bladder Management			
H. Bowel Management			
Mobility Transfer:			
I. Bed, Chair, W/Chair			
J. Toilet			
K. Tub, Shower			
Locomotion			
L. Walk/Wheel Chair	W/C	W/C	W/C
M. Stairs			
Communication			
N. Comprehension	a/v	a/v	a/v
O. Expression	a/v	a/v	a/v
Social Cognition			
P. Social Interaction			
Q. Problem Solving			
R. Memory			
Total			

Figure 8-2
Treatment plan.
(Capistrano-by-the-Sea Hospital, California)

```
STAFF MEMBER  STEVE SUMPTER, M.S., C.T.R.S.          DEPT.  REHABILITATION
PROBLEM NO                       DECREASED FUNCTIONAL, COPING SKILLS, AND SOCIAL SKILLS
MANIFESTATIONS:  SOCIAL ISOLATION, DIFFICULTY EXPRESSING FEELINGS, INABILITY TO
                 RELAX, MINIMAL RISK TAKING, LIMITED TASK COMPLETION, EASILY BORED,
                 DECREASED SELF-ESTEEM, DISORGANIZED THINKING AND DECISION-MAKING.
STRENGTHS USED IN PLAN:

DISCHARGE CRITERIA/GOAL:  PATIENT WILL DEMONSTRATE HEALTHIER WAYS TO COPE.
```

DATE	PLAN OBJECTIVES	INTERVENTION APPROACH/ACTIONS	EVALUATE PROGRESS STATEMENT
	Pt. will participate in all Rehabilitation Groups on a daily basis by:	Orient patient to the Rehabilitation schedule, monitor attendance, and encourage participation in all ordered groups.	
	Pt will demonstrate improved ability to complete assigned tasks, take risks, self structure, and discuss anxieties related to participation in these groups by:	Assist patient in evaluating the therapeutic value of activities such as: Craft Workshop, Art Experience, Leisure Skills, Outings and Group Recreation for involvement in after discharge. Identify ways to enhance the value of leisure in developing improved leisure skills.	
	Pt. will discuss a D/C Plan and Leisure Time Plan using information from program participation by:	Meet with patients on 1:1 basis to assess their plan prior to discharge.	

Documentation of Outcomes

A third key stage of therapeutic recreation service in the clinical setting involves documentation—the systematic observation of patient or client involvement and the evaluation of program outcomes. Typically, this documentation includes the following elements:

1. *Recording Participation.* Each session should be carefully observed and promptly described in a written report—often making use of a rating form that simplifies the process and describes participation and level of group involvement.

2. *Success in Meeting Behavioral Objectives.* Since these usually deal with overt behaviors, such as learning a skill, demonstrating knowledge, or developing positive interactions with others, they can readily be scored on scales that indicate degrees of change in behavior or the positive accomplishment of objectives. Usually, these involve precise objectives that can be concretely observed and measured.
3. *Meeting Broader Attitudinal or Behavioral Goals.* At regular intervals, documentation should involve making broader judgments about the progress of the patient or client in meeting the overall attitudinal, cognitive, or behavioral goals that have been identified in the treatment plan.

In general, documentation should confine itself to observable phenomena, rather than subjective judgments or interpretations of the therapeutic recreation process. It should be informative, brief, and precise and should avoid jargon or overly technical terms.

Publication of Findings

Most summaries of patient or client progress in therapeutic recreation are used "in-house" and are not shared with other professionals. However, case studies or findings of carefully monitored programs serving such population groups as individuals with spinal cord or head trauma, mental illness or mental retardation, substance abuse, or other disabilities are frequently reported in the *Therapeutic Recreation Journal*.

Known as *efficacy research,* the findings of hundred of such reports were summarized by a Temple University team of educators in a three-year project funded by the National Institute on Disability and Rehabilitation Research of the U.S. Department of Education. Coyle, Kinney, Riley, and Shank documented the positive outcomes of therapeutic recreation service in six major areas of personal and societal benefits, with emphasis on rehabilitation outcomes that could be closely linked to medical treatment approaches.[4]

Guidelines for Clinical Practice

The most authoritative set of guidelines for treatment-oriented practitioners was published by the National Therapeutic Recreation Society in 1995.[5] This manual contains standards and criteria for eight important elements in therapeutic recreation service. While designed to apply to the overall field, regardless of setting, its primary focus is on clinical-practice programs.

The eight standards of practice deal with (1) Scope of Service; (2) Mission and Purpose, Goals and Objectives; (3) Individual Treatment/Program Plan; (4) Documentation; (5) Plan of Operation; (6) Personnel Qualifications; (7) Ethical Responsibilities; and (8) Evaluation and Research.

Expansion of Special Recreation Programs

During the last years of the 20th century, a number of trends affecting the overall health care system in the United States tended to constrict the growth of clinically based therapeutic recreation service.

First, during the 1970s and 1980s, many large state-supported institutions that served primarily mentally ill and mentally retarded populations were sharply reduced in size and in some cases terminated. This came about as a consequence of the national effort, in both the

United States and Canada, to "deinstitutionalize" the care of hundreds of thousands of such individuals by getting them out of the huge, impersonal, custodial institutions where many of them were permanently confined, and returning them to community life.

Changes in Managed Care. Another important trend in the 1990s involved the nation's growing reliance on the managed health-care system and its dependence on insurance-based coverage of treatment costs through third-party reimbursement practices.

Through this decade, many hospitals experienced fiscal crises and takeovers, and others were forced to reduce emergency services and cut back on their staffs and specialized programs. There was considerable pressure to reduce the length of patient stays in hospitals, and often to deny payment for services that had formerly been covered. Many hospitals and rehabilitation centers were forced to reduce their services, and in many cases, only the most critical treatment services were funded adequately—which inevitably had an impact on adjunctive services such as therapeutic recreation.[6]

Factors Promoting Special Recreation

At the same time, several factors encouraged the establishment of community-based special recreation programs serving persons with disabilities. First, deinstitutionalization led to greater numbers of such individuals living in community setting. While the overall response to this trend, in terms of providing adequate funding for residential and other services, was clearly insufficient, many hospitals and rehabilitation centers did establish aftercare or post-discharge units to that provided people varied services, including recreation.

The society at large became much more aware of the great number of disabled persons in the population at large and determined to provide fuller resources and opportunities to meet their needs. The therapeutic and recreation field itself acted as a vigorous advocate for such priorities, and different categories of disabled persons, such as individuals with hearing disabilities or mental illness, fought for fuller public support. The passage of the Americans with Disabilities Act in 1990 was a major force in stimulating public awareness and support for special services. Growing numbers of agencies of all types began to develop programs and facilities to provide special recreation opportunities for persons with disabilities. In some cases, they focused on a particular category of disability or a defined age group. In others, they covered a wide range of impairments and target populations.

By the mid- to late-1990s, the types of agencies providing special recreation included the following:

1. Public recreation and park departments that are sponsored by government on federal, state, and local levels, and that increasingly are initiating programs to serve disabled persons.
2. Voluntary, nonprofit organizations, such as YMCAs and YWCAs or Boy and Girl Scout groups, which serve the public at large, but may also provide services for disabled individuals.
3. Specialized community organizations that have been formed to provide education, counseling, vocational training and other services, including recreation, for a particular category of disabled persons, such as visually impaired or mentally retarded persons.

4. Colleges and universities that offer adapted physical education and other specialized recreation opportunities to their disabled students, sometimes in connection with their professional curricula.
5. Hospitals or rehabilitation centers that frequently establish outpatient or satellite programs to serve their own discharged patients/clients or other disabled persons living in the community.
6. Group homes or other transitional residential facilities for developmentally disabled or other special populations that provide a range of support services for them.
7. Special recreation agencies that have been established primarily to provide varied leisure services to a wide range of disabled persons living in the community.
8. Community councils or boards that coordinate the efforts of various civic agencies and social groups in meeting the human-service needs of disabled residents.
9. Consortiums of public agencies representing two or more communities that provide special recreation through joint sponsorship arrangements.

In some cases, such organizations designed facilities and planned programs to serve segregated groups of individuals with disabilities. However, the strong thrust at century's end was to integrate disabled individuals with nondisabled individuals to whatever extent possible. "Mainstreaming," "normalization," and "least-restrictive environment" became slogans guiding most such agencies, and the concept of "handicap" was set aside in favor of a much more positive view of the potential of persons with disabilities in all spheres of community life.

Examples of Community-Based Special Recreation

Many county and municipal recreation and park departments designed and built new playgrounds or other leisure facilities to provide enhanced opportunities for such individuals to enjoy varied forms of play—along with their families and friends. Accessibility for persons with physical disabilities became a requirement for all new construction, and many older facilities were remodeled to encourage their involvement.

A growing number of public departments established special programs to serve different groups of disabled persons with a wide range of services, including the input of other community organization. Fig. 8-3 illustrates special youth programs offered by the Parks and Leisure Activities Department in Las Vegas, Nevada, and its Leisure Buddies/P.A.L. program, designed to promote integrated play for both disabled and nondisabled persons. This department offers parties, celebrations, carnivals, and trips throughout the year, as well as camps for developmentally disabled youth and adults. It also offers wheelchair basketball and "quad" rugby competition carried on in collaboration with the national organization, Disabled Sports U.S.A.

A second example of diverse special recreation programming is shown in Fig. 8-4. The Long Beach, California, Department of Parks, Recreation and Marine sponsors a great variety of activities for physically challenged, visually impaired, deaf seniors and other groups and incorporates services offered by other agencies in such areas as alcohol and drug-abuse rehabilitation, job training, deaf telephone assistance, or energy rebate assistance.

Coordinating Role of Public Departments. In addition to sponsoring their own special services for disabled persons, many public recreation and park departments today play a

Figure 8-3
Adaptive Recreation Program, Las Vegas

Lorenzi Adaptive Recreation Center

- **Lorenzi Adaptive Recreation Center** is a year round recreation program offered for youth, 7-21 years of age. Its purpose is to provide planned recreation experiences for youth with and without disabilities. The activities are designed to maintain and increase the participant's recreational and leisure skills. In addition, the Center's goals are to meet the physical, emotional, social and intellectual needs of each participant.

- **Teen Club** offers services that are an extension of the regular programming at the Lorenzi Adaptive Recreation Center. These services include a variety of therapeutic and educational groups to promote a healthy, independent and well-balanced leisure life-style.

- **Teen Club** provides the opportunity for adolescents and children to transition from school into the community through community reintegration programs.

- **Teen Club** outings held once a week. Outings may include community tours, learning how to use the CAT bus system, as well as attending a matinee or paddling a canoe. Teen Club promotes independence and choice through a variety of programs.

- **Youth Council** is another program extended from the regular programming at Lorenzi Adaptive Recreation Center. This program gives youth, ages 11-17, a chance to make a positive impact on their community while having a great time in the process.

- **Youth Council** meets once a month to set their monthly goals and plan for upcoming events. Youth Council's three main focuses are outings, service projects, and fund-raising which may include pizza and bowling, sporting events, dances, dinners, canned food drives, trips to local attractions, nursing homes, hospitals, etc.

- **Lorenzi Youth Council** is one of eleven Youth Councils within the City of Las Vegas.

- **Leisure Buddies/P.A.L. (Partners Assisting with Leisure)** is for people of all ages and ability levels.

- **Leisure Buddies/P.A.L.** provides an opportunity for people in the community and persons with disabilities to assist one another in a variety of recreational settings such as canoeing, swimming, bowling, crafts and a number of other recreational programs offered through the City of Las Vegas, Clark County and the City of Henderson.

- **Leisure Buddies/P.A.L.** program provides an opportunity for both the Leisure Buddy and the PAL to have fun, make new friends and get involved in something they enjoy.

Figure 8-4
Special recreation activities in Long Beach.

See pg. 52 for Youth Sports League information at this site.

Night-lighted Game Courts. Roller Hockey court available for rental.

East Bay Alcooholics Anonymous Meetings. Su, 9 a.m.-6 p.m.

South Coast Orchid Society. Meets on 3rd M of each mo., 6:30-10:30 p.m.

Long Beach Coordinating Council. Meets 4th Th of each mo., 9-11:30 a.m.

 Citywide recreation activities and classes for individuals with disabilities.

Adaptive Recreation in Special Environments (ARISE). Ages 9 and up. This after-school program for people with disabilities includes arts, music, dance, sports, special events and excursions. M-F, 2-5 p.m. at Stearns Champions Park. Summer hours: M-F, 1-5 p.m. For information, call Adaptive.

California Pools for the Handicapped, Inc. Therapeutic swimming for all ages. Facilities include wheelchair ramps, stairs and lifts. People with arthritis meet Tu/Th from 9-10 a.m. and a low-impact aerobics class is conducted W/F from 9-10 a.m. General pool hours are Tu-F, 9 a.m.-4 p.m. and Sa, 9 a.m.-2 p.m. For details, call 537-2224.

Citizens' Advisory Commission on Disabilities (CACOD). Meets the 2nd Th of mo. at 2:30 p.m. at City Hall. Recreation, employment, architectural barrier, transportation, health, housing and social services committees are held the 4th Thursday of the month. For information, call Dolores Barrows at 570-6304.

Community Advisory Committee for the Handicapped (CAC). A support group for parents who have special education students in the Long Beach Unified School District. Call 436-9931, ext. 1311.

Square Dance Class. Ages 15 and up. An 8-week program (Jan. 6-Mar. 10 and Mar. 17-May 12) for people with developmental disabilities. M, 7-9 p.m. Fee is **$16** at Stearns Champions Community Center. Call Adaptive for more information.

Deaf Telephone Communication Center (TTY). Information and referral services available by calling 436-6706.

Dining Out Program. Ages 18 and up. Dinner program for young adults with developmental disabilities at local restaurants. Participants pay own meal costs. 1st and 3rd W of mo., 6:30-9:30 p.m. For reservations, call 570-1687 after 2 p.m., M-F.

Energy Rebate Program. Disabled residents receive tax breaks on utility fees. For details, call these centers: Central Facilities, North Facilities, West Facilities, Senior Center and Houghton Park.

Girl & Boy Scouts. 1-3 p.m. 1st Sa of mo. at Stearns Champions Park.

Indoor Sports and Games for Disabled Adults. Second Sa of mo., 1:30-6:30 p.m. and 4th Sa of mo., 1:30-6:30 p.m. at Stearns Champions Park.

Lip Reading. Sponsored by Long Beach City College. Th, 10 a.m.-Noon at the Senior Center. For more, call 570-3500.

Long Beach Alcohol and Drug Abuse Rehabilitation Program. An outpatient program that provides confidential treatment and prevention of alcoholism and other drug problems. For information, call 570-4100.

Long Beach Early Intervention Council. Made up of parents and service agencies that represent infants and toddlers with special needs. For details, call the council at 985-8481.

Mommy and Me Aquatics. Five-week course introduces kids with disabilities, ages 5-8, to water safety and beginning swimming. One-hour, twice weekly. Call Special Olympics at 421-2882 for details.

Movie Night Out. Young adults with developmental disabilities ages 18 and up. Evenings out to the theatre in small groups. Must pay your own ticket and snack costs. 2nd W of mo., 6-10 p.m. For details, call Adaptive.

Quad Rugby. Offered in cooperation wtih Long Beach Memorial Rehabilitation Hospital. For information, call 933-9043 or Adaptive.

Recreation for the Visually Impaired. Adults. Tu, 9 a.m.-3 p.m. at the Senior Center. For details, call 570-3500.

Residential Camp for Developmentally Disabled. Ages 16 and up. Winter camp is **$150** and runs in February. Summer camp is **$250** and runs in June.

Sailing for the Physically Challenged. For beginners and intermediates. Rigging modification, cockpit adaptation and techniques for those with physical disabilities. Contact Duncan Milne at (714) 722-5371 for details. Class free to all qualified disabled persons.

Sign Language Introduction. Call Adaptive for time & dates.

Special Events Nite. Ages 18 and up. Monthly activities such as plays, baseball games and ice skating. Call Adaptive.

Special Olympics Practice. Includes swimming and seasonal team sports on Tu/Th, 6:45-8:30 p.m. Call 421-2882 for registration.

Stroke Activity Center. Social rehabilitation for stroke patients. W, 8:30 a.m.-2:30 p.m. at El Dorado Park West Community Center. Call 570-1630 or 427-8712.

Summer Youth Employment Training Program (SYETP). Ages 14-21. SYETP 1st Step program for youth with disabilities. Work experience and job training provided. Call Adaptive for details by March 15.

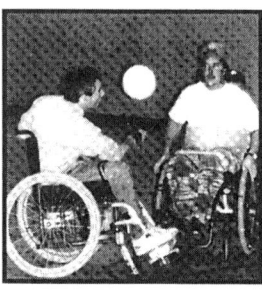

leading role in coordinating the work of other community agencies in functions relating to recreation. For example, the Montgomery County, Maryland, Department of Recreation works closely with other community organizations in promoting summer camping for children and teenagers with disabilities (Fig. 8-5).

Programs of Nonprofit Organizations

Many nonprofit community agencies today provide special services for children, youth, and adults with disabilities. They include the following types: (1) general youth-serving organizations, such as the Boy or Girl Scouts, the Ys, or Boys and Girls Clubs, which establish special units for disabled participants; (2) national organizations that promote a particular type of activity or serve a specific population, such as Special Olympics, Very Special Arts; and Wheelchair Sports, USA; and (3) individual organizations in a single community or region that offer diversified recreation and related program services, such as RCH, Inc., in San Francisco, and the South East Consortium for Special Services, Inc., in Westchester County, New York.

Figure 8-5
Brochures illustrate role of Montgomery County, Maryland, Recreation Department in promoting special camping programs.

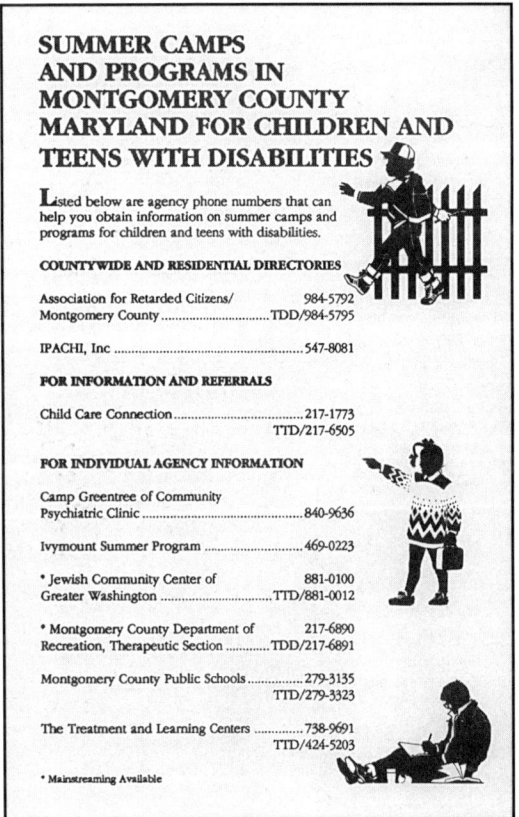

Special Olympics. This remarkable program was founded in 1968, when Eunice Kennedy Shriver organized the First International Special Olympics Games at Soldier Field in Chicago. Today it serves over one million children and adults who have mental retardation with year-round sports training and athletic competition. Special Olympics programs, which include special units for severely retarded individuals, have been established in all 50 status and in about 25,000 communities and are often cosponsored by local school districts.

Around the world, there are accredited Special Olympics programs in almost 150 nations, with more than 16,000 games and tournaments being held each year. Over half a million volunteers provide leadership in the Special Olympics, and the organization's Unified Sports program promotes the integration of individuals with mental retardation in school and community sports activities. Fund-raising, volunteers, and the contributions of many community organizations help assure the success of the Special Olympics on many levels.

Wheelchair Sports, USA. As a member of the U.S. Olympic Committee family, Wheelchair Sports, USA, serves as the international, sanctioning body for wheelchair sports and promotes local, national, and international competition in twelve activities, including water-skiing, sled hockey, basketball, quad rugby, archery, fencing, and track and field, which are directed by separate groups in these sports.

WSUSA also acts as the coordinating body for the Regional Sports Organization and organizes the U.S. international team that competes every four years in the Paralympics that are held at the winter and summer cities of the Olympic Games.

Very Special Arts. This is an international nonprofit organization that offers arts education for persons—especially children and youth—with disabilities. Each year over 1.5 million Americans participate in Very Special Arts programs, including music, dance, and drama, in all 50 states and in 65 other countries around the world.

An affiliate of the John F. Kennedy Center for the Performing Arts, Very Special Arts also sponsors activities in the visual arts and creative writing and works in cooperation with local educational and cultural institutions, volunteers, parents, and artists.

RCH, Inc. Founded in the San Francisco Bay area in 1952 as a demonstration project to meet the needs of a small group of disabled persons, this organization has become a leading center of therapeutic recreation services, working with thousands of individuals of all ages and many types of disabilities.

With funding from the San Francisco Recreation and Park Department and other state and federal agencies, RCH, Inc., offers, in addition to camping and varied recreational activities, transportation, food services, vocational rehabilitation and supported employment programs, day activity programs for seniors, respite care assistance, and other social services. At its 40th anniversary in 1992, RCH, Inc., was serving 1,800 residents of the area, with a staff of 120 full-time workers and an annual budget of $4 million based on a unique public-private sponsorship arrangement.

South East Consortium. Another emerging pattern in special recreation is for a number of communities or social-service organizations to join together within a region, using joint staffing and facilities resources and a mixture of public and philanthropic fund-raising support to provide special recreation.

The South East Consortium for Special Services, Inc., in lower Westchester County, New York, is a nonprofit organization serving 12 towns and villages with comprehensive recreation services. Like RCH, Inc., it serves people with varied disabilities and of different age groups, and places special emphasis on normalization—that is, on integrating disabled

Competitors give their all in Special Olympics meets. Medical and other volunteers provide needed assistance to young athletes.

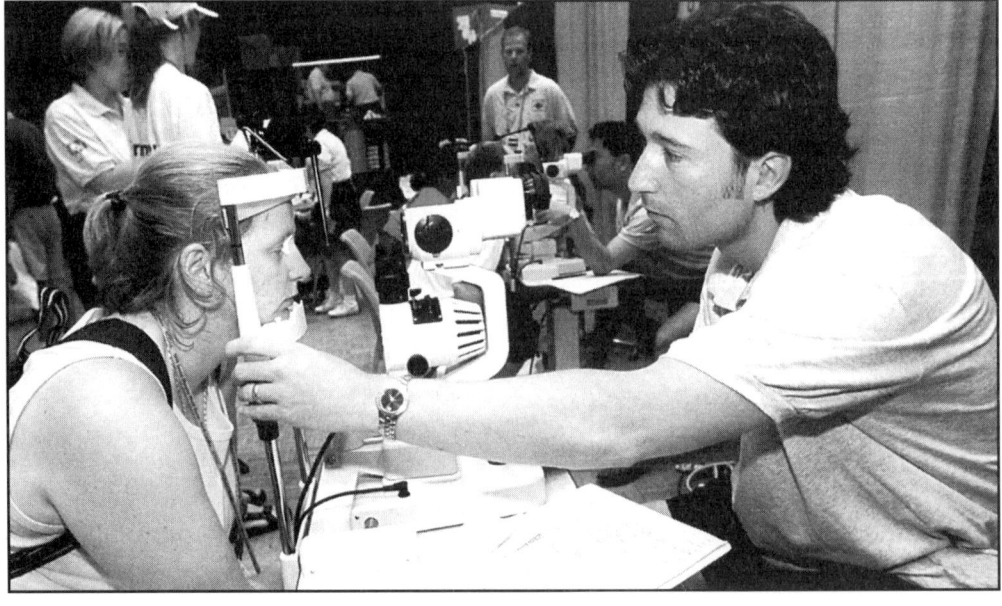

participants with nondisabled individuals to the extent possible, in participating in popular kinds of hobbies, social events, and other pastimes (See Fig. 8-7). While the consortium charges participants for many program activities, scholarships are available for those who cannot pay, And the overall agency is clearly charitable and tax exempt.

Like other special recreation agencies, the South East Consortium also works closely with other organizations serving disabled persons, and provides staffed leisure activities in eleven residential facilities for developmentally disabled teens and adults.

Commercial Recreation Businesses

Initially, most for-profit leisure-service enterprises did not welcome participants with disabilities, partly because they felt that it would be too difficult to serve them, and partly because they feared negligence lawsuits in the event of accidents and injuries. They may also have believed that other patrons would find the presence of persons with disabilities disturbing, and that it would hurt "business."

Today, under legal pressure to serve disabled persons, and partly because they recognize that many of them represent an important marketing target, many recreation businesses make a special point of attracting such participants. This is particularly true of cruise lines, theme parks, and resorts, which frequently organize special programs and group trips for physically disabled persons.

A good example of such marketing efforts is Dollywood (see page 199), which has made special facility adaptations to serve impaired individuals, Staff are trained to serve disabled guests efficiently and courteously, and manuals and printed guides indicate which rides or other attractions may readily be used by physically disabled persons without difficulty, and which may have special requirements with respect to mobility or other physical factors.

Employment and Professional Development

Although accurate statistics of all the individuals employed in therapeutic recreation service are difficult to obtain, reports by the *Occupational Outlook Handbook* published by the U.S. Department of Labor have indicated that approximately 38,000 specialists work in this field—chiefly in nursing homes or long-term care facilities, psychiatric hospitals, rehabilitation centers, and other specialty hospitals.

If one were to add all the full- or part-time individuals employed in nonprofit organizations, commercial businesses, correctional institutions, and even campus recreation programs—which frequently offer special programs for disabled persons—the likelihood is that the total would be twice that number.

Fig. 8-8 shows examples of advertisements for therapeutic recreation personnel that appeared in the health care employment section of the New York Times during the mid-l990s. Many other job notices of this type appear in the newsletters of professional societies, or are on display at professional conferences.

What kinds of education, prior experience, and professional skills should applicants for such positions have? Obviously, individuals who have majored in therapeutic recreation service in accredited colleges or university departments offering a specialty in this field would be best qualified.

Figure 8-7
Examples of the variety of outings and events sponsored for disabled participants by South East Consortium.

TEEN/ADULT VACATIONS

ECO MARINER'S VACATION DAYS
PROGRAM SUPERVISORS:
AMY CARO (TEEN)
SIA TOFANO (ADULT)
Anchors Away! This summer teenagers and adults can climb aboard the 80 foot, three masted schooner, **The Sound Waters** for adventures they will never forget. Exploring the waters of Long Island Sound on this Coast Guard safety certified vessel, mariners will experience seamanship, navigation, map skills, ecological programs and the beauty of sailing. Participants will experience five full days of sailing and one overnight of camping along the Long Island Shore.

WHO:	ALL DISABILITIES, Ages 13 - Adult
PLACE:	Yacht Haven Marine Center, Stamford, Conn.
DATES:	Monday, Aug. 21 - Friday, Aug. 25
TIME:	9:30 a.m. - 4:30 p.m. The bus leaves SEC at 8:45 am and returns to SEC at 5:15 pm.
CODE:	SAIL 350
FEE:	$350.00
NOTE:	**Participants must bring bag lunches and drink.**

MYSTIC COAST EXCURSION
PROGRAM SUPERVISOR: SIA TOFANO
Come aboard and cruise with us along the Mystic Coast. We will visit the U.S.S. Nautilus submarine and climb the medieval stairs of Gillette Castle. We will hop onto a steam train then take a boat ride to listen to music at Harkness Park. Lastly we will walk the decks of the Charles W. Morgan at Mystic Seaport. **Don't miss this trip!**

WHO:	ALL DISABILITIES, Ages 16 - Adult
PLACE:	Mystic, Conn.
DATES:	Friday, July 15 - Sunday, July 17
TIME:	Van leaves SEC office at 4:30 P.M. on Friday and returns 8:30 p.m. Sunday.
CODE:	MYST 350
FEE:	$275.00
NOTE:	Two continental breakfasts are included in fee. All other meals and snacks are not included.

"FOR CHOCOLATE LOVERS WITH SIMPLE TASTES"
PENNSYLVANIA DUTCH/HERSHEY PARK
PROGRAM SUPERVISOR: SIA TOFANO
If you love chocolate kisses, picture book farms and down home cookin', this trip is for you. We will stroll the streets of of Hershey where chocolate flows and roses grow. We will visit magnificent gardens, a major theme park, a zoo and a chocolate factory. Right next door we will visit Amish Country where America's first pretzel came from, ride an old fashion steam train and sample a traditional Pennsylvania Dutch meal. So, **if you are a chocolate lover with simple tastes, you will love this trip!**

WHO:	ALL DISABILITIES, Ages 16 - Adult
PLACE:	Hershey, Pennsylvania
DATES:	Sat., August 12 - Tues., Aug. 15
TIME:	Van leaves SEC office at 9:00 a.m. on Saturday and returns at 10:30 p.m Tues.
CODE:	COCO 350
FEE:	$465.00
NOTE:	Three Continental Breakfasts and one traditional Pennsylvania Dutch Meal included in fee. All other meals and snacks not included.

Certification in Therapeutic Recreation

In the past, many states offered registration in the specialized field of therapeutic recreation as a means of identifying qualified practitioners. This process was supplanted in the 1980s by a new certification plan based on a combination of education and experience, adopted by the National Council for Therapeutic Recreation Certification. As shown in Fig. 8-9, alternative paths are offered for two certification levels: professional and paraprofessional.

Today, many government and nonprofit organizations require that job candidates be certified, and in many cases, state health departments or civil service—boards require this certification for professional-level positions.

Figure 8-8
Newspaper advertisements for therapeutic recreation positions.

Job Competencies in Therapeutic Recreation

Beyond the issues of professionalization and certification, what kinds of job responsibilities do therapeutic recreation practitioners have and what skills or personal qualities do they need to carry them out successfully? A number of research studies have examined these questions systematically. A comprehensive study of the job functions of therapeutic recreation specialists was conducted in 1958 by the Educational Testing Service in Princeton, New

Figure 8-9
Certification paths in therapeutic recreation.

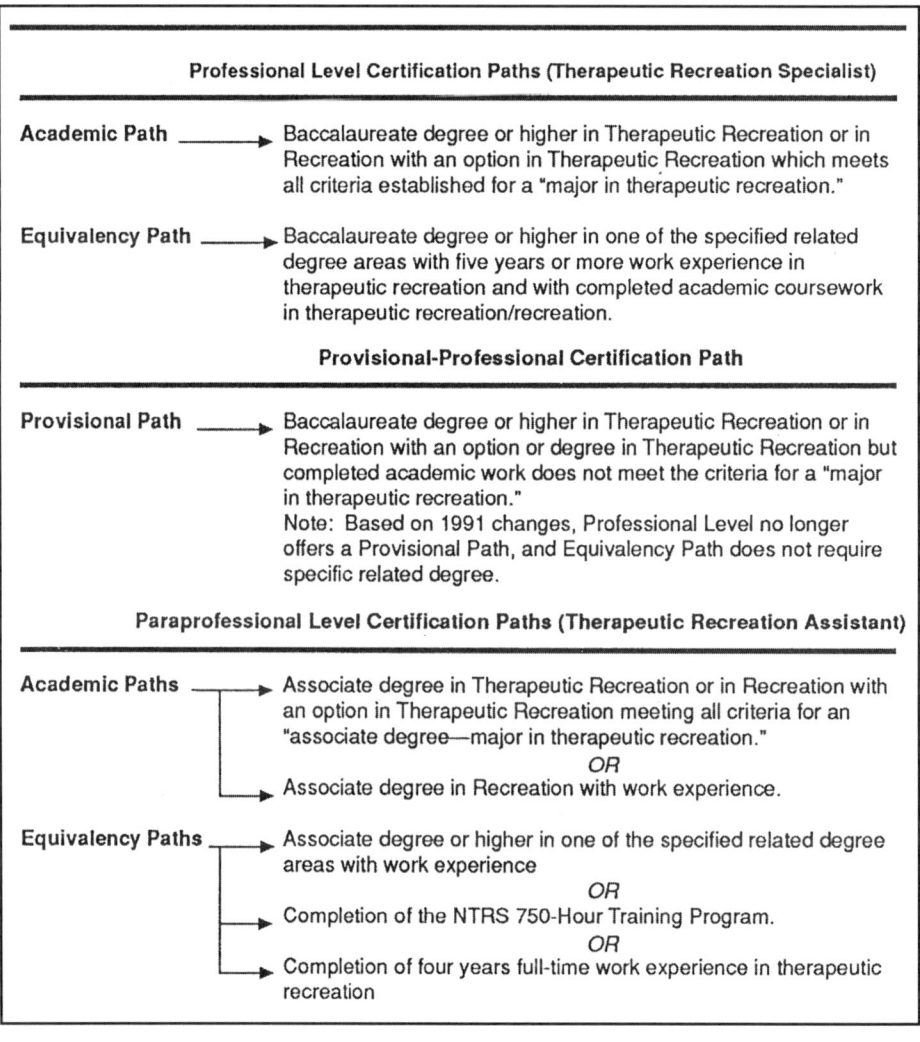

Jersey. It identified a set of job responsibilities that were the most highly rated by a large sample of certified professionals throughout the United States (see Fig. 8-10).

Still other studies have examined the competencies needed to serve special populations. These include such personal elements as having positive attitudes toward disabled persons, knowledge of facility design and accessibility, leadership and supervisory skills, characteristics of special populations, and awareness of trends and issues in the field.

In addition to such findings, the National Therapeutic Recreation Society has prepared a useful manual, *Preparing for a Career in Therapeutic Recreation.*

Figure 8-10
Key functions of therapeutic recreation specialists.

1. Implement programs for groups and individuals.
2. Identify and analyze agency/department and community resources.
3. Exchange information with team members regarding client/patient's functioning and progress, and revise program.
4. Integrate the information collected for use in planning a program for the client/patient.
5. Observe client/patient's behavior to assess physical, social, emotional, cognitive, and leisure functioning.
6. Develop and document individualized program/treatment goals and plan based on assessment and consistent with professional guidelines.
7. Interview client/patient and significant others to assess physical, social, emotional, cognitive, and leisure functioning.
8. Implement individualized program/treatment plan.

Suggested Questions for Class Discussion or Essay Examinations

1. What are the three main elements or stages in the leisurability model of therapeutic services that was originally suggested by Gunn and Peterson?
2. This chapter identifies two major thrusts in purposeful recreation programming for persons with disabilities today. What are these? Briefly describe each one and indicate its primary purposes and the settings in which it is typically carried out.
3. Describe the role of assessment in the clinical model of therapeutic recreation. If you were to deal with a particular area of disability (e.g., mental illness, developmental disability, or stroke recovery patients), what kinds of information would you seek, and what measurement tools or processes would you use?
4. This chapter provides several examples of community-based recreation programs for persons with disability. They may be carried out under different kinds of structures or administrative sponsorship. Identify and briefly describe two of these approaches.

5. Therapeutic recreation service is usually recognized as one of the most highly professionalized disciplines within the overall field of organized leisure services. What does this mean, and what are some of the key hallmarks of professionalism?

Footnotes

[1] *Philosophical position statement.* National Therapeutic Recreation Society, adopted May 1982.

[2] *Staff manual.* Piersol Rehabilitation Center. Philadelphia, Pa.: University of Pennsylvania Hospital, n.d.

[3] Kinney, W. B. (1980). Clinical assessment in mental health settings. *Therapeutic Recreation Journal.* 4th Q., 39.

[4] Coyle, C., Kinney, W. B., Riley, B., and Shank, J. (1994). *Benefits of therapeutic recreation: A Consensus view.* Temple University and National Institute on Disability and Rehabilitation Research.

[5] *Standards of practice for therapeutic recreation services and annotated bibliography.* (1995), Arlington, Va.: Therapeutic Recreation Society.

[6] Stark, K. (1997). Talk isn't cheap, forcing changes in psychiatry. *Philadelphia Inquirer.* Sept. 14, E-1.

Chapter 9

Sports Management Today

Introduction

Sports represent a huge force in the lives of millions of Americans. This field has immense economic implications in terms of attendance revenues, the manufacture and sale of goods and equipment, television income, and the millions of jobs it sustains. However, beyond this, sports have tremendous appeal for individuals and families of every background and socioeconomic level. It offers active participation and serves as a spectator-based form of entertainment that often commands a high degree of emotional attachment to favorite teams or athletes.

This chapter defines sports and shows their scope through statistics that show the extent of current involvement and spectatorship. It describes the different kinds of organizations that sponsor sports programs within the nation's leisure-service system and presents the varied professional roles and functions required to manage sports programs of every type. It then discusses a number of problems linked to sports management today, and concludes by giving a comprehensive picture of sports as a promising career field for young people.

Sports in American Life: Scope and Variety

As a key area of participation in the leisure-service system in the United States today, sports are sponsored by many different kinds of public, nonprofit, commercial and other organizations.

Sports are closely linked to such institutions as education, business and industry, politics, and popular entertainment and offer a rich opportunity for personal and group development and for families to develop strong ties through sharing leisure interests. Sports may be experienced as casual, spontaneous, and relaxed forms of play in a neighborhood or community setting. They may also be highly organized and demanding pursuits, carried on by well-paid professionals before huge audiences.

Sports Defined

How are sports to be defined? While this may seem to be an unnecessary question, the reality is that the term "sport" is often applied to a wide range of physical activities, including many outdoor recreation and fitness pursuits, as shown in Table 9-1.

Different authors suggest different definitions. For example, Hess, Markson, and Stein describe sports as

> (1) Activities with clear performance standards; (2) involving competition through physical exertion; (3) governed by norms defining role relationships; (4) typically performed by members of organized groups; (5) with the goal of achieving a reward; (6) through the defeat of other participants.[1]

Other authors suggest that sports are activities that demand physical exertion and skill, involve a contest or competition, and are carried on within a framework of rules and fair play. While the term "athletics" is often used instead of "sports," it tends to be applied more often to organized team sports in schools or colleges, and less often to such individual sports as tennis and golf or other recreational pursuits, such as skiing or swimming.

Although each sport is a form of physical activity, not all physical activities should be regarded as sports. For example, activities such as walking for exercise or camping, although listed in Table 9-1, are not commonly thought of as sports. Similarly, even competitive activities like ballroom dance contests, synchronized swimming, and cheerleading meets might not be regarded as sports, at least within the popular meaning of the term. Nor should professional wrestling, which is really a rehearsed show, be considered a legitimate sport.

Scope of Sports Involvement

Sports are played on many levels of skill and intensity and are sponsored by many types of leisure-service organizations. They range from an informal neighborhood basketball game for children and youth to the Little League Baseball World Series, from a table tennis tournament in a senior center to World Cup soccer.

One major segment of a sports sponsorship consists of schools and colleges that provide instruction in basic sports skills as part of physical education. They also sponsor intramural and club sports, as well as interscholastic and intercollegiate varsity competition.

Another major segment of sports participation is represented by nonprofit youth-serving organizations, such as Little League Baseball, the American Youth Soccer Organization, Pop Warner Football, the Police Athletic League, and numerous religious-sponsored groups, such as the Catholic Youth Organization. Youth-oriented affiliates of national organizations in other sports, such as bowling, tennis, and golf, also promote widespread participation in American communities.

Thousands of teams and leagues serving all age groups are organized by volunteer groups of community residents, often in cooperation with public recreation and park departments. On the professional level, popular teams compete in baseball, football, basketball, and ice hockey, while individual competitors take part in hundreds of tennis, golf, winter sports

Table 9-1
Participation in selected sports activities.
(Number participating in previous year, at least once.
Persons over age of 7; in thousands).

Activity	All Persons		Sex	
	Number	Rank	Male	Female
Total	237,745	(X)	115,443	122,301
Aerobic exercise	24,119	11	5,314	18,805
Backpacking	11,469	22	7,240	4,229
Badminton	6,084	28	2,909	3,175
Baseball	14,823	18	11,610	3,213
Basketball	33,281	9	22,375	10,906
Bicycle riding	53,342	3	28,595	24,747
Billiards	34,477	8	21,841	12,636
Bowling	42,895	6	22,579	20,316
Calisthenics	10,064	25	5,023	5,041
Camping	44,695	5	24,102	20,593
Exercise walking	73,307	1	26,666	46,641
Exercising with equipment	47,823	4	22,200	25,622
Fishing, freshwater	40,208	7	27,160	13,048
Fishing, saltwater	11,045	23	7,926	3,119
Football, touch	11,645	20	9,603	2,042
Golf	23,082	12	18,219	4,863
Hiking	26,457	10	14,465	11,992
Hunting with firearms	19,251	15	16,317	2,933
Martial arts	4,673	30	3,286	5,251
Raquetball	5,582	29	3,768	1,814
Running/jogging	22,239	13	12,320	9,919
Skiing, downhill	10,466	24	6,277	4,188
Skiing, cross-country	3,385	21	1,820	1,566
Soccer	13,876	19	8,626	5,251
Softball	19,873	14	10,837	9,035
Swimming	60,223	2	29,145	31,078
Table tennis	9,542	26	5,907	3,635
Target shooting	15,695	17	11,097	4,598
Tennis	11,486	21	6,381	5,105
Volleyball	18,535	16	8,970	9,565

(Source: Statistical Abstract of the United States (1999) and National Sporting Goods Association.)

events, and similar contests each year. In dozens of other, less popular sports, hundreds of thousands of additional players compete on amateur, semi-professional and professional levels.

Growth in Participation

Among American youth 12 years of age and younger, the most popular team sports during the 1990s were basketball (9.7 million participants), soccer (7.7 million), softball (5.3 million), baseball (5.1 million), and volleyball (5 million).

In high schools, millions of boys and girls play on intramural teams and take part in interscholastic competition. The most popular sports for boys are 11-man football, basketball, outdoor track and field, and baseball, with between 13,000 and 17,000 secondary schools offering each of these sports. Among girls' teams, basketball, outdoor track and field, volleyball and softball are the most popular sports.

Most recreational sports have gained steadily in participation over the past several decades. Amateur softball play increased from 16 million participants in 1970 to 42 million in 1996, while golf play rose from 11.2 million in 1970 to 24.7 million in 1996. Even recreational tennis, which had declined in popularity during the 1980s and early 1990s, was reported to have made a strong comeback in the late 1990s.[2]

Attendance at College and Professional Sports Events. Similarly, spectator statistics at many college and professional sports events has risen steadily over the past two decades (see Table 9-2).

Table 9-2
Selected Spectator Sports Attendance: 1985–96

Sport Category	Unit	1985	1990	1996
Baseball Major League Attendance	1,000	47,742	55,512	61,665
Basketball—NCAA				
Men's Colleges	Number	753	767	866
Attendance	1,000	26,584	28,741	28,225
Professional	Number	24	27	29
Attendance	1,000	11,534	18,586	21,797
Football, NCAA Colleges	Number	509	533	566
Attendance	1,000	34,952	35,330	36,083
National Football League Attendance	1,000	14,058	17,666	
National Hockey League Attendance	1,000	12,774	13,786	17,105

(Source: Statistical Abstract of the United States, 1999.)

Gains for Girls and Women in Sport

A striking aspect of sports' expanding popularity in American life has involved the dramatic growth of participation by girls and women resulting from the passage of Title IX of the Educational Amendments Act of 1772. By 1978, there was a sevenfold increase in the number of girls playing high school sport (Table 9-3)

Similar gains occurred in intercollegiate athletics, where athletic scholarships for women had been almost non-existent before Title IX. Today, there are over 10,000 scholarships available for female athletes.[3]

Table 9-3
Participation of girls and women in high school and college sports competition.

Level	1971–72	1977–1978	1997–98
High School	294,015	2,083,040	2,570,333
College	31,582	64,375	135,110

(Sources: National Federation of State High Schools Associations and National Collegiate Athletic Association.)

In addition to these changes, there has been a remarkable surge in the number of older women taking part in varied sports and fitness activities. Growing numbers of women have been successful in such internationally popular sports as professional tennis and golf. In addition, female professional leagues have been formed in basketball and soccer.

However, the struggle to gain equal support for girls and women in high school and college sports continues. Fig. 9-1 shows 10 criteria used by educators promoting gender equity to judge whether female athletes are receiving institutional support comparable to that given to male athletes.

In addition to the progress they have made in school and college sports, women have also become increasingly active in the important field of sports journalism, working as reporters, columnists, and television and radio commentators.

Minority-Group Participants in Sport

Clearly, one of the important contributions of organized sports in American life has been the opportunity it has provided for young men and women of minority racial and ethnic backgrounds to achieve national visibility and financial success.

Since the admission of Jackie Robinson to the formerly segregated major leagues in baseball, African-American athletes have emerged as leading college and professional athletes in football, baseball, and basketball. Similarly, Hispanic-American players and athletes from

**Figure 9-1
Title IX compliance checklist.
(Questions developed by Vivian Acosta and Linda Carpenter, professors at Brooklyn College, New York. "Yes" responses to any of these questions indicate that Title IX violations may exist.)**

✔ The boys' basketball team plays at the prime time of 7 P.M. and the girls' team plays at 5 P.M. as the warm-up game.

✔ My daughter's team uses the larger locker room of the entire student body; some of the boys' teams have separate locker room facilities.

✔ Transportation to the games is provided by vans driven by the coaches for the girls' teams; buses with drivers are used for the boys' teams.

✔ Our booster club buys shoes for our football team but our female athletes buy their own shoes.

✔ The coach of our baseball team is full time; the coach for our softball team is part time. We have 10 teams for boys and 10 for girls; we have 10 head coaches for the girls, and 10 head coaches plus 6 assistant coaches for the boys.

✔ When budget constraints require our school to downsize its program, it cut an equal number of boys' and girls' teams.

✔ The cheerleaders and pep band attend the boys' games but not the girls' games.

✔ Letters and trophies are presented to male athletes at a traditional banquet; certificates are given to female athletes at the last game.

✔ We have lights and a dugout on our baseball field; our softball field has neither.

✔ The boys practice in the new gym and the girls practice in the old gym.

---

various Latin-American countries—ranging from Roberto Clemente to Sammy Sosa—have achieved stardom on many professional baseball teams.

While minority-group individuals in the past had relatively little involvement in such "country club" sports as tennis and golf, because of their costs and social exclusion, today the major national organizations in these fields are making a concerted effort to interest inner-city, minority-group youngsters in joining them. The remarkable success of Tiger Woods in golf, and the Williams sisters, Serena and Venus, in tennis has contributed significantly to this drive.

Even in such specialized areas of outdoor sports as skiing, in which there have been few African-American competitors, today young black athletes are beginning to emerge. For example, 20-year-old Andre Horton and his 17-year-old sister, Suki, are primed to become the first African Americans on the United States Ski and Snowboard Team—with encouragement from the major professional skiing associations.[4]

A Nonprofit Organizations Promoting Recreational Sports

In addition to school and college sports sponsorship, another important segment of the organized leisure-service field consists of nonprofit groups that conduct major sports instruction and competition programs for both youth and adults.

Their contribution to the world of sports is immense. They not only provide youngsters with beginning skills and enthusiasm for active participation in sports that many continue through youth and adulthood, but they also help to build the audience for college and professional competition that sustains the entire sports enterprise.

Little League Baseball

Founded in 1939 in Williamsport, Pennsylvania, with three teams representing small local businesses, Little League Baseball today represents the world's largest sports program for children and youth, with over 3 million children competing in over 80 countries. From its inception, the goal of Little League Baseball has been to help youngsters develop citizenship, discipline, teamwork, and physical well-being through sports that emphasize team play rather than individual achievement. To accomplish this goal, the Little League organization sets clearly defined rules for each community, team, and player, and provides a detailed operating manual that is brought up to date each year. In a statement of its guidelines, it is made clear that

> Little League programs operate within specific boundaries for each league's territory, to permit participation by all eligible youngsters within the boundaries. Adults in communities where no chartered Little League program exists can organize a program, with help from Little League headquarters.
>
> Although leagues may assess a registration fee used to purchase uniforms and equipment, maintain fields, etc. [See page 19] the fee cannot be a prerequisite for playing.

The Little League philosophy does not permit any eligible candidate to be turned away, and rules require that every child plays in every game—as part of a policy to ensure that a win-at-all-costs philosophy does not dominate competition. Although most people know Little League through the major division for 9- to 12-year-olds, there are actually several other groupings: T-ball for 5- and 6-year-olds, minor league play for less experienced 7- to 12-year olds, and junior and senior Leagues, in both baseball and softball, for older players. While some girls play in Little League Baseball, they are more fully involved in softball leagues.

Risk management and safety practices are stressed in Little League programs, and player accident and liability insurance coverage is available through Little League headquarters.

Pop Warner Football

Another example of a leading nonprofit, national organization promoting team sports for children and youth is Pop Warner Little Scholars. Committed to promoting academic performance as well as sports performance, this organization was founded during the Great Depression with just four teams. Today, it boasts over 5,000 tackle teams, 4,000 cheerleading squads, and 700 flag football teams, with programs in 38 states, Mexico, and Japan.

Pop Warner Football's purposes are to increase participation in youth football and team spirit, to maximize safety and fun for all, and to instill lifelong values of teamwork, dedication, and athletics. Its rules include the following: no cutting, no tryouts, mandatory play for all team members, and no individual awards for outstanding play. Teams are organized in seven age ranges and weight-balanced classes, from Mitey-Mite to Bantam, and play with strict mandatory equipment and under rules that result in Pop Warner's having a far lower injury rate than school-organized competition.

Pop Warner provides a low-cost insurance program, featuring medical and general liability, and offers regional coaching clinics. It coordinates national Punt, Pass and Kick Competition and sponsors December Superbowl, National Cheer and Dance Championships in Walt Disney World, Florida, as well as an All-American scholar-athlete program.

National Bowling Organizations

While other team sports tend to be limited to youth and young adult participation, bowling represents one of the major sports that can be carried on throughout ones life. Both as an amateur recreational activity and as a form of professional competition, it is coordinated in the United States by USA Bowling in Greendale, Wisconsin, an umbrella organization that includes the American Bowling Congress, the Women's International Bowling Congress, and the Young American Bowling Alliance.

All three organizations seek to promote bowling on all levels through sanctioned leagues operating under standardized tenpin bowling rules. They sponsor leagues, tournaments, and instructional programs and inspect and certify lanes and equipment, along with assisting in fund-raising, insurance coverage, and other administrative functions. Although bowling's popularity declined after its post–World War II heights of participation, it is estimated that as many as 91 million people bowl at least once a year, with 222 million individuals bowling at some point in their lifetime.

While the best-known association in this area is the American Bowling Congress, a key force in promoting the growth of new tenpin bowlers is the Young American Bowling Alliance. With assistance from the Bowling Proprietors Association of America, this organization carries on the following promotional functions:

> It offers program material for organizing leagues, including schedules, handicap tables, award applications, membership cards, record forms, and secretary's handbook.
>
> Extensive awards program, featuring emblems, plaques, medals and certificates for individual and team accomplishments. Awards are determined by age classification for Bantam, Prep, Junior, Major and Senior members.[5]

The Young American Bowling Alliance also recruits and trains thousands of young people for leadership roles in this field. More than 15,000 coaches and league officials provide beginning and advanced instruction. Coaching schools provide training for adults and league assistants, and teach juniors to become student coaches. As part of this process, they serve on association committees, plan and conduct tournaments and assist in instructing disabled bowlers.

In addition to such national programs, numerous other organizations promote youth sports in such areas as tennis (Figure 9-2) and track and field (Figure 9-3).

Economic Importance of Sport

Over the past several decades, the emergence of sports as a major area of public leisure interest and involvement has resulted in its becoming a huge economic force, both in the United States and worldwide.

In 1986, a new publication, *Sports Inc.*, reported that the sports industry had become the nation's 25th biggest enterprise. As measured by Wharton Economic Forecasting Associates, its key spending areas included

> ... leisure and participant sports, ranging from $4.3 million in Babe Ruth baseball team fees to $1.1 billion in ski-lift tickets, $3.9 billion in greens fees and $4.9 billion in health-and-fitness clubs, Equipment' clothing and footwear for players generated an additional $15 billion in revenues.[6]

Figure 9-2
U.S. Tennis Association promotes this sport on all age levels and places a strong emphasis on introducing it to youth in inner-city leagues.

Figure 9-3
Thousands of public and nonprofit community organizations work with the National Recreation and Park Association in cosponsoring Hershey's Track and Field Youth Program.

"More Than a Track Meet"

Hershey's™ Track & Field Youth Program is a playground program designed to introduce children between the ages of 9 and 14 to physical fitness through basic track and field events, such as running, jumping and throwing. It emphasizes participation, friendship and sportsmanship. It is truly "More Than a Track Meet!"

If you would like more information on how you can offer this program in your community, please contact:

NRPA National Programs Office
22377 Belmont Ridge Road
Ashburn, VA 20148
Phone: 1-800-649-3042

Rafer Johnson, Olympic Gold Medalist, serves as the North American spokesperson for the program. Rafer is a charter member of the National Track and Field Hall of Fame. He had the honor of being the final torch bearer at the 1984 Los Angeles Olympic Games, and started the Olympic torch "Run to Atlanta" in 1996.

Rafer Johnson, Olympic Gold Medalist ▶

At that time, gate receipts for college and professional sports brought in $3.1 billion, vendor sales yielded $1.9 billion, sports related advertising in print media amounted to $3.6 billion, and corporations sponsored $800 million worth of sports events.

Through the 1980s and early 1990s, total spending on sports, including fitness and selected outdoor recreation activities, was estimated as ranging from $50 billion to $100 billion a year. In the late 1990s, it was reported that the annual amount for all aspects of sports involvement—including amateur and professional sports, facility and event management, the manufacture and sale of sporting goods, sports for people with disabilities, and international sports—had risen to $212.5 billion, making it larger than the automobile industry.

Examples of the economic impact of sports are shown in Table 9-4, which illustrates the growth of sporting goods sales during the 1990s. Figure 9-4 summarizes the multibillion-dollar boom in building sports stadiums in the early years of the 21st century.

Such examples of sports' growth as an industry are reinforced by the huge sums paid by television networks for broadcasting rights for major-college and professional games, plus the multimillion-dollar contracts for even moderately skilled big-league athletes. The examples also make it clear that the sports field, in general, is the source for well-paid jobs encompassing a huge variety of specializations.

In addition to such reports, *Street and Smith's SportsBusiness Journal* regularly gives Nielsen reports on the top-rated sports television shows and their audiences and shows the stock market performance trends of the major corporations that constitute the huge sports industry today.

Career Development in Sports

Inevitably, the growing public interest and involvement in sports led to an increased awareness of the wide range of job possibilities they offered.

In a leading text on sports management, Chelladurai points out that this field is relatively new compared with other disciplines and occupational fields. It came about, he writes, as an offshoot

> ... of the older field called *physical education*. In earlier days, a specialized field within physical education was called *administration of physical education,* which was concerned with management of physical education and sport in educational institutions. Subsequently, as the intercollegiate athletic programs and intramural programs grew in size and stature, specializations were developed to address the concerns of these programs.[7]

Along with the growing interest in this field, a number of research studies began to examine the roles and job responsibilities of intercollegiate athletic directors and professional sports managers. For example, Quain and Parks carried out a systematic analysis of job opportunities and work functions in six related career areas:

(1) the physical fitness industry; (2) sports promotion and media operations; (3) sports marketing; (4) sports administration, including varied management functions; (5) sports directing in school and college settings; and (6) aquatics program management.[8] Gradually,

Table 9-4
Sporting goods sales: 1990 to 1998

Selected product category	1990	1994	1998 proj.
Sales, all products	48,250	53,453	66,495
Annual percent change	-0.7	8.8	3.7
Percent of retail sales	2.6	2.4	2.5
Athletic and sports clothing	10,130	9,521	12,412
Athletic and sport footwear	11,654	11.120	13,687
Walking shoes	2,950	2,534	3,397
Gym shoes, sneakers	2,536	1,869	2,059
Jogging and running shoes	1,110	1,069	1,586
Tennis shoes	740	556	556
Aerobic shoes	611	356	342
Basketball shoes	918	867	1,066
Cross training shoes	679	1,101	1,377
Golf shoes	226	238	265
Athletic and sport equipment	11,964	15,257	18,225
Firearms and hunting	2,202	3,490	2,639
Exercise equipment	1,824	2,449	2,889
Golf	1,219	1,342	4,033
Camping	1,072	1,017	1,198
Fishing tackle	776	717	687
Snow skiing	606	652	752
In-line skating and wheel sports	(NA)	545	530
Tennis	287	257	335
Archery	265	306	292
Baseball and softball	217	295	301
Water skis	88	51	55
Bowling accessories	155	157	157
Recreational transport	14,502	17,555	22,171
Pleasure boats	7,644	7,679	10,636
Recreational vehicles	4,113	5,690	7,389
Bicycles and supplies	2,423	3,470	3,187
Snowmobiles	322	715	960

(Source: National Sports Goods Assoc., Mt. Prospect, Illinois, and Statistical Abstract of the United States, 1999.) (Billions of dollars).

Figure 9-4
Partial listing of new sports stadium construction in 1993–2003. (Source: Street and Smith's *SportsBusiness Journal*, Mar. 5, 2000)

No Timeout in Sports Building Boom

For 1999 through 2003, $7.9 billion has been committed for 81 sports-related projects in the U.S. and Canada. In 1999-2000, $3.29 billion will be spent for 35 new and renovated venues.

In the Midwest, more than $2 billion will be spent for 5 sports stadiums to be completed through 2002 in Detroit, Milwaukee, Cleveland, Cincinnati and Columbus (Ohio). Sports/concert arenas are opening in 8 cities: Indianapolis, St. Paul, Prospect Heights (Ill.), Flint (Mich.), St. Charles (Mo.), Columbus and Cincinnati (Ohio), and Green Bay, Wis.

As colleges and universities look for more outside revenue, the market for new and expanded arenas, multipurpose facilities and stadiums is very active. From 1999 through 2001, at least 21 new and expanded projects—with construction and design cost of more than $884 million— will be added.

Openings of major pro facilities include:
- **Toronto's** $189 million (U.S.), 19,900-capacity Air Canada Centre for NBA Raptors and NHL Maple Leafs
- **Seattle's** $517 million, 47,000-seat Safeco Field for MLB Mariners, and
- **Seattle's** $430 million, 72,000-seat football/soccer stadium for NFL Seahawks opens Aug. 2002
- **Nashville's** $292 million, 67,000-seat East Bank Stadium for the NFL Tennessee Oilers
- **In Flushing (NY),** $500 million, 60,000-capacity New Shea Stadium for MLB Mets
- **Raleigh's** $155 million, 21,000-capacity Entertainment & Sports Arena on the NC State campus for the NHL Carolina Hurricanes and N.C. State University Wolfpack
- **Minnesota's** $130 million St. Paul Arena opens in September 2000 as new home of the NHL Wild. Seating of 18,600 for hockey, 19,400 for concerts, with 74 suites and 3,000 club seats.
- **New Orleans'** $110 million, 20,000-seat Arena (ECHL Brass & Tulane Univ. USA Conf. Green Wave).
- **Indianapolis'** $183 million, 20,000-capacity Conseco Fieldhouse (NBA Indiana Pacers, IHL Indianapolis Ice, Ellerbe Becket);
- **Miami's** $160 million, 20,000-capacity American Airlines Arena (NBA Heat) offi cially opens Dec. 31 with Millennium Eve Concert with top names.
- **Dallas** summer 2001 NBA Mavericks, NHL Stars 19,000 concerts/basketball, 18,000 hockey

Ohio will add five:
- **Cincinnati's** $280 million 65,500-seat Paul Brown Stadium is on track for August 2000 bow as the new home of the NFL Bengals
- **Cincinnati's** $297 million, 45,000-seat Cincinnati Reds MLB Ballpark
- **Cleveland's** $247 million, 72,000-seat Browns Stadium for its replacement NFL team
- **Columbus** $150 million Nationwide Arena opens September 2000 as home of expansion NHL Blue Jackets. Seating is 20,000 for concerts, 19,500 for basketball and 18,500 for hockey, with 52 suites, 26 loge boxes, 120 club service seats and lounge.

the field grew to embrace professional sports management, including facility management, events management, marketing, sponsorship structures, and sports law.

Higher Education Programs in Sports Management

As increasing numbers of college departments and schools of health, physical education, and recreation began to offer courses and then separate degree options in sports management, the National Association for Sports and Physical Education (NASPE) and the North American Society for Sport Management (NASSM) conducted a study in 1986 to identify the curricular programs in this field. Initially, it found 86 such degree programs. By the time its survey was completed in 1990, there were 181 such curricula. By the late 1990s, the number had risen to 200.

As public interest in this field grew rapidly, numerous texts were published that presented its job possibilities in glowing terms and identified a variety of other specialized career areas. In 1991, for example, Shelly Field listed 73 specific job titles under eleven different employment headings, These included (1) career opportunities for professional athletes; (2) jobs with professional sports teams, as scouts, coaches, and ticket managers; (3) sports business jobs, such as sports agents, events coordinators, or publicists; (4) school and college coaching jobs; (5) officiating positions; (6) sports journalism jobs; (7) recreation and fitness jobs; and several other specialties in sports such as boxing or wrestling, racing, wholesaling and retailing, and sports medicine.[9]

Through the 1920s, other investigators developed detailed breakdowns of job categories in sports under several different career headings. Literally hundreds of specific job roles were identified, ranging from scoreboard operator or public-address announcer to executive titles such as league commissioner or radio producer. Other positions, for which college courses in sports management would not be particularly helpful—as well as others that could be reached only after years of professional experience—were also identified.

However, college study in a curriculum that meets the standards developed by the NASPE and the NASSM, with core courses in such areas as organizational skills, marketing, finance, ethics, economics and law, is clearly an appropriate first step toward achieving a successful career in sports management.

Special Aspects of the Sports Management Field

In addition to the theoretical aspects of sports management—or the practical skills that can be learned both in courses and in internships and field work—those considering entering this field should be aware of certain special aspects that make it different from other elements in the leisure-service system.

First, sports differ from most other kinds of business ventures in that it is extremely difficult to predict the outcomes of given programs or enterprises. Parks, Zanger, and Quarterman point out that the reason for this is

> . . . the spontaneous nature of the activity, the inconsistency of events, and the uncertainty surrounding the results. Sports marketers, therefore, face unique challenges dictated by the nature of the enterprise.[10]

Factors creating such uncertainty range from shifts in public interest and support to the difficulty in predicting the performance of athletes in college or professional sports, plus the impact of injuries that may hamper a team's performance.

Another unique aspect of sports is that they do not depend, as most businesses do, on financial income derived from the direct sale of a product or service. Instead, sports income is gained from a great variety of extraneous sources: television rights, concessions, parking, merchandise sales, rental and licensing fees, and—in the case of collegiate and public recreation programs—from student or user fees, memberships, and donations.

Finally, sports represent a difficult field to enter, particularly on the professional level, in that hiring practices often favor individuals who have starred in college or professional sports, and thus have a high degree of visibility. While this basis for selection is logical in terms of coaching or managing job requirements, it should be less relevant for many other positions in the field, where knowledge of finance, marketing, public relations, or events management should receive major emphasis.

Other Problem Areas

A unique aspect of sport in contemporary American life is that, while it is generally thought of in positive, idealistic terms as a means of promoting good character, self-discipline, and citizenship—and as a means of sustaining health and physical fitness—too often these values are not realized.

Instead, fans and young players are often shocked by revelations about the criminal behavior of college or professional athletes, the recruitment and academic coddling scandals in many institutions, and the realization, when teams move from city to city, or when favorite professional athletes are suddenly traded, that sport often is, in the disillusioned fan's words—"just a business."

Health and Injury Concerns. The value of sports in promoting fitness and overall health is challenged when studies reveal the considerable number of serious concussions and other injuries that occur, particularly in major contact sports. In some sports, such as varsity wrestling, deaths-occurring from drastic weight-loss efforts before important bouts have recently received attention and call for stronger regulations.

Character-Building. This important aspect of sports comes under criticism when hazing in schools and colleges routinely results in young athletes being cruelly brutalized and even sexually mistreated. This hazing is encouraged because of a mistaken belief that such punishment, handed down by older players to younger ones, builds team loyalty and aggressive manliness needed in such sports as ice hockey and football.[11]

Bribery and Betting. In high-pressure college and professional sports, two other negative influences are bribery and betting. For example, the intensive campaign of bribery that swayed the International Olympic Committee to assign the 2002 Winter Olympics to Salt Lake City, Utah, created an international scandal.[12] Shortly thereafter, it was revealed that three million Americans were betting through on-line pools on the annual NCAA Basketball Tournament on the Internet, despite the long-recognized danger posed by organized gambling to the integrity of sports.

Pressures on Young Athletes

Finally, the ways in which organized sports for children and youth are often presented in communities large and small deserves attention. Too often, adults place tremendous pressure on youngsters to win—often to the point that boys and girls quit organized sports at the age of 12 or 13, because they no longer meet their needs for fun, healthy exercise, skill improvement, and relaxed recreation. Not infrequently, parents and coaches flagrantly abuse officials, and coaches and in some cases threaten and physically attack them.[13]

Need for Ethical Values in Sport

None of these abuses are inherent in sports. They come about in part because of the pressures to win that are part of society itself. This notion becomes increasingly powerful as young players move up the ladder of recreational sports leagues, junior high and secondary school sports, and college athletic programs.

On the positive side, a number of national organizations, such as the Coalition of Americans to Protect Sports, Parents and Coaches in Sports, and the National Alliance of Youth Sports, have done research, organized conferences, and fought to restore positive values and policies to youthful competition. Promoting "child-centered coaching" and rules to prevent child abuse and overly violent play leading to injuries, they are having a growing impact on the management of recreational sports for youth—often in cooperation with organizations such as Little League, which seek to eliminate negative coaching practices and parental pressures.

Many religious-affiliated sponsors of youth sports have also promoted more positive values and policies to overcome the negative aspects of win-at-all-costs coaching. The Catholic Youth Organization frequently sponsors coaching clinics and symposiums that stress sound sports management approaches. The Church of Jesus Christ of Latter-Day Saints (Mormon Church) gives strong support to youth sports directed by positive religious values, as part of its overall mission, and as a means of strengthening the attachment of young people to the church.

Career Opportunities in Sports

Clearly, the sports field holds an immense attraction for many hundreds of thousands of young Americans who have had positive experiences on community or school teams in their lives. In a realistic text on job opportunities in this field, W. R. Heitzmann comments that the exciting and glamorous lives we see professional athletes leading represent for many the pinnacle of sports Achievement. But, he continues:

> . . . these high-profile, much sought after jobs are not the only positions available in this ever-expanding career field. Sports and athletics require much more than the fan entertainment the athletes offer to make sports successful at all levels of competition.

> The job opportunities that service sports and athletics in general outnumber those of athletes many times over. From physical education in the school setting to coaching peewees or managing the big leagues, from sports medicine to sports officiating, the peripheral jobs supporting the players are the real substance of sports and athletics the world over.[14]

Heitzmann goes on to say that athletes who can no longer compete on the professional level, teaching-minded individuals who wish to show others how to play, and sports enthusiasts who just want to be near the action all gravitate toward jobs in this field for the same basic reason: their love of sports.

As Chapter 11 will show in fuller detail, the individual who seeks to explore sports leadership as a career field will need to begin preparation at an early stage, and decide what aspect of the field appeals to him or her. Figure 9-5 illustrates one area of potential employment, showing job listings for several different positions in a university department of intercollegiate athletics. Figure 9-6, in contrast, shows examples of advertised job-openings

Figure 9-5
Examples of job openings in sports management on the college and university level.

The University of New Mexico
Department of Intercollegiate Athletics

Are You Interested in Living and Working in the Land of Enchantment?

The University of New Mexico, a NCAA Division 1-A institution and member of the Mountain West Conference is currently soliciting applications and nominations for the following positions:

Assistant Strength and Conditioning Coach. This is a full-time position reporting to the head strength and condition coach. Responsibilities include but are not limited to designing, implementing, and supervising training routines for male and female student-athletes in 21 intercollegiate sports. Required qualifications include a Bachelor's Degree and one to three years experience directly related to the duties and responsibilities specified.

Senior Academic Advisor. This is a full-time position reporting to the assistant athletic director for academic services. Responsibilities include but are not limited to: assisting student-athletes with all facets of academic advisement (class scheduling, tutoring, degree and career planning, etc.); monitoring of compliance with all NCAA rules related to academic eligibility; and support of life skills program. Required qualifications include Bachelor's Degree and one to three years experience directly related to the duties and responsibilities specified.

Assistant Director, Facilities/Operations. This is a full-time position reporting to the director of facilities/operations. Responsibilities include but are not limited to assisting director in the development, planning coordination and management of facilities and event operations. Facilities include the world famous "Pit", University Stadium (football), baseball, softball, tennis and track and field venues. Required qualifications include a Bachelor's Degree and one to three years experience directly related to the duties and responsibilities specified. Knowledge of building and facilities maintenance, safety and security; ability to schedule events and/or facilities usage; ability to supervise and train staff including organizing, prioritizing, scheduling work assignments, and records maintenance skills; experience in examining and developing policies, procedures and strategic initiatives which will enhance facility/event operations preferred.

Assistant Director of Marketing. This is a full-time position reporting to the director of marketing. Duties include but are not limited to: developing and implementing marketing plans for a variety of men's and women's sports; selling and servicing of corporate sponsorships; group and corporate ticket sales; presentation of games and special events; community relations; and supervision of students, interns and volunteers. Required qualifications include a Bachelor's Degree and a minimum of six months experience directly related to the duties and responsibilities specified.

To apply, log on to the university's website: www.unm.edu and send resumes by February 29, 2000 to: Sylvia Lopez, Personnel Coordinator, University of New Mexico Athletics Department, South Campus, Albuquerque, NM 87131-0041.

The University of New Mexico is an Equal Opportunity/Affirmative Action Employer.

Figure 9-6
Examples of job openings in professional sports management, chiefly in marketing and sales.

CAREER OPPORTUNITIES

BUFFALO SPORTS ENTERPRISES, INC.

Buffalo Sports Enterprises has just secured an ABA professional basketball franchise for the WNY market. We are a progressive, customer/fan and sponsor focused organization committed to developing a winning basketball team. We have 2 positions open, both offer a competitive salary with benefits.

SPORTS GENERAL MANAGER

We seek an experienced sports manager who has experience in all sports operations including: ticket sales, sponsorship sales, media, player relations and contracts, game operations and sports (basketball helpful but not necessary) operations. We offer a great opportunity for someone to help build something wonderful for WNY. Hard work, good values and a strong sense of ethics necessary. Reply with resume and salary history to:
Chairman
ABA Buffalo, Inc.
c/o Buffalo Sports Enterprises, Inc.
661 Delaware Avenue
Buffalo, NY 14202

BASKETBALL HEAD COACH

We are seeking an experienced Head Basketball Coach with a proven track record in coaching, player evaluation and of course winning games. We offer a great opportunity for someone to help build this franchise from the ground up. Reply with resume, coaching statistics and background, and salary history to:
Chairman
ABA Buffalo, Inc.
c/o Buffalo Sports Enterprises, Inc.
661 Delaware Avenue
Buffalo, NY 14202

SCHAFER CORPORATION, a leader in sports video editing equipment, is seeking a salesperson with a football/basketball background to work in our Chelmsford, MA office. 30-40% travel required. BS degree required. Proficiency with Windows 98 and computer hardware is preferred. We offer a professional working environment, competitive salary and superior benefits. Fax or email your resume with salary requirements to 978-256-1404 or ldibene@schafercorp.com Schafer is an affirmative action, equal opportunity employer.

The Buccaneer Marketing Department has immediate openings for 2 positions:

NEW PARTNER DEVELOPMENT

Seeking aggressive sales person with minimum three years sales results. This salary plus commission position must be able to work long hours. A background in media or sports sales a plus.

MARKETING MANAGER

This service-oriented position requires strong relationship and sales promotion skills. Three years of proven sales promotion and client service skills a must. The ideal candidate will have a background in consumer and/or business to business promotions.

Please mail resume, Indicating position and salary history, to:
One Buccaneer Place
Attn: Human Resources
(Indicate New Partner Development or Marketing Manager)
Tampa, FL 33607
Absolutely No Phone Calls
EOE M/F/V/H

MIAMI FUSION

SALES MANAGER - Position requires a highly motivated individual with strong communication skills. Right person must have a strong desire to accomplish goals. The ability to develop relationship is key. Bachelor's degree required. **Objectives:** Sell season tickets • Sell group tickets • Sell mini plans. Compensation: very competitive...salary + commission. Forward resume to Mike Stanfield Director of Ticket Sales @ Fax: 954-733-6105

Sunshine Network,

Florida's #1 sports network, and one of the Nation's premiere Regional Sports Networks, is looking for talented salespeople to be based in either our Orlando or Hollywood, FL offices. You must possess strong sales skills, the desire to succeed, and love of sports.

Please send your resume to: **Director of Sales, Sunshine Network, 4000 Hollywood Blvd., #715-s, Hollywood, FL 33021. Fax 954-967-5699. E-mail: llazerson@sunshinenetwork.com phone 945-967-5680**

in professional sports, that place a strong emphasis on business-related functions such as marketing and sales operations.

All of the other kinds of sports organizations described in this chapter, from nonprofit youth-serving sports leagues to the management of commercial golf, tennis, or ski centers, also offer numerous job opportunities. While many of these are entry-level jobs, they all offer the potential for advancement to higher supervisory or executive positions.

Suggested Questions for Class Discussion or Essay-Examinations

1. Define *sports* as you understand them, distinguishing them from *athletics* and *games*. What forms of competitive physical activities would you *not* consider examples of sports?
2. The tendency is to show the importance of sports in monetary terms (i.e., the amount of money spent on them), or in terms of the number of people who either take part in them or watch them. Can you think of another, more meaningful way to demonstrate its importance of sports today?
3. This chapter emphasizes the extent to which women and girls, during the past three decades, have progressed toward equality in sports participation and support. Why is this so important? Do you believe that women and men should be given exactly the same amount of support in college sports today? Justify your answer.
4. Select one of the national organizations that sponsor or promote a specific form of sport that is described in this chapter. What services does it offer, and why is this type of organization important in the total leisure-service system?
5. Despite the undisputed popularity of sports in today's society, many critics believe that sports are afflicted with a number of abuses and negative influences. What are these, and what role can members of the leisure-service profession—particularly recreation leaders and managers—play to counter these negative factors?

Footnotes

[1] Hess, B., Markson, E., and Stein, P. (1988). *Sociology.* New York: Macmillan, 571.
[2] Christophe, A. (1999). What a racket. *Parks and Recreation.* Oct., 54.
[3] See Lough, N. (Ed.). (1998). Promotion of sports for girls and women. Special Feature, in *Journal of Physical Education, Recreation and Dance,* May–June, 25–35.
[4] Lloyd, B. (2000). Black brother-sister duo pursue Olympics. *New York Times.* Feb. 17, D-5.
[5] Putting on the media blitz. (1999). *Annual Report, American Bowling Congress.*
[6] Sport your economy. (1987). *U.S. News and World Report.* Dec. 7, 59.
[7] Chelladurai, P. (1996). In Parkhouse, B. (Ed.). *The management of sport: Its foundation and applications.* St. Louis: C.V. Mosby and National Association for Sport and Recreation, 13.
[8] Quain, R., and Parks, J. (1986), Sport management survey; employment perspectives. *Journal of Physical Education, Recreation and Dance.* Apr., 18–21.
[9] Field, S. (1991). *Career opportunities in the sports industry.* New York: Facts on File Publishers.
[10] Parks, J., Zanger, B., and Quarterman, J. (Eds.). (1998). *Contemporary sports management.* Champaign, Illinois: Human Kinetics Press, 5.

[11] Cavanaugh, J. (2000). Six wrestlers in Connecticut are charged in hazing case. *New York Times.* Feb. 17, D-2.
[12] Ragavan, C. (1999), Let the scandal inquiries begin. *U.S. News and World Report,* Jan. 11, 33.
[13] Kozlowski, J. (1999). Sports league held liable for brutal attack on coach. *Parks and Recreation,* Nov., 45–52. See also: Ferguson, A. (1999). Crazy culture of kids sports. *Time.* July 12, 52–60.
[14] Heitzman, W. R. (1993). *Opportunities in sports and athletic careers.* Lincolnwood, Illinois: VGM Career Horizons, *ix.*

Chapter 10

Travel, Tourism, and Hospitality

Introduction

Travel, tourism, and hospitality represent a key component of the leisure-service field and certainly offer one of the most popular forms of recreation for Americans. At the same time, they constitute a huge industry that far outweighs any other aspect of leisure involvement in terms of money spent and the numbers of persons employed in it.

This chapter defines the terms *travel, tourism* and *hospitality* and identifies their key elements, as well as the social and economic trends that influence them today. It goes on to discuss several different kinds of tourist attractions and services—theme parks and, water-play parks, cruise ships, and other waterborne forms of leisure travel, adventure travel, and "eco-tourism"—as well as cultural, religious, historical, and environmental travel motivations.

The interaction of different types of agencies in developing and marketing tourism ventures is discussed, and the chapter ends with an overview of career opportunities in this diverse field.

Basic Concepts of Travel, Tourism, and Hospitality

Obviously, the three terms discussed in this chapter are connected, in that the tourist must use travel to get to his or her destination, and normally must depend on hospitality services while there. However, all three terms have distinctly different meanings.

Travel, for example, might apply to any movement from one location to another. However, in economic reporting it is used to describe trips taken over a minimum distance that are not part of one's customary routine. McIntosh, Goeldner, and Ritchie point out that the term *traveler* is usually defined as "any person on a trip between two or more countries or between two or more localities within his/her country of usual residence."[1] They then state that *tourism* comprises

> . . . the activities of persons traveling to and staying in places outside their usual environment for not more than one consecutive year for leisure, business or other purposes.[2]

This definition broadens the meaning of tourism beyond the idea of "pleasure travel," in that one may be a tourist while traveling on business. One might also be traveling for religious purposes (e.g., to worship at a holy shrine) or for educational, family-related or other practical purposes. As Table 10-1 shows, travel to visit friends or for other pleasure-related lessons comprises a major portion of all trips. Even business travel (e.g., as in a trip to a convention) is often mingled with recreational activity.

The third term, *hospitality,* has its roots in the Latin word *hospitare* meaning "to receive as a guest." Its basic elements are the provision of accommodations or lodging, accompanied by food and beverages. Typically, hospitality includes varied forms of entertainment or recreation and might also involve transportation assistance or other services designed to make the visitor's stay more comfortable.

Each of these elements includes a considerable number of separate operations or services and is customarily linked to others in packaged trips or tours.

Table 10-1
Travel by U.S. residents: 1985–97
[In millions: 497.8 equals 497,800,000]

Type of Trip	1985	1990	1995	1997
All travel: Total trips	497.8	589.4	669.7	715.9
Person trips	808.3	956.0	1,172.6	1256.1
Business travel: Total trips:	156.6	182.8	207.8	207.4
Person trips	156.6	182.8	207.8	207.4
Pleasure travel: Total trips	301.2	361.1	413.0	443.2
Person trips	539.5	649.4	809.5	862.4
Vacation travel: Total trips	264.5	328.7	349.7	388.6
Person trips	487.8	591.6	680.4	751.8

(Sources: Travel Industry Association of America, Washington D.C., and *Statistical Abstract of the United States,* 1999.)

Travel may be carried on by airplane, cruise ship, railroad, tour bus, automobile, or by more primitive or simpler means such as horseback, bicycle, canoe, kayak, or by foot.

Tourism comprises a host of different enterprises and attractions ranging from theme parks and water-play parks, national or state parks or historic monuments, major sports events or cultural festivals, visits to foreign lands or exotic settings, professional conventions and business meetings, shopping areas, gambling casinos, weddings and funerals, and numerous other destinations.

Hospitality may include hotels, resorts, bed-and-breakfast lodging, camps, or the provision of food and beverages and other forms of personal assistance. As Chapter 7 suggests, hospitality is also an important function in different private-membership settings such as country clubs, yacht clubs, and other resort-like communities that offer dining rooms, restaurants, bars and night clubs as part of their appeal for members.

All of these services, taken together—along with travel agents and other organizations that plan, sponsor and promote travel tours—comprise the overall "tourism industry."

Scope of Tourism Today

Various statistical reports confirm that travel and tourism have become an immense industry, that involves many hundreds of billions of dollars. For example, the Travel Industry Association (TIA) reported that expenditures rose from $489 billion in 1996 to $502 billion in 1997 in the United States alone. In 1998 the trend continued, with pleasure travel increasing by over 10 percent for the first half of the year accounting for over 70 percent of all travel in the United States during this period.[3]

Worldwide, the statistics are equally impressive. On a global scale,

> . . . 635 million people traveled to a foreign country in 1998, spending US $439 billion. International tourism receipts combined with passenger transport totaled more than US $504 billion—making tourism the world's #1 export earner, ahead of automotive products, chemicals, petroleum and food.[4]

While some may challenge the accuracy of such statistical reports, either in the overall recreation and leisure field or in separate areas such as tourism,[5] methods of measuring tourism's economic impact have become increasingly sophisticated, with both government agencies and industry analysts developing new systems for arriving at total spending figures. A tourism satellite account (TSA) methodology has increasingly been adopted by leading industrial nations, permitting them to arrive at standardized statistics for measuring the domestic impact of tourism, its contribution to employment, tax income, manufacture of goods and food, and even its effect on each nation's balance of payments.[6]

It was reported in 1998 that, by using such methods, the direct and indirect impact of travel and tourism was found to represent more than 11 percent of the world's gross domestic product (GDP) and would rise by 12.5 percent or more during the next decade. It was reported that, at the time, there were 79.2 million jobs in the tourism industry itself and 231 million jobs that depended to a large degree on its needs and revenues—figures predicted to rise substantially by 2010.[7]

Trends Promoting Tourism

What accounts for the tremendous growth that has taken place in worldwide tourism over the past few decades? A number of demographic trends, along with economic prosperity and the increasing availability of vacations, weekend opportunities for travel, and the expansion of relatively inexpensive and convenient packaged tours and cruises, have contributed to this striking development.

Demographic Factors

The sheer growth in population over the past half century represents a major factor in promoting the volume of pleasure travel that has just been summarized.

Each age group—children, adults, and senior citizens has become increasingly involved in leisure travel. While Americans from the ages of 25 to 34 take more pleasure trips than those in other age groups, family travel has climbed steadily, with U.S. adults with children accounting for 74 percent of all vacation travel today. To underscore this point, 47 percent of baby boomers born in the decades after World War II take family vacations each year.

A huge tourism market can be found in the growing numbers of Americans in their late middle-age years who are approaching retirement and have the capability for travel. In addition, the postretirement group of senior citizens will expand steadily, not only in the United States but throughout the world.

The impact of civil rights laws, affirmative action, and the steady increase in the number of financially comfortable minority-group families has meant that millions of African Americans and other racial minorities now have the economic capability for travel, as well as the opportunity to travel safely in areas of the country that once refused to accommodate them. Finally, as described in Chapter 8, many disabled individuals who formerly could not travel conveniently now enjoy tourist trips both in the United States and abroad.

Discretionary Time

Economic reports have indicated that a high percentage of employees, businesspersons, and professionals are working longer hours today than in the 1970s and 1980s (see page 000). One effect of this trend has been that these people tend to take shorter, more active and concentrated vacations and weekend trips.

For example, the number of weekend trips taken by Americans jumped by 70 percent between 1986 and 1996, and those trips comprised more than half of all U.S. travel. In 1996, statistics indicated that 604 million weekend person-trips were taken, almost 80 percent of them for purposes of pleasure.

Growth of Tourism Sponsors

A key factor in this development has been the emergence of a variety of different types of agencies and groups that plan and sponsor short-term trips and vacations. For example, many public recreation and park departments organize trips for their residents, sometimes for senior citizens, family groups, or other special groups of individuals. As Chapter 6 points out, many armed forces and employee service units organize inexpensive short trips and tours. Religious agencies frequently sponsor tours to holy lands, and colleges and universities today organize short vacation trips, for both their students and their alumni.

Other Factors: Destinations and Travel Technology

A key element in the dramatic growth of tourism has been the increasing variety of destinations and attractions that appeal to travelers around the world.

In sociopolitical terms, the end of the Cold War and the consequent removal of barriers to travel imposed by Soviet-bloc nations means that millions of travelers from Western countries are now able to explore historic and culturally fascinating lands that, in many cases, their families had emigrated from in the distant past. Also, many veterans of past wars travel to historic battlefields where they had fought for their country—and often are welcomed by the local citizenry, whom they had liberated.

One factor in promoting the growth of tourism involves the role of government on all levels. Various federal commerce and land-management bureaus promote tourism travel, and state travel offices spend over $500 million annually on tourism promotion. Illinois, Hawaii, and Texas have the highest travel budgets, followed by Florida and Pennsylvania—with tourism-related fees, lottery revenues, and highway and motor vehicle funds providing the bulk of support for such advertising.

In addition, many county and municipal recreation and park departments sponsor special events to attract visitors. They also host tours so travel agents can promote local tourist attractions.

Diversified Travel Interests

In search of cultural and historical knowledge, 53 million American adults visited museums and historic sites in a recent year, and 33 million adults attended cultural events such as theater and music festivals while traveling.

Sports represent a strong attraction to tourists, with Americans taking 60 million trips per year to attend sports events either as participants or spectators. Additional numbers enjoy tennis, golf, and similar pastimes while on vacation. Nearly 30 million American adults visited a national park within a recent year. One-third of adults take camping vacations annually, many of them in recreation vehicles, which have made family travel increasingly convenient. An estimated 31 million adults enjoy such adventure pursuits as white-water rafting, scuba diving, and mountain biking. Even shopping has become a popular tourism motivation, with about 37 percent of travelers visiting discount outlets en route to their destination.[8]

All of these varied travel pursuits today have been made increasingly accessible and convenient both by the commercial organizations that provide the bulk of tourism attractions and by the airlines, cruise ship companies, tour operators and travel agencies that package tripe and accommodations within a wide range of price levels. Often such packages include flights to Europe, for example, combined with hotel stays that are so reasonable that millions of travelers can afford them—travelers who never would have been able to enjoy such trips in the past.

Impact of the Internet

New forms of technology play an important role in facilitating travel arrangements. With the growth of electronic marketing, millions of travelers can now explore new destinations and search for the best services and lowest costs through their computers. In 1998, about 20 percent of travel products were offered on-line, with ten Web sites accounting for 50 percent of all such sales—and these numbers are rapidly growing.[9] For example, Internet users booked $276 million in travel on-line in 1996, including air travel, hotel rooms, car rentals, and other expenses. In 1997, sales tripled to $827 million. It is estimated that by 2002, the total will be nearly $9 billion—with heavily increased spending on Web site advertising.

Internet marketing will be especially useful in attracting overseas visitors to U.S. tourism destinations. The number of non-U.S. Internet users is expected to climb to 143 million by 2002, up from 16.4 million in 1997. Web sites will become increasingly global, thus making it easier for overseas travelers to explore destinations and make purchases from abroad.

Structure of the Tourism Industry

Tourism may be examined in several different ways by reviewing the roles and motivations of different elements within the overall travel, tourism, and hospitality system or the different perspectives of groups that play a part in it.

McIntosh, Goeldner, and Ritchie identity four different perspectives on tourism, including the following:

- The *tourist,* who seeks various psychic and physical experiences, ranging from change of scenery or aesthetic or cultural involvement to exposure to exotic environments or the opportunity for varied forms of play or social involvement.
- The *businesses* that provide tourist attractions, goods, and services in order to make a profit, along with other types of cultural or environmental organizations, such as museums, performing arts companies, historic mansions, or botanical gardens that, while nonprofit, seek income from visitors in order to sustain their operations.
- The *government* of the host community or area which encourages tourism as a "wealth factor" in the economy of its jurisdiction as a source of business enterprise, employment, and tax revenues.
- The *host community,* including local residents who usually view tourism as a positive factor in terms of providing employment, but who also may resent tourists from other regions when they create overcrowding and a burden on local resources, or when they are insensitive to local values and customs.[10]

Basic Components of Tourism

Like the overall leisure-service system itself, tourism may be seen as a complex system composed of many different parts. However, these may be broken down into three major elements: transportation, accommodations, and attractions.

Transportation, as indicated, may include a variety of modes of land, air, and sea travel and two or more forms of travel on a single tour or cruise. It may also include arrangements for local travel carried on independently by a tourist, once the destination has been reached.

In addition to the actual provision of airplane, ship, and other forms of transport, this function also involves travel agencies, tour operators, Internet Web services, travel counselors, car rental agencies, insurance companies, and other companies or services that facilitate the trip itself.

Accommodations are commonly referred to as lodging and food and beverage services. However, they may also range from campsite rentals to full-service resort or cruise ship

Figure 10-1
Examples of tourism brochures prepared by the Kamloops, British Columbia, Canada, Recreation and Park Department.

accommodations and possibly involve stays in a hunting lodge or tent during backpack or horseback trips, or even lodging in a castle or historic chateau.

Accommodations may also involve special guide services, child care arrangements, assistance by a concierge in making theater or concert reservations, health care aid, and similar forms of support.

Attractions represent the most varied of the three functions, in that they may consist of active forms of recreation, sightseeing, entertainment, thrill rides, or any of the other specialized experiences that tourists seek.

Many resorts or cruise ships today offer sophisticated Broadway-type shows, gambling casinos, and optional side trips to unusual landmarks, folk performances, shopping centers, scenic beaches, and similar settings. In some cases, such as the Elderhostel movement serving older men and women, an educational program and the opportunity to live in a foreign

Figure 10-2
Contents page of a brochure produced by the Valley Forge Convention and Visitors Bureau promoting tourism in this historic region.

college or university environment may represent the unique attraction that is sought. In other cases, the highlight of a trip may involve exploring an ancient archaeological dig or seeing wild creatures in their exotic environment.

As Chapter 5 suggests, many trips are undertaken in pursuit of wilderness-based pastimes, such as hunting, fishing, mountain climbing, and other forms of risk recreation.

To illustrate the way in which these various elements of travel, tourism, and hospitality fit together, this chapter now examines several major types of tourism destinations or forms of organized attractions.

Theme Parks

Theme parks, as we know them today, descended from a long-standing type of American recreational enterprise—amusement parks. Most of these parks were originally built around large cities, as subsidiary ventures linked to transportation businesses, such as railroad and trolley-car lines, excursion boats, and similar companies.

Historically, amusement parks featured a mix of roller coasters and other novelty, or "thrill" rides, such as Ferris wheels, whirligigs, miniature car "racetracks" and tunnels of love. They also featured game booths, fun houses, freak shows, and other exotic displays (including in some cases strippers or belly dancers), beer gardens, and restaurants.

Disneyland. In the years following World War II, such parks became increasingly run-down and tawdry, and lost their appeal to many families. Then, in 1955, Walt Disney, creator of popular animated films, established Disneyland in Anaheim, California.

A huge success, with its wholesome and appealing atmosphere and cleverly designed rides and attractions—many of which featured Mickey and Minnie Mouse, Pluto, and other Disney cartoon characters—Disneyland set in motion a wave of other modern family fun complexes that also became major tourist destinations.

Called "theme parks" because they tended to be based on popular themes, such as fairy tales, history, stories from children's literature, unusual locales, live animal or sea creature displays, these ventures gained instant popularity.

Among the most successful early theme parks were the Bally Corporation's Six Flags chain, Busch Entertainment's Park Continent and Olde Country, and the Marriott Corporation's Great America chain. In time, Disney added Disney World, in Lake Buena Vista near Orlando, Florida, which was followed by theme parks in France and Japan. Through the 1980s and 1990s, the Disney Company continued to add exciting and innovative new attractions—Future World and World Showcase in the EPCOT (Experimental Prototype Community of Tomorrow) complex, the Disney MGM Studios, and a host of other separate attractions—a Cirque du Soleil show, created especially for Disney, Disney's Typhoon Lagoon, River Country, Blizzard Beach, Fort Wilderness Resort and Campground, Animal Kingdom, and numerous other attractions.

Disney's unique contribution was to develop entirely new and technologically advanced environments and management systems. The goal was to capture every aspect of the tourist enterprise, from restaurants, spas, hotels, sports facilities, stores, and other businesses to a major new cruise line.

Popularity of Theme Parks

By the mid-1990s, theme parks had gained immense popularity throughout the United States, with attendance and revenues rocketing skyward—like the daring rides they featured—from coast to coast. U.S. News and World Report described the trend in 1995, predicting that about 255 million thrill seekers would visit North American theme parks that year compared to 151 million annually in the 1970s:

> Total park revenues are expected to reach $5 billion this year, compared with $321 million in 1970 . . . . This summer, 45 state-of-the-art roller coasters will be introduced in 41 theme parks, and theme-park operators will invest nearly $1 billion in new and existing facilities. The real excitement will come from attractions that try to translate into rides the thrills from movies and T.V. . . .
>
> At four Sea World parks, owned by Busch, guests can watch a stunt show with buzzing speedboats based on "Baywatch," the popular T.V. series. The Six Flags chain, a group of 11 regional parks owned in part by Time Warner, has tied into entertainment in a big way [with rides and shows linked to blockbuster movies].[11]

Imaginative technology has been used to create spectacular shows, as well as frightening new rides. At Orlando's newest theme park in 1999, Universal's Islands of Adventure, $2.9 billion was spent to create rides that could not have been imagined in the early days of amusement parks. On its Spider-Man ride, visitors are strapped into a cab that lurches and twists in the dark, while 3-D images of destruction explode from 25 huge movie: screens, accompanied by brilliant fire and water effects:

> Spider-Man Jumps onto the hood of the [cab], Doctor Octopus shakes
> it like a gorilla with a new toy, Hobgoblin tosses flaming pumpkins, Hydro Man spritzes everyone and the [cab] plummets what feels like hundreds of feet from the sky into concrete canyons . . .[12]

Besides the four top Disney parks, other leading North American parks at the end of the 1990s included Universal Studios Florida, Seaworld Florida, Busch Gardens in Tampa Bay, Six Flags Great Adventure in New Jersey, Knott's Berry Farm and SeaWorld in California, and Cedar Point in Ohio.

Dollywood. Not all theme parks rely primarily on such spectacular rides and shows. For example, Dollywood, a complex of shops, rides, entertainment events, craftsmen's centers, restaurants, theaters, and other showplaces, is heavily based primarily on the image of Dolly Parton, the popular country singer and movie star. Situated in the Great Smoky Mountain National Park region, Dollywood features gospel singing performances, harvest celebrations, a "showcase" series of country performers, and similar attractions attuned to its traditional Appalachian mountain setting (Figure 10-3).

Despite its informal, down-home image, Dollywood is a sophisticated operation, complete with effective advertising and public relations strategies; a complex schedule of performances and events from April through December; a moderate one-price daily admission ticket that includes most shows, rides, craft showcases, and special events; and carefully developed employee management practices (see page 235).

Figure 10-3
Dollywood Theme Park brochure.

Waterparks

A special segment of the theme park industry that has been enjoying considerable recent growth consists of waterparks—amusement destinations that rely on a combination of wave pools, twisting slides, chutes and rides, and other water-based play facilities and shows. There are about 1,000 waterparks today that provide aquatic entertainment across the nation, chiefly in states with warmer climates.

In the late 1990s, the waterpark industry logged seven straight years of attendance growth, with over 62 million visitors annually. In 1998 and 1999, more than 20 new parks were opened, and many existing parks added new rides or doubled their overall facilities. Thousands of waterpark operators attend conventions of the American Waterpark Association each year, viewing the latest technology and learning how to increase attendance and revenues.

Cruise Lines

A second major sector of tourism attractions is provided by more than 200 cruise ship lines that offer a bewildering variety of vacation options afloat, ranging from small sail-driven schooners to giant, luxurious ocean liners.

The North American cruise industry anticipated breaking the six million–passenger mark for the first time in 2000, having committed itself to building and refurbishing more than 60 ships by 2004. In 1999 12 new ships—including three by Holland America line—joined the North American fleet, adding more than 17,500 new berths for the 57 million Americans who have indicated their intention to take cruises within the next five years.

North American cruises—including Caribbean, Alaska, Bermuda, and trans-Canada routes—represent the largest portion of money spent on vacation cruise, with short cruises becoming increasingly popular.

In 2000, approximately two million passengers took more than 1,300 cruises of five days or less, in some cases flying to a convenient port of embarkation. This is in sharp contrast to the pattern of vacation cruises several decades ago, when cruises were much longer—often involving extended ocean voyages—and could be afforded only by well-to-do customers.

Today, many middle-class individuals and families are able to take short, relatively inexpensive cruises, often availing themselves of the discounts that have become increasingly available as the growth in the number of berths has resulted in stiffer industry competition. However, such cruises are by no means lacking in luxury in terms of accommodations and recreational amenities. John Walker writes:

> Being on a cruise ship is like being on a floating resort. Accommodations range from luxurious suites to [much smaller] cabins. Attractions and distractions range from early morning workouts to fabulous meals, with nightlife consisting of dancing, cabarets, and possibly gambling. Day life might involve relaxation, visits to the beauty parlor, organized games, or simply reclining in a deck chair by the pool reading a novel. Nonstop entertainment includes language classes, charm classes, port-of-call briefing, cooking, dances, bridge, table tennis, shuffleboard, and more.[13]

This description illustrates the point that while tourism may be viewed as one element within the overall leisure-service system, recreation itself is often simply one aspect of tourism's hospitality function.

Increasingly, the newer ships being built not only have greater passenger capacity, but also facilities that would do justice to the most elaborate land resorts—impressive lounges, dining rooms, fitness studios, pools, and indoor atriums that stretch several stories high. Two of the new ships, Royal Caribbean International's 142,000-ton, 3,114-passenger Voyager of the Seas and Explorer of the Seas, both have an ice-skating rink, an inline skating track and a rock-climbing wall. The Explorer also has a marine laboratory and classroom.

Other Cruise Experiences

In some cases, cruise packages include land-based options. For example, Princess Cruises offers a cruise-tour package to Glacier Bay in the Gulf of Alaska, including a private rail car trip to spectacular wilderness lodge settings.

Windjammer Barefoot Cruises, Ltd., schedules sailing vacations to more than 60 ports-of-call throughout the Bahamas, Virgin Islands, Windward and Leeward Islands, and Venezuela, reaching remote, exotic and ecologically rich locations often inaccessible to larger cruise ships. Its recreational opportunities include a host of nautical and land-based pastimes (Figure 10-4).

On a lesser scale, many companies offer shorter or less ambitious boating leisure experiences, both inland and along coastal waters. The Delta Queen Steamboat Co. in New Orleans, for example, offers paddle-wheeler vacation trips up and down the Mississippi River, visiting old mansions and historic sites.

Figure 10-4
Optional excursions and recreational activities available on Windjammer cruises.

So what tall ship should I sail on? Each Windjammer ship has its own unique personality and itinerary. Whether you're single, newlyweds, or retired; Windjammer has something for everyone. We make it easy for you to decide by checking off your interests below.

Excursion	**Activities**
Island tours	snorkerling
Rainforest hikes	Swimming
Parasailing	Sun bathing
Mountain bike riding	Beach volleyball
Kayaking	Celestial navigation class
Deep sea fishing	Navigation class
Bird watching	Knot tieing class
Scuba diving	Exercise class
Snorkel safaris	Local bands
Dolphin encounters	Partying
Historic forts/ruins	Fun & games
Nature walks	Beach parties at night
Waterfall hikes	
Cultural tours	
Jeep safaris	

Special Destinations and Leisure Interests

A third major area of tourism involves trips that are taken to satisfy a particular form of leisure interest or personal motivation. Such trips are usually based on interests such as sports, cultural pursuits and the arts, history, nature, religion, and adventure.

In many cases, individuals or groups make their own travel arrangements and are independent in the activities they pursue. In other cases, they are part of organized tours or trips that schedule transportation arrangements, secure accommodations, apply for group visas, or handle dozens of other necessary tasks.

Sports Spectatorship

Millions of individuals travel each year to such major events as championship boxing matches, the Super Bowl, the World Series, the Grey Cup, the World Cup, the Olympics, Wimbledon or U.S. Open tennis tournaments, the Indianapolis 500, or dozens of other famous competitive events.

Many other individuals blend their vacation travel with visits to major sports halls of fame, such as the major league baseball, professional football, basketball, and hockey halls in Cooperstown, New York; Canton, Ohio; Springfield, Massachusetts; and Toronto, Canada. Still others schedule their late-winter or spring vacations in the South or Southwest so they can watch their favorite baseball teams in spring training—a special kind of appeal that is often promoted by local convention bureaus and municipal recreation and park agencies.

Travel to Pursue Outdoor Adventure

Today, a considerable amount of organized tourism is based on the widespread desire for outdoor adventure. In addition to the types of camping, skiing, backpacking or water-based recreation that may be undertaken close to home, millions of Americans venture on longer trips to pursue their outdoor recreational hobbies.

Chapter 5 described the role of numerous hunting outfitters that offer accommodations, guide services, and easily accessible big game in the United States and Canada. For those with more ambitious or varied hunting ambitions, some companies today arrange tours to more distant and exotic environments, as shown in Figure 10-5.

Women have increasingly become involved in many different forms of adventure recreation. Woodswomen, Inc., located in Minneapolis, sponsors a wide range of instructional programs in outdoor leadership skills, as well as trips to such unusual settings as Mount Kilimanjaro and the Serengeti desert in Africa, trekking expeditions in the Himalayan mountains, visits to the Mayan ruins and ancient shrines in Mexico, and explorations in the Galapagos Islands off the coast of South America (see Fig. 10-6).

Closer to home, popular tourist destinations in wilderness settings often involve stays at Western dude ranches, backpacking and horseback tours of mountain areas, and—in an unusual example of delving into the ways of the old West—the opportunity to participate in a cattle drive conducted each year in ranch territory close to Kamloops, British Columbia, Canada. (see Figure 10-7).

Figure 10-5
Brochures promoting big-game hunting for exotic species in Africa, New Zealand, Nepal, and other distant lands.

Figure 10-6
Brochure illustrating outdoor adventure trips sponsored by Woodswomen, Inc.

Call 800-279-0555 or 612-822-3809 to register!

	Trip	Dates	Level	Location	Price
Leadership	BWCA Leadership	May 30-June 6	WJ/L	MN	$725
	Northwest Mountain Leadership	July 18-24	HA/L	WA	$835
	Grand Canyon Leadership	Sept 12-18	HA/L	AZ	$795
Multi-Activity	Vacation in Cozumel	Mar 7-13	R	Mexico	$945
	Red Cedar Trail Festival	June 19-21	S/WJ	WI	$195
	Autumn on Cape Cod	Oct 2-8	R	MA	$1295
Rock Climbing	Joshua Tree Rock Climbing	Apr 2-9	WJ/HA	CA	$850
	Beginning Rock Climbing	April 25, May 30, June 13 or July 11	S	MN	$55
	Movement on the Rocks	June 14 or July 12	S	MN	$55
	North Shore Rock Climbing- NEW	June 25-28	ET	MN	$475
Skiing & Snowshoeing	Beginning Cross-country Ski	Jan 10, 24 or Feb 7	S	MN	$39
	Beginning Cross-country Ski-NEW	Jan 25	S	CO	$39
	Intermediate Cross-country Ski	Jan 25	S	MN	$39
	CO Beginning Snowshoe	Feb 14	S	CO	$39
	Sierra Ski & Telemark- NEW	Mar 1-7	ET	CA	$995
Wildlife Adventures & Safari	Exploring the Galapagos Islands	Feb 26-Mar 9 or June 11-22	R	Ecuador	$3450
	Kilimanjaro and the Serengeti	Oct 19-Nov 8	ET/WJ	Africa	$5250
Women & Kids	Camping Adventure	June 9-10 or July 17-18	S/WJ	MN	$55
	Canoe Day on Mpls Lakes	June 17 or Aug 4	S	MN	$35
	Rock Climbing	June 18, 23, July 9	S	MN	$35
	Northwoods Canoe (age 9+)	June 28-July 2	S/WJ	MN	$345
	Canoe Day on the Mississippi	July 10	S	MN	$35
	Canoe Expedition (age 9+)	Aug 5-8	S/WJ	WI	$160
	Raft & Camp Adventure (age 12+)	Aug 11-13	S/WJ	MN	$160

Whirlwind Tourism

In a new, popular form of adventure recreation, growing number of thrill-seekers today are enjoying tornado chasing. Dan McGraw writes that, while it sounds completely crazy, storm-chasing tours are rapidly gaining popularity among those whose favorite TV show is the five-day forecast on the Weather Channel:

> About a half-dozen companies will take vacationers out in search of 100 mph winds, baseball-size hail, and the occasional funnel cloud. Prices range from $1,500 to $2,000 for 10 days to two weeks. The tours operate in prime tornado season, from April through June. All the companies have Internet sites, and most tours fill up several months in advance.[14]

Figure 10-7
An unusual Western adventure event—a charity-sponsored cattle drive conducted annually in Kamloops, British Columbia, Canada.

Cultural and Historical Travel Attractions

Another major type of destination for tourist visits consists of cultural programs, festivals, performances, and the arts. Throughout North America and Europe, for example, each year there are hundreds of arts festivals, including music, opera, dance, and theater performances, which draw huge numbers of visitors.

Fine arts are featured in many outstanding museums, and often the special exhibitions of leading artists draw many thousands of visitors over a two- or three-month period.

Similarly, natural history museums, planetariums, botanical gardens, and zoos are popular tourist destinations.

Heritage Destinations

Numerous communities have taken artifacts of the past, such as abandoned prisons, factories, coal mines, and railroads, and have revived them as fascinating tourist destinations. Often they have historical value and deep meaning for the present as well. Such is the case with old slave plantations, critical battle sites, and other places that contributed to the nation's rich past.

In many cases, government recreation and park agencies have joined with nonprofit foundations to develop and promote such facilities. In a number of Canadian provinces, so-called "heritage" tourism, which celebrates the lives and cultures of the nation's original Indian and Inuit (Eskimo) tribes, as well as other national groups that settled the land, has become key thrust of government cultural and leisure-service agencies.

Educational and Religious Destinations

Many individuals today—particularly older, retired persons—take advantage of their expanded leisure time to travel to colleges or universities in both the United States and abroad, to take specially organized classes in areas of personal interest.

Elderhostel, the leading organization in this field, packages hundreds of such tours or stays each year, providing inexpensive opportunities to live on campus, using dormitories and food services, while taking classes and exploring new and different environments.

Similarly, Hostelling International—American Youth Hostels (HI-AYH) offers a network of 150 low-cost, dormitory-style international youth hostels and hundreds of hostel-based education programs that provide opportunities for people of all ages to experience diverse cultures and become exposed to new and varied environments.

A nonprofit membership organization founded in 1934 to promote international understanding through educational travel, HI-AYH, with its main office in Washington, D.C., is composed of 38 local councils throughout the United States, each responsible for its own development, maintenance, operation and fund-raising. Overall, it operates hostels in more than 70 countries and conducts a broad-based cultural exchange program.

During the 1980s and 1990s, interest grew in religious-oriented travel, with tours highlighting important Christian, Jewish, Muslim, and Buddhist sites. The old dream of spiritual pilgrimage is one that travelers are fulfilling in rapidly growing numbers. For many people, such trips involve far more than a "go-there, see-that" kind of tour. Instead, many visitors to holy lands and sacred places are seeking deeply meaningful spiritual experiences. In 1999, Judi Dash wrote that religious tourism had become a billion-dollar a-year business and had created a boom for tour companies specializing in religious themes. She continued:

> During 2000, which Pope John Paul II has declared a special Great Jubilee year, with indulgences granted Catholics who Journey to major holy shrines, as many as 30 million pilgrims are expected to visit Rome and a record four million— including the Pope—to visit Israel.[15]

Tourism and International Understanding

Such travel experiences affirm the increasing importance of tourism at a time when social scientists and futurologists predict that the world will become more and more "global."

As barriers among nations are breached, people of every background will become increasingly interdependent in terms of business ventures that cross borders and the swelling flow of information through the Internet. While other forms of leisure—such as international sports competition and the exchange of entertainment products such as movies, television shows, and popular music—contribute to this growing inter-dependence, tourism represents probably the richest potential in terms of improving international relationships at people-centered, grassroots levels.

David Edgell, an official with the U.S. Travel and Tourism Administration, sums up the optimistic views of many:

> International tourism in the twenty-first century will be a major vehicle for fulfilling the aspirations of mankind in its quest for a higher quality of life . . . and hopefully laying the groundwork for a peaceful society through global touristic contact. Tourism also has the potential to be one of the most important stimulants for global improvement in the social, cultural economic, political and economic dimensions of future lifestyles.[16]

It should be noted that not all appraisals of tourism's impact on international relations or its contributions to host countries are equally positive. As the volume of recreational travel has continued to grow steadily, numerous critics have expressed concern about its impact.

Social and Environmental Effects of Tourism

Some observers have commented that the attitudes of tourists (mostly white and relatively prosperous) toward the residents of islands in the Caribbean visited by their cruise lines (mostly black and poor) have essentially colonial overtones.

Economic studies have shown that very little income from tourism goes directly to the residents of such host countries and that, even when they are employed in the tourist industry, either on cruise ships or in resorts, their jobs tend to be overwhelmingly menial and poorly paid.

In many cases, tourism in poor nations or regions of the world is actually predatory and is often manifested in the growing trend for pedophiles to prowl through such countries as Thailand, the Philippines, and Central and South American lands where poverty-stricken children may be easily exploited sexually.[17]

From an environmental perspective, varied forms of tourism and outdoor recreation travel frequently contribute to pollution and other destructive effects on ocean waters, wilderness, and wildlife. In the summer of 1999, there was a continuing controversy between residents of several towns along Alaska's coastline and major cruise lines, such as Royal Caribbean, concerning the dumping of toxic chemicals and other wastes in close-by ocean waters. Douglas Frantz writes:

> Fed up with giant ships that discharge waste into their waterways and with tourists who flood their downtown, residents of Juneau, the state capital, in early October

approved a $5 tax on every passenger. A bit farther north, the small town of Haines voted to limit the number of cruise ships allowed at its dock. And some Juneau residents have called for one cruise line to be barred from the state's waters.[18]

In terms of the impact of the growing use of snowmobiles, all-terrain vehicles, and mountain bikes on wilderness environments and backcountry areas, Ewert and Shultis have identified both positive and negative effects. The favorable outcomes include greater support and awareness of backcountry recreation and protected areas, as well as the obvious economic benefits, such as job creation for local residents. The negative outcomes include user conflicts and overcrowding of wilderness areas, along with increased erosion, air and water pollution, and wildlife disturbance.[19]

Reliance on Eco-Tourism. A powerful thrust in recent years has involved the trend toward eco-tourism in certain areas of outdoor recreation. Simply defined, this consists of uses of the nature environment that are sensitive to its needs, that are unobtrusive and nondestructive and that, in fact, often center on learning about the history and ecological processes within a given region or wilderness area.

Recently, this approach has been applied to tourism in distant lands. In Africa, for example, the Conservation Corporation of Africa (Conscorp) operates 22 small, isolated, and expensive lodges that are widely scattered in wildlife-rich regions. Conscorp offers typically luxurious guest accommodations, but with a new eco-tourist approach that respects and promotes the well-being of the tribespeople in surrounding villages. Douglas McNeil writes:

> Conscorp builds schools and clinics near its lodges, and it employs as many local people as possible, not just as cooks and chambermaids, but as builders, ironworkers and trackers. It buys materials for local artists and sells their work in its curio shops. It hires people to clear trees, then buys the charcoal they produce from the wood they carry home.[20]

Conscorp's philosophy is partly idealistic and partly practical. It is based on the hope that the bigger the stake local people have in their lodges, the less likely they will be to poach, take the company to court, or even object when an occasional elephant herd destroys their corn fields.

Gambling as a Tourism Attraction

Linked to the discussion of tourism from a social-welfare or environmental perspective, it is impossible to ignore the huge influence of organized, legal gambling as a tourist attraction.

Over the past three decades, many states and cities have established lotteries, approved casinos, and generally accepted what was once a morally disapproved and legally prosecuted pastime (Figure 10-8). They have done so in an effort to stimulate their economies, attract visitors, build employment, and boost tax revenues. Indian tribes from coast to coast have established giant casinos, usually with outside funding and technical assistance. Gambling on riverboats, on the Internet, and on international airline flights, and cruise ships and in dozens of other kinds of venues has become a giant industry, closely linked to tourism as a form of special attraction.

This trend has been controversial; conservative forces in a number of areas of the country have resisted the growth of gambling, arguing that it is immoral on religious grounds, that

Figure 10-8
This brochure promoting riverboat gambling on the Mississippi River in the early 1990s depicts "gaming" as a family-friendly, folksy recreational pastime.

it is essentially a tax on the poor, and that it leads too often to addiction and crime, while failing to bring the hoped-for economic rewards. While many of the major casinos, particularly in Atlantic City and Las Vegas, have continued to do well and have built multibillion-dollar combined resorts and casinos, others have faltered under intense competition.

Gambling, or "gaming," as its sponsors prefer to call it, is clearly an important element in the organized leisure-service system. However, few professional preparation curricula in colleges and universities deal with it, other than as a subject of sociological investigation or, in a few community colleges, as a field of technical training for jobs in casinos.

Jobs and Career Opportunities in Tourism

From a broader perspective, it is widely recognized that travel, tourism, and hospitality services are responsible for millions of jobs today, ranging from the most limited forms of poorly paid work in hotels, restaurants, and other tourist attractions to extremely lucrative positions in management posts.

A number of authors have presented breakdowns of the kinds of jobs found in the tourist industry today. Some have done this in terms of either the separate branches of the field where travel, tourist, and hospitality services are provided, or the major kinds of job categories found in tourism (see Figures 10-9A and B).

Other authors have listed many dozens of job titles within a host of specialized roles on ships and in theme parks, restaurants, hotels, travel agencies, and other settings. Their range and variety are illustrated in the following examples:

Cruise lines usually hire in the following areas: food and food service staff; entertainment and musicians; deck and cabin stewards and stewardesses; bartenders and cocktail servers; retail and gift store clerks; fitness and gym instructors; youth counselors and children's group leaders; office personnel; tour guides for land activities; casino dealers and equipment maintenance personnel; and numerous other positions apart from those among the ship's actual crew.

Figure 10-9A
Types of agencies providing employment in travel, tourism, and hospitality.

Theme parks
Water-play parks
Sports arenas
Social and residential clubs
Tour operator
Travel agencies
Corporate and convention meeting centers
Convention and visitors bureaus
Travel companies: airlines, railroads, motorcoach

Cruise ship lines
Catering companies
Festival managers
Special events and exposition companies
Campgrounds and hostels
Destination resorts
Casinos
Bed- and-breakfast businesses
Hunting, fishing, and outdoor recreation companies
Museums, zoos, aquariums

Figure 10-9B
Major areas of job responsibility.

Sales and marketing
Promotion and advertising
Customer relations
Personnel management
Event planning and scheduling
Fiscal management and accounting
Insurance and liability

Risk management and security functions
Facility operations and maintenance
Market research
Occupational health and safety
General management

Management-level positions in hotels and resorts include such job titles as food and beverage service manager; club or lounge manager; convention manager or coordinator; front desk clerk; rental car agency manager; marina manager; executive housekeeper; concierge, and guest-services manager; reservations manager; controller/auditor; social director; human resources manager; and social director or attraction manager.

In theme parks and water-play parks, entry-level or technician positions might include such titles as receptionists and cashiers; guards and security personnel; show performers; animal trainers or health care personnel; cashiers; ride attendants and technicians; housekeeping personnel; and finance or administrative assistants. On more advanced levels, positions would include human resources specialists and payroll managers; software engineers and systems analysts; finance and accounting specialists; special-events managers and show producers; facility designers; legal and paralegal staff; public relations and advertising specialists; marketing and sales directors; and merchandising specialists.

Future Perspectives in Travel, Tourism, and Hospitality

In general, authorities in this field are highly optimistic about the future, and they predict a continued expansion of travel and tourism operations, along with steadily rising attendance and revenue statistics. In the late 1990s, for example, the World Travel and Tourism Council, the official international organization in this field, described travel and tourism as:

> The world's largest industry, with approximately $3.8 trillion in gross output in 1997 and an expected $7.1 trillion by the year 2007;

> The world's leading industrial contribution, producing more than ten percent of the world's Gross National Product (GNP);

> A leading producer of tax revenues, and employer of 262 million people, or ten percent of the global workforce, and

> Expected to grow faster than any other sector of world employment.[21]

Critical Views

However, a growing number of economists and industry observers are more cautious in their analysis of the field's future prospects. Reviewing the remarkable explosion of the cruise industry, which increased in sales volume tenfold over the 1980s and 1990s, John Greenwald pointed out that the major cruise lines—including the Walt Disney Company's—had ordered an astonishing $10 billion worth of floating pleasure palaces at the turn of the century. He asks:

> A fleet of monster ships is steaming into a high-sea showdown. They're loaded for fun. But can they all make money? [22]

Faced with increasing competition, cruise lines have many berths to fill and are offering incentives to fill them. Few passengers today pay the full listed price for a voyage.

Increasingly, the strategy of cruise lines has been to attract customers at low daily shipboard rates and then give them every opportunity to spend freely in bars, shops, and casinos while on board. Today, the second major source of cruise line income, after ticket revenues, is the sale of beverages.

The reality is that many other forms of popular tourism have become increasingly expensive. In theme parks, for example, the cost of what had once been a relatively modest family outing has climbed steadily. One traveler commented that when he and his wife and two children visited Busch Gardens in Tampa a few years ago, they were stunned by the cost of four tickets—$152. Today, the cost would be $176, including taxes. After consulting several travel agents, Kathleen Shea wrote in March 2000:

> For a family of three, four days at Disney World would cost about $1,800 for a no-frills non-Disney hotel room, airfare, and park admission, including round-trip tickets for $229 each.[23]

Many families spend several thousands dollars for a week's vacation, which includes visits to several theme parks. Obviously, the nation's ability to sustain such discretionary areas of spending will depend on its continuing the wave of prosperity of the past several years—and its commitment to what a leading economist has called "luxury fever"—the willingness to spend lavishly on nonessentials. At the same time, the surge in the total number of tourist attractions and expensive new ventures raises additional questions. Gregg Zoroya writes, in *USA Today:*

> Orlando is hotter than ever. Its insatiable appetite for new and expanded fun zones—more than 80 now exist in and around the city—and white-hot competition between its two theme-park giants, Disney and Universal, has experts drooling with anticipation. But even advocates warn that Orlando is becoming too much for tourists to easily absorb.[24]

Competition and Consolidation in Tourism

Over and above such concerns, the reality is that the entire tourism field has moved into an era of intense competition, mergers, and takeovers. Robin Knight reports in *Time* that airlines are coalescing into huge conglomerates that coordinate flights, share revenues, and set fares jointly. Hotel groups and tour operators are merging across national borders. Travel agents, cruise lines, car-rental firms, and rail and ferry companies are all forming giant groupings. They use the strategy of global ownership, with its wide scope and numerous resources, in an effort to avoid being marginalized in today's competitive environment.

Knight cites examples of these trends in different areas of the travel,tourism, and hospitality field:

> Consolidation is the name of the tourism game. Four giant alliances, led by Star . . . account for more than 60 percent of world airline traffic today . . . Star is run by a management board and boasts integrated check-ins and sales forces . . . An increasingly contentious wave of mergers and takeovers since 1997 has left 80 percent of the British package-holiday business in the hands of just four companies.

> Travel agents . . . are fighting for their future in an increasingly hostile environment. Both tour operators and airlines have cut agents' commissions from 10 percent to 7 percent. Agencies' core business is also under pressure from the Internet and its ability to reflect modern lifestyles [as many travelers take] several short and impromptu breaks throughout the year [or seek] specialized tourism, such as golf tours and culinary holidays.[25]

There is growing evidence that the tremendous surge in expanding tourist enterprises described earlier has created a serious overabundance of attractions, while the number of consumers seem to be declining in certain areas of participation. In the highly competitive theme-park field, with Disney and Universal battling to establish new ventures, some authorities predict a bloodletting of mammoth proportions.

Bernard Baumohl comments that the building boom at century's end took place just as consumer demand for theme parks was softening:

> Attendance at the three older Disney parks dropped about 10 percent last year, according to *Amusement Business,* a trade magazine. The number of visitors at Universal Studios Florida and Sea World was flat in 1998, at 8.9 million and 4.9 million, respectively. The economic slump overseas slashed tourism to Orlando [and experts] wonder whether the whole theme-park business is maturing, as the children of U.S. by baby boomers get older and hence reduce the number of repeat trips.[26]

Obviously, such reports are in sharp contrast to the optimistic projections of representatives of the travel and tourism industry that were cited earlier in this chapter. Whether they are true, and whether the reported "glut" in cruise ships, theme parks, gambling casinos and other resorts will prove risky, if the economy suffers a downturn or American families become more conservative in their spending, only the future will decide. For now, it is clear that from a career perspective, tourism continues to represent a major, diversified area of job opportunity in the leisure-service field.

Suggestions for Class Discussions or Essay Examinations

1. The travel, tourism, and hospitality field has become widely recognized as a major economic force both nationally and internationally. What accounts for its immense popularity in terms of the appeal of tourism and other social or demographic changes? How do public recreation and park agencies fit into this picture? What is the contribution of the Internet?
2. Theme parks have grown steadily in numbers and technological sophistication since the 1950s. What does the term "theme" imply, and what are some of the special themes or types of parks today? What was Disney's unique contribution to this sector of the tourism field?
3. Cruise lines have also grown tremendously in numbers of ships, their variety of attractions, and the sheer volume of cruises taken today. How has the nature of pleasure cruising changed, and what are some of the appealing elements of modern cruise ships? Using examples from this chapter, can you contrast some of the different styles of cruising?
4. Much tourism is also based on the very specific interests and motivations of travelers and the ability of companies to package trips to meet theme special needs. Cite several different such types of destinations or special travel themes, as described in the text (examples: adventure recreation, religious destinations). Are there special tourism packages designed for different populations in age and gender groups? What are some examples?
5. This chapter warns that despite the healthy growth of this field, some critics believe that there may be a glut of theme parks, cruise ships, and other tourist attractions. What might happen in the tourism industry if today's flourishing economy takes a downturn?

Footnotes

[1] McIntosh, R., Goeldner, C., and Brent Ritchie, J. (1995). *Tourism principles, practices, philosophies.* New York: John Wiley. 11.

[2] *Ibid.*

[3] Industry continues to set records. (1998). *Travel and Tourism Executive Report.* Vol. XIX (5), 1.

[4] A worldwide TSA: Finding a way to measure tourism's economic impact. (1999). *Leisure Industry/Recreation News,* 11.

[5] Crossley, J.C., and Jamieson, L.M. (1993). *Introduction to commercial and entrepreneurial recreation.* Champaign, Ill.: Sagamore Publishing, 17.

[6] A worldwide TSA . . . *op. cit.*

[7] WTTC economic impact report on global tourism. (1998). *Travel and Tourism Executive Report.* Vol. XIX (7), 7.

[8] Statistics summarized from several issues of *Travel and Tourism Executive Report,* 1998 and 1999.

[9] Marketing and selling electronically. (1998). *Travel and Tourism Executive Report.* Vol. XIX (7), 1.

[10] McIntosh et al., op. cit., 9-10.

[11] McGraw, D (1995). America's theme parks ride high. *U.S. News and World Report.* June 26, 50.

[12] Corliss, R. (1999). Thrill park. *Time.* May 31, 82.

[13] Walker, J.R. (1999). *Introduction to hospitality.* Upper Saddle River, N.J.: Prentice Hall, 42.

[14] McGraw, D. (1998). Whirlwind tourism. *U.S News and World Report,* 58.
[15] Dash, J. (1999). Journeys of faith. *Philadelphia Inquirer.*
[16] See Holecek, D., in Van Lier and Taylor p. 17
[17] Roche, T. (1999). Tourists who prey on kids. *Time.* Feb. 15, 58.
[18] Frantz, D. (1999). Alaskans choose sides in battle over cruise ships. New York Times. Nov. 29, A-1.
[19] Ewert, A., and Shultis, J. (1999). Technology and backcountry recreation. *Journal of Physical Education, Recreation and Dance.* Oct., 23.
[20] McNeil, D. (1997). Packaging luxury with wildlife. *New York Times.* June 25, B-1.
[21] 262 million jobs, $3.8 trillion from travel and tourism worldwide. (1997). *Travel and Tourism Executive Report,* No. 4, 3.
[22] Greenwald, J. (1998). Cruise lines go overboard. *Time.* May 11, 42.
[23] Shea, K. (2000). Thrills and bills. *Philadelphia Inquirer.* Mar. 12, L-1
[24] Zoroya, G. (1999). Orlando overload: How much is too much at rapidly expanding theme parks? *USA Today.* May 10, 8-B.
[25] Knight, R. (1999). The new age of travel. *Time.* July 12, 45.
[26] Baumohl, B. (1999). A new park theme: Glut. Time. May 21, 84.

Chapter 11

Career Perspectives in Leisure-Service Agencies

Introduction

Having examined the ten major types of leisure-service organizations in America today, we now focus more sharply on the field from a career perspective.

In so doing, the authors will address the reader directly. If you are planning to begin a career in this field, or if you are already enrolled in a college or university degree program in recreation, park, and leisure studies, this chapter is intended to help you make intelligent choices in working toward your ultimate goals.

To be successful in any of the specialized areas of leisure services described in this book, you need to have an accurate understanding of the field itself, and of the special rewards and demands found in the different service areas. You also need to have a realistic understanding of your own personality and career goals, your strengths and weaknesses, and what you need to do to build a strong base for future accomplishment.

This chapter should help you by providing guidelines for personal self-assessment and suggestions for early preparation for entry into the field, for internship and job-search strategies, and for continuing development and professional affiliation.

Leisure Services: Their Rewards and Demands

What makes working in the overall leisure-service field or in any of its subsystems an appealing and realistic occupational goal for many young people?

It is an overall field of service that may be viewed both as an industry and as an important element of social or community service. It provides the opportunity for personal growth, for the deep satisfactions that come from meeting challenges successfully, and for achievement and recognition by others. For those who have a special interest in sports, the creative arts, outdoor recreation, involvement in nature, working closely with people, and making a contribution to people's lives, it offers specialized career roles that meet such individual needs and interests.

Personal Qualities of Leisure-Service Professionals

As this chapter will show, the specialized types of leisure-service organizations described earlier have markedly different goals and expectations of their employees. However, they also tend to value a number of important personal traits that are important in all areas of recreation management. Samuels and Foucar-Szocki write:

> People who do best in hospitality, recreation, tourism and functionally related professions are generally outgoing, have a good sense of humor, a good deal of energy, like to work with people, and do not like to sit behind a desk for excessive periods of time. [The field needs] creative people and people who can easily solve problems as managers, marketers, program leaders, and developers. They . . . should be service oriented almost to excess.[1]

In addition to such traits, successful leisure-service professionals, whatever their specific job focus, tend to have the following kinds of skills and personal qualities.

Initiative and Energy. Unlike other, more routine occupational fields in which job functions are clearly defined and repetitious, leadership in any of the specialized leisure-service disciplines requires the ability to take the initiative in seeking out new challenges or problems, and the creative energy needed to solve or master them.

Linked to these qualities is the sheer willingness to work hard and, when necessary, put in long hours. Realistically, other people's free hours often are the recreation professional's working hours. In some job situations, it is not uncommon for program specialists to work during the day with office-related responsibilities and then to supervise programs carried on during the evening hours—or to work regularly on weekends and holidays, when many recreational events are scheduled.

Organizational Skills. Although play and recreation may appear to be informal or highly spontaneous kinds of activities, to manage any recreational enterprise successfully requires a high level of organizational skills. The ability to plan wisely, to use good judgment and make sound decisions, to see both the broad picture and the smaller details, and to follow through conscientiously on all job responsibilities is a key requirement for success in this field.

People-Centered Qualities. At every level, leisure-service leadership involves working with people. Whether working with youthful participants in a community center, patrons in a theme park, representatives of community groups, or co-workers, people-centered qualities and skills are critical. These qualities include a genuine respect and liking for others and tolerance for their differences, as well as the ability to listen to and empathize with them, and to command their respect and trust.

In professional terms, successful leaders must also be committed to meeting the needs of patrons or customers as fully as possible. They must also be able to work harmoniously with their bosses and subordinates and with representatives of other organizations or community agencies. Qualities that contribute to such effectiveness include tact and sensitivity, patience and humor, emotional balance and self-understanding, and the ability to communicate effectively.

Recreation-Related Values. As earlier chapters of this text point out, while recreation, parks and leisure services represent an immensely diversified field, all of their component disciplines have a common, shared focus on the provision of satisfying and constructive leisure experience.

Given this reality, people who seek careers in any of the leisure-related occupations should have a meaningful background of involvement in varied recreational pursuits—ideally including the playing of leadership roles as a volunteer coach or club officer. Linked to this background, individuals who enter the field should have a sound personal philosophy that recognizes the importance of recreation and leisure in contemporary life and the need to achieve the best possible benefits and outcomes for participants and the community at large through organized programs.

Other Background Factors

Along with these general qualities, a number of other important factors contribute to your ability to land a good job in the field to begin with, or to perform successfully over time. Obviously, for an individual who plans to work in a field such as sports management, extensive experience in varied athletic programs will be helpful—particularly if it involves such elements as coaching, scheduling, league or facility operations, and fund-raising. For a man or a woman who hopes to work in a nonprofit youth-serving agency, a background in Boys and Girls Clubs, Ys, or similar organizations that depend on group leadership responsibilities will have provided useful knowledge and skills.

Clearly, any leisure-service organization conducting a job search will look for such background experiences in candidates. In addition, many positions in the field involve other kinds of roles—as salespersons and marketing specialists; human-resource managers; public relations or advertising managers; risk-management specialists; and supervisors with problem-solving, conflict resolution, or counseling skills.

Need for Self-Assessment

Realistically, very few young people who are planning to enter the leisure-service field are likely to possess all the personal qualities and skills that have just been described.

As you look at them, however, can you rate yourself accurately and objectively with respect to each of the areas presented-in terms of your own strengths and weaknesses?

Some people are able to rate themselves intuitively and to see themselves very clearly. Most people, however, require help from others, such as teachers, past supervisors, co-workers, and even friends, in order to get an accurate picture of themselves. Seagle, Smith, and Dalton have devised a set of questions, exercises, and instruments to help leisure-service students prepare for internships in the field. To begin, they maintain that one of the most important questions to ask yourself at the outset has to do with your level of self-confidence. They write:

> First, it is important to take a look at how you feel about your own abilities. If you believe in yourself, you are likely to have positive feelings about yourself and project a positive image to others,
>
> Since this is vital to your professional future, you need to take some time to assess your self-confidence. Specifically, you need to identify positive and negative statements (internal messages) that you make to yourself. It is especially important to note any negative statements and find ways to change them into positive ones.[2]

Seagle and his co-authors suggest that it is necessary to examine your personal philosophy or system of values as they affect your vocational goals, along with your personal interests and needs and other traits or professionally related skills that might affect your career development.

To assess these areas systematically, they present a series of exercises and rating scales intended to help individuals gain a comprehensive picture of their own strengths and weaknesses. Excerpts from two such scales are shown in Figure 11-1 and Figure 11-2.[3] While designed primarily to help recreation and leisure- studies students to prepare for internship assignments, they also apply to young people who are examining themselves in terms of possible career choices.

Figure 11-1
Professional skills assessment.
(Note: These items are excerpted from a much longer list of skills.)

Professional Skills	I Already Possess	I Already Possess but Need to Refine	I Need to Acquire	Not Needed for Internship
Analyzing Budgeting Communicating (Oral) (Written) Computing Decision-Making Delegating Goal Setting Initiating Marketing Negotiating Organizing Planning Problem-Solving Selling Team Building				

Figure 11-2
Personality traits assessment.

Personality Traits Skills	I Already Am Possess	I Already Am but Need to Refine	I Need to Become	Not Needed for Internship
Able to say no Accepting of Criticism Considerate of others Cooperative Creative Enthusiastic Ethical Hard worker Honest' Open Minded Patient Punctual Reliable				

Working on Self-Improvement

Realistically, it may be difficult for most individuals to see themselves with a completely unbiased and accurate eye, with respect to their own personality traits. Instead, the most promising setting for conducting this kind of self-analysis might be a class in leadership and group dynamics, in which small-group members are encouraged to share views of each other's performance in assigned tasks.

As far as the rating of professional skills is concerned, many of the listed items, such as "analyzing," "budgeting," "delegating," and "marketing," would only come into play in a real work setting and would therefore not be meaningful to young men and women at an early stage of study in a leisure-services curriculum.

Nonetheless, the process described by Seagle and his co-authors is helpful in that it identifies many of the key questions you might want to ask to help determine your own suitability for work in the leisure-service field.

Setting Personal Targets

The purpose of self-assessment as part of making career choices is obviously not simply to get a grade or rating on a set of items. Instead, its purpose is to help you set a direction for yourself, and to recognize major areas of personal strength and weakness.

With respect to one's personality traits, the idea of remaking one's total character is unrealistic. Our basic values and ways of interacting with others tend to be fairly deeply rooted and not easily changed-even if it were desirable to do this. However, it is possible to recognize specific behavioral traits that are positive and helpful, and others that are not.

If you were to recognize, with the help of others, that you used certain nonproductive means of responding to stressful situations or working with others in a team setting, it would be possible to set specific goals, or behavioral "targets'" and to strive consciously to improve in these areas. At the same time, if you lacked certain basic professionally related skills, you might plan to work on these deficits by taking classes to build needed competence, by attending workshops or clinics, or by volunteering to assist in an agency on specific tasks having to do with computerized budgeting or scheduling, marketing or advertising functions, or similar skill areas.

Assuming that your self-assessment also revealed some very positive qualities and skills, it could encourage your determination to strengthen these elements even more, and to give you needed confidence and direction in your career planning.

Making Career Choices

A second important purpose of the self-assessment process is to help you determine the career direction that you want to take, so that the best possible match is made between your needs and interests, personal qualities and values, and professional skills and the demands of a given leisure-service specialization.

While some beginning students in a college or university leisure studies curriculum may have already determined that they want to major in armed forces recreation, therapeutic recreation, sports marketing, or some other specialized field, many others may not have made such an early decision. Obviously, the choice of a career specialization depends heavily on the program options offered within the curriculum you are enrolled in. If your interest is in working with at-risk youth in an urban ghetto, there would be little point in taking a degree in a department that specializes in preparing outdoor recreation personnel, such as park or forest rangers.

However, assuming that you are in a position to choose from several degree options, it is helpful to review the 10 types of agencies described in chapters 3 through 10, to determine how their characteristics and staffing needs dovetail with your personal qualities and skills.

Key Characteristics of Agencies

What follows is a brief summary or recap of the goals, program elements and staffing practices of the major types of leisure-service agencies. Next, a number of examples of job descriptions and recruitment and hiring practices drawn from throughout the field are presented.

Public, Governmental Agencies. Tax-supported recreation and park departments, particularly on the local level, are geared to serve a broad cross section of the population with varied facilities and program elements. Their job openings range from seasonal or part-time activity specialists and program aides to upper-level division heads and agency directors.

Most positions in the public sector are classified under civil service regulations and policies, and promotions and other personnel actions are usually governed by precisely defined policies and personnel manuals. Hiring in this field is fairly stable, and since the fiscal cutbacks of the 1980s, public recreation and park workforces have remained relatively intact.

Nonprofit Agencies. In most such organizations, the social goals of youth-serving programs or other special interest agencies are of primary concern. Whether sponsored by religious denominations or secular boards, nonprofit agencies must have a high standard of purpose and staff performance with a strong, concurrent emphasis on maintaining community support and fiscal stability.

From a career point of view, youth-serving organizations and similar nonprofit groups offer a wide range of often-overlooked job possibilities.

Commercial Recreation. This diversified field differs sharply from the preceding two in terms of its essential purpose. With profit its key priority, job skills involving effective marketing, financial management, and customer service are critical qualities if one is to succeed in commercial recreation.

Armed Forces Recreation. As a branch of the government's civil service structure, military Morale, Welfare, and Recreation programs tend to be highly bureaucratic; they have a complex chain of command, sharply defined policies, and professional titles and job roles.

At the same time, armed forces recreation involves a great variety of challenging program elements and the opportunity for creative staff performance. Among all the categories of specialized leisure-service described in this text—with the possible exception of the travel, tourism, and hospitality field—it offers the best opportunity for living and working in exciting and exotic settings around the world.

Recreation and Employee Services. As Chapter 5 demonstrates, in this field recreation represents only one of a battery of important service functions and must be clearly responsible for meeting the important goals of sponsoring companies—in measurable terms, where possible.

Employee service programs, whether involving health and fitness, stress management, discount buying and company stores, or sports leagues and social events, must contribute to such objectives as improving job performance and company morale and reducing health care and insurance costs.

Campus Recreation. As indicated earlier, programs in this field tend to be structured in two categories: (1) sports and outdoor recreation-related services, and (2) more general social or special-interest clubs and activities that are part of the student life spectrum and are usually housed in student union or residence-hall settings.

Hiring in campus programs often depends heavily on the use of graduate students as instructors or as leaders in other roles, along with full-time, continuing-program directors who frequently have academic connections as well.

Private-Membership Groups. While there are thousands of individuals working in this field, in country clubs or other types of clubs and in retirement and other residential communities, in general, they do not identify with the leisure-service profession or join its organizations.

Instead, employees in private-membership settings tend to have a high level of performance and leadership skills in sports such as golf and tennis, and to be responsible for recreation services as part of a larger management role involving facility management and other functions.

Therapeutic Recreation Service. In contrast, this field tends to be highly professionalized in terms of specialized preparation; membership in national or state societies; and certification based on education, experience, and examination performance.

While a substantial number of therapeutic recreation professionals work in treatment settings, the strong thrust today is toward expanding special recreation programs for persons with disabilities living in the community.

Sports Management. This field is unique in that sports represent an important element in every other type of leisure-service agency's program, especially public, nonprofit, commercial, and campus recreation units.

While the most visible aspect of sports involves the leading college or professional players, teams, and coaches, there is a huge structure of clubs, leagues, and instructional programs that serves all age levels on an amateur basis in communities throughout the nation. Going far beyond the popular team sports or high-powered golf or tennis competition, dozens of other sports appeal to both participant and spectator interest.

Travel, Tourism, and Hospitality. This final area of leisure-service management is like sports because of its varied attractions and different companies that serve public needs.

As Chapter 10 points out, many jobs in the tourism field involve fairly routine or mechanical service functions in restaurants, hotels, cruise ships, and theme parks that do not require a background in higher education or specialized skills. At a second level of employment, jobs that require a degree of expertise in such areas as personnel management, the operation of shows or attractions, scheduling and conduct of trips and tours, risk management, and financial operations, are somewhat better paid and provide the opportunity for advancement to higher levels of responsibility.

Analyzing Job Opportunities: Five Factors

Summing up, the 10 categories of recreation, park and leisure-service agencies described in this book vary greatly in their goals and operational practices, as well as their personnel policies and hiring practices.

If you were to analyze them to determine which area of specialization were to make the most sense for you, in terms of making a career choice and entering a degree program that equips you to work in it, which factors would be critical? Five elements need to be considered:.

1. Nature of the Work Involved. Recognizing that it is not possible to say at an early stage that a position in a given field would demand a set of specific job functions, you would want to know whether the overall thrust of the field would be appealing to and compatible for you. To use some simple examples, working as a forest ranger would be quite different from serving as a pit boss in a gambling casino; and both of those jobs would differ greatly from that of a therapeutic recreation specialist working with developmentally disabled youth and adults. It would be important at the outset to know that a particular field would be meaningful and attractive to you.

2. Would You Be Right for the Field? A closely related question has to do with the issue of your personal qualities and skills at this point. If a particular area of work were to demand high-pressure involvement with the public in a marketing or sales role, would you be comfortable with that? If it were to demand a degree of physical risk or advanced computer-based or financial- management skills, would that suit your temperament or present capabilities? Turning the question around, would a particular field take advantage of your personal strengths and the facilities that you would bring to the table?

3. Opportunity for Education or Other Experience. Assuming that you are attracted to a given field or specialization, would the opportunity for specialized training in it be available at the institution you are presently attending, or would you have to transfer to another? Would this be essential for you to enter the field successfully?

If you wanted to gain direct experience in a given field while attending college, would there be programs or organizations reasonably close by, where you might do volunteer or part-time paid or seasonal work in order to upgrade your skills and résumé? While it would be possible for you to wait for a formal internship that would help you to gain such experience, it would be wise to explore the field directly at an early point to make sure it is right for you.

4. Long-Term Potential of the Field. Is it possible for you at this point to judge whether working in a given area of specialization, such as public recreation and parks or campus recreation would provide you with the long-term potential for personal growth and advancement that you desire?

In a related question, could you make a reasonably sound determination about the prospects of a given field over the long haul? While some areas of leisure-service management, such as public recreation and parks and nonprofit agencies, have a strong degree of permanency, other fields may be threatened by sharp economic or social changes or shifts in public tastes or family needs. Is long-term security important to you, or would you be threatened if it weren't?

5. Employment Outlook. Finally, can you determine the level of hiring or the opportunity for advancement in a given field at present or in the near future? While it may seem difficult to make such determinations, job listings and notices which will be illustrated later in this chapter can give you a reasonable picture of the kinds of job prospects that might be available for you when you are ready for full-time employment.

Gathering Evidence over Time

Obviously, there are no easy answers to several of these questions. Some require making subjective judgments that would be based heavily on guesswork. Others would involve speculating about the future, and basing that speculation on limited available evidence.

Nonetheless, if you are considering making a decision at this point about your career focus or destination, these questions are the kinds of issues that you should explore.

What is important is that, at this point, you lay a solid foundation for a future career in terms of your own needs and interests, personal qualities and skills, and begin to gain helpful job experience and personal contacts so that when you are ready to move into full-time, year-round employment, you do it from a position of strength.

Examples of Present-Day Employment

To enrich your understanding of career possibilities, the following section of this chapter presents a number of examples of job openings and hiring practices that are drawn from representative leisure-service agencies.

First, many public recreation and park departments have an extensive listing of job titles, with full details of their work functions, qualifications, civil service grades, (if required), salary ranges, and other necessary information. For example, the Community Services Department of the City of Scottsdale, Arizona, has position statements for such titles as *Assistant Pool Manager, Parks and Trails Planner, Lifeguard/Instructor, Recreation Coordinator,* several grades of *Recreation Leader, Stadium Coordinator, Recreation Specialist,* and numerous other full-time or part-time seasonal jobs (Figure 11-6).

Positions in U.S. Navy Morale, Welfare And Recreation programs include such titles as *Club Manager, Caterer, Food and Beverage Manager, Child Development Center Manager, Family Home care Coordinator, Supervisory Recreation Specialist, Outdoor Recreation Specialist, Athletics Specialist, Arts and Crafts Director, Physical Fitness Specialist, Auto Hobby Shop Manager, Marina Manager, Computer Operator, Bowling Center Manager,* and dozens of others. Position descriptions for each such title are the same throughout the system, although individual bases may have widely differing personnel needs.

Within each specialized area of the leisure-service field, it is possible to obtain similar breakdowns of job titles and personnel classification systems, although in some areas—such as private-membership organizations—these would tend to be less formally structured.

Position Descriptions and Job Notices

A number of position descriptions and job notices were presented in earlier chapters of this text (see pages 60, 61, and 185).

To provide a fuller picture of typical positions, which may range from entry-level jobs or internships to management-level positions, several additional examples are provided in Figures 11-3 through 11-8.

Such recruitment notices may be distributed in a variety of ways: (1) in direct response to individuals inquiring about job openings; (2) in mailings to college and university departments offering degrees in recreation, park, and leisure services, (3) in the newsletters or job listings of professional societies, particularly state recreation and park associations; (4) at job fairs or placement booths at professional conferences; (5) as follow-up notifications of full-time openings sent to individuals who have had earlier seasonal or part-time work experience with an organization; or (6) in paid advertisements in trade newspapers or professional magazines.

Some large-scale national organizations maintain job listings that they publish periodically, which present details of job openings, including job title; civil service grade (if governmental); name and location of organization; description of work functions; required education, experience, or certification, salary range; date of scheduled appointment; and deadline for submission of applications.

Use of Internet to Publicize Job Openings

Increasingly, numerous job openings are being listed in the Web pages of professional societies, placement-service companies, and major chains of hotels, cruise-line organizations, and similar businesses. With the low unemployment rate and job market of the late 1990s and early 2000s, hotels, restaurants, and similar businesses must constantly hire personnel for service jobs and rely heavily on the Internet to recruit personnel. In some cases, such services are without charge; in others, particularly for upper-level, more highly paid positions, there are placement fees.

There are numerous listings on the Web pages of professional societies, service organizations, and varied businesses that maintain Web sites both to provide general information about their operations and to offer placement assistance to job candidates (see Figure 11-9). Many other organizations use the Internet to present general recruitment messages, following up with more detailed announcements of specific job openings, locations, functions, and hiring requirements, as shown in Figures 11-10 to Figures 11-12.

Figure 11-3
General notice for park ranger positions in the National Park Service (first page only). See also page 60.

The National Park Service — Careers

Park Rangers

Park Rangers perform a wide variety of duties in managing parks, historical sites, and recreational areas. Many wear a prescribed uniform.

- Career Guide
- General Information
- Seasonal Employment
- Internships
- Volunteers in Parks
- Contacts
- OPM Job Announcements

Duties
Park Rangers supervise, manage and perform work in the conservation and use of resources in national parks and other federally-managed areas. Park Rangers carry out various tasks associated with forest or structural fire control; protection of property; gathering and dissemination of natural, historical, or scientific information; development of interpretive material for the natural, historical, or cultural features of an era; demonstration of folk art and crafts; enforcement of laws and regulations; investigation of violations, complaints, trespass/encroachment, and accidents; search and rescue; and management of historical, cultural, and natural resources, such as wildlife, forests, lakeshores, seashores, historic buildings, battlefields, archaeological properties, and recreation areas. They also operate campgrounds, including such tasks as assigning sites, replenishing firewood, performing safety inspections, providing information to visitors, and leading guided tours. Differences in the exact nature of duties depend on the grade of position, the site's size and specific needs.

Location
Park Rangers work in urban, suburban, and rural areas. More than half of the Park Rangers work in areas east of the Mississippi River. Much of their work is performed outdoors, but often Rangers must work in offices, especially as they advance and assume more managerial responsibilities. During their careers, most Rangers can expect to be assigned to several different parts of the country. While we try take into account each employee's preference, we do not guarantee that a ranger will remain stationed in only one area.

Training
The orientation and training a Ranger receives on the job is sometimes supplemented with formal training courses. Training for duties which are unique to the Park Service is available at the Horace M. Albright Training Center at Grand Canyon National Park, AZ, and the Stephen T. Mather Training Center at Harpers Ferry, WV. In addition, the Park service makes use of the Training Center in Brunswick, GA. Performance is evaluated critically on a continuing basis and only those who prove completely satisfactory in every respect are retained in the park management career field.

Career Potential
Depending upon qualifications Park Rangers begin their service at various grades. From the

http://www.nps.gov/personnel/rangers.htm   10/27/1999

Figure 11-4
General notice for professional positions in Boy Scouting, listing major job functions.

The Professional in Scouting

The Boy Scouts of America provides a program for young people that builds desirable qualities of character, trains in the responsibilities of participating citizenship, and develops their personal fitness. Scouting serves more than 4 million young men and women in every part of the country through more than 300 local council service centers. Nearly 4,000 professional Scouters lead, guide, and train more than a million volunteers. Scouting is a volunteer organization. The professional staff has the responsibility for working with volunteer committees and community leaders to recruit, train, guide, and inspire them to become involved in the program of Scouting.

RESPONSIBILITIES

The professional Scouter in an entry-level position is assigned to a district or service area within a local council. The job responsibilities are broad and varied. Duties include promoting, supervising, and working in the district or service area through volunteers. Different aspects of the professional Scouter's job include:

- **Sales.** The professional Scouter is responsible, through volunteers, for extending Scouting to religious, civic, fraternal, educational, or other community-based organizations.
- **Service.** Major emphasis is placed on service. The professional staff ensures that all Scouting units are served through volunteer commissioners, regular roundtable meetings, training events, and activities.
- **Finance.** The professional Scouter has responsibility for securing adequate financial support for Scouting in the assigned area. Working with volunteers, professionals recruit leadership for the Friends of Scouting and finance campaign efforts to meet the financial needs of the council.
- **Administration.** The professional Scouter administers the Scouting program in the assigned district or service area.
- **Public Relations.** Professional Scouters must recognize the importance of good working relationships with other professionals and with volunteers. Scouting depends on community support and acceptance. Professional leaders must have good communication skills and be able to tell Scouting's story to the public.

If you are an adult and a college graduate, you may qualify to become a BSA professional. For more information call or visit a local council service center of the Boy Scouts of America

The Boy Scouts of America   http://www.bsa.scouting.org

Figure 11-5
Examples of Job Listings in U.S. Navy MWR Job Opportunity Bulletin, Millington, Tennessee, January 2000.
(Note: Full listing includes required qualifications for positions and procedures for applying.)

RECREATION SPECIALIST GS-0188-07
Reference No. 99-10-611
Announcement No. 9PS1657

      MWR DEPT. NAVAL SUPPORT ACTIVITY MONTEREY BAY, Monterey, CA
      Starting Salary. $26,998.00 per year. Area of Consideration: All Appointable Eligibles Worldwide. Relocation Expenses: Not Authorized. Functions: Plans, markets and conducts an ongoing program to provide physical conditioning programs for active duty, retired military, family members and DOD employees. Motivates and educates participants on proper physical fitness through the development of promotional literature, lectures, classes, workshops and events. Counsels individuals on proper diet and nutrition.

MARINA MANAGER, NF 1101-03/04 (Pending Classification)
Reference No. 99-12-632
Announcement No. MWR 11-00

      MWR DEPARTMENT, NAS Jacksonville, FL
      Salary Range: $25,000 - $35,000 Per Annum. Area of Consideration: Worldwide. Relocation Expenses Negotiable. Open Until Filled. MAJOR DUTIES: Incumbent will supervise, operate and maintain the Marina facility, associated Marina programs and outdoor recreation areas and programs. Will be responsible for rentals, resale, purchasing of all supplies and equipment, preparation of budget and operating within budgetary limits, supervision, scheduling and evaluation of employees, ensuring compliance for all fire, safety, security and sanitation inspections of facilities.

MWR Director, NF 1101-05
Reference No. 00-01-643
Announcement No. 00-01-643

      MWR Dept., Naval Submarine Base, Kings Bay, GA
      Salary Range: Negotiable, $55,004-$71,503. Relocation Expenses: Negotiable. Opening Date: 5 Jan 00. Closing Date 31 Jan 00. Area of Consideration: All Sources. MAJOR DUTIES AND RESPONSIBLITIES: Directs and manages a comprehensive and diverse MWR Department providing programs, services, facilities and products to improve the quality of life, morale and well-being of authorized personnel. Ensures that all department activities function as a unit with the common goals of providing high standards of programs, services or products for the patron. Incumbent fosters and aggressively promotes a climate of mutual support and cooperation consistent with total quality management philosophies and processes. Ensures initiation, implementation, and evaluation of market analyses, cost benefit analyses, and product analyses in order to continuously improve the efficiency, acceptability, overall quality and satisfaction of patrons.

Figure 11-6
Partial listing of temporary, part-time, and seasonal positions under title of Recreation Specialist, in Scottsdale, Arizona, Community Maintenance and Recreation Division.

DESCRIPTION FOR EACH POSITION:

~ **Adapted Recreation Specialist** - Provides assistance to children, teens, or adults with disabilities in recreation programs. Includes social skill instruction and coaching, teaches activity skills, and provides additional supervision to ensure safe and successful participation in an inclusive recreation class or program. May include providing support with independent living skills such as restroom assistance, feeding, and changing of clothes. Requires CPR certification.

~ **Adult Flag Football Official** - Officiates Adult Flag Football games, maintains control of game and participants. Keeps score and running clock on field. National Intramural Recreational Sports Association training for football provided and required of all officials.

~ **Adult Power Volleyball Official** - Officiates Adult Power Volleyball games, maintains control of games and participants. Keeps scores on card and flips score. National Intramural Recreational Sports Association and N.F.H.S. training provided and required of all officials.

~ **Adult/Youth Sports Site Supervisor** - Maintains game site during adult or youth sports games. Set-ups and clean-ups; assigns staff to game field/court, monitors scorekeepers, officials, and coaches; resolves issues as they arise, ensures site is safe and clean for participants; enforces site rules.

~ **Adult/Youth Sports Scorekeeper** – Keeps score at youth or adult sports games. Records fouls, points, and penalties on log sheet and keeps parents/participants informed of score.

~ **Data Entry Specialist** – Answers registration phones calls, inputs registrations from mail, telephone and fax. Provides touch-tone registration access information to participants. Matches registration receipts and sends them out. Maintains participant information in database. Inputs program maintenance information into the Data Entry System. Informs participants of program changes, cancellations or additions. Researches balances dues to notify participants of moneys owed.

~ **Elementary Youth Sports Coach** - Coaches youth at a school site teaching fundamentals in the following sports: flag football, volleyball, basketball, track and roller hockey. Supervises youth participants, ensures participants are safe, teaches participants fundamentals and sportsmanship, communicates with parents, attends games and communicates with school on a regular basis. National Youth Sports Coaches Association certification and training provided and required of all coaches.

~ **Elementary Youth Sports Official** - Officiates youth sports (track, football or basketball) in a game setting with 4th-8th graders. Maintains control of game while instructing participants on proper procedures and rules. National Youth Sports Officials Association training and certification required and provided by Youth Activities Program.

~ **Events Specialist** - Assists with city wide special events such as Mighty Mud Mania, Wet and Wild Water Day, and others. Sets-up & prepares for events; prepares signs & awards, assists with publicity, and a wide variety of other duties, depending on the event. **Recreation Intern** Each internship is unique and is setup to meet goals of the department, as well as the student. Interns will be involved in a wide variety of programs, parks, and events, depending on the time of year or semester of internship.

~ **Specialty Class Instructor** – Provides Leisure Ed/Special Interest Classes for our Preschool, Summer and Outdoor Programs. **Preschool** - Plans and facilitates a 2 to 3 hour socialization class for up to 10 children ages 3 to 5. Plans activities (indoor and outdoor) to include introduction to social skills, craft and games activities, and provides supervision to ensure safe and enjoyable participation in class. **Summer** - Plans and facilitates 2 to 3 hour classes for school age children early morning and late afternoon, before and after our traditional summer program times of 10 to 4. Supervises youth participants, ensuring participants are safe, communicates with parents, and plans and facilitates a variety of activities for the participants. **Outdoor**- Guides participants in outdoor, day and evening activities (day hikes, day trips and camping). Ensures participants are safe, drives 15 passenger vans, leads hiking activities or guides participants in day excursions.

~ **Train Guide/Ticket Taker** - Assists McCormick-Stillman Railroad Park's railroad exhibit by taking tickets, conducting tours, and assisting the public. Good customer service skills and the ability to do light cleaning are required. Railroad knowledge a bonus, but not required.

Figure 11-7
Examples of several job openings in municipal recreation and park agencies, publicized by Pennsylvania Recreation and Park Society.

Recreation Program Coordinator - Elizabethtown Area Recreation Commission. Position involves planning, organization and administering of seasonal programs. Additional duties include writing news releases, program registration, developing reports, and coordination and supervision of activities. Computer knowledge helpful. Position includes day/evening and weekend hours. Graduation from a four year college with a degree in Parks and Recreation, Leisure Services or related field recommended. Excellent benefits. Salary negotiable, commensurate with experience. Closing date: Wednesday, January 19, 2000. Send resume to: Elizabethtown Area Recreation Commission, 600 E. High Street, Elizabethtown, PA 17022, Attn: Barry L. Acker, Director.

Recreation Program Coordinator: Whitemarsh Township is seeking a program coordinator to fill this newly created position. This full-time position's responsibilities include: the planning, implementation and coordinating of existing programs and development of new programs, management of part-time staff for individual programs, scheduling of park and recreation facilities for a year-round community recreation based program. Position requirements are as follows: bachelor's degree in Parks and Recreation or related field and practical experience with implementation of programs, computer skills, and customer service. Salary ranges from $20,000 to $25,000 with full benefit package, DOQ. To apply, send resume, and references to: Douglas W. Knauss, Park and Recreation Coordinator, 616 Germantown Pike, Lafayette Hill, PA 19444. Position open until filled.

Teen Recreation Specialists - Lancaster Recreation Commission - Seeking a talented and energetic individual to conduct adventure, recreation and educational activities for teenagers and work with teachers, parents and volunteers. Schedule varies weekly to include day, after school, and evening and weekend hours. A BS in Recreation and Parks, Social work, or a related field is preferred. Starting salary is dependent on experience. Send resumes with three reference contacts to Lancaster Recreation Commission, 525 Fairview Avenue, Lancaster, PA 17603.

Dozens of other placement services provide guidance and direct contact with the full range of job opportunities in both domestic and international settings.

For example, the Club Managers' Association of America provides mid-management career listings for corporate- and member-owned clubs in seven regions of the United States and abroad, giving full details about the clubs themselves (facilities, membership characteristics, program features, and financial status) and about the job openings themselves.

The American Hotel and Motel Association (AHMA) is the trade association representing the multibillion-dollar lodging industry. As a federation of state lodging associations, representing some 11,000 businesses worldwide, the AHMA offers research, training, and educational materials in all aspects of the field, add assists in personnel placement as well.

Numerous other professional societies and trade associations (see Appendix A) offer similar services for each sector of the overall leisure-service field.

Figure 11-8
Example of internship position with Pop Warner Little Scholars to work on Punt, Pass & Kick Competition.

POP WARNER LITTLE SCHOLARS, INC.
586 Middletown Boulevard, Suite C-100
Langhorne, PA 19047

PH   215 752 2691
FAX 215 752 2879
E-MAIL headquarters@popwarner.net
WEB SITE www.popwarner.com

Pop Warner Little Scholars, Inc.
Intern Job Description

TITLE: Intern

REPORTS TO: Office Administrator

RESPONSIBLE FOR: Coordinating Punt, Pass & Kick (PPK) Competition, Assist with and Analyze Awards Banquet, Supply Mailing to local leagues

PRINCIPLE JOB OBJECTIVES:

Work with local Pop Warner programs in organizing PPK competitions and sending out supplies.

Assist office administrator with final preparation for Pop Warner Little Scholars Awards Banquet. Solicit ads for program book, survey analysis and follow-up.

Coordinate mailing of annual supplies to Pop Warner Leagues throughout country.

SPECIFIC RESPONSIBILITIES:

PUNT, PASS & KICK Program

- Contact new groups to get involved.
- Assist with organization of local and sectional championships.
- Assist in marketing program with help from NFL Properties.

Pop Warner Little Scholars Banquet

- Assist office administrator in final preparation for banquet.
- Contact sponsors for ad placement in program book.
- Survey analysis and follow-up after banquet

Annual Super Bowl Preparation

- Develop list of special guests and corporate sponsors
- Assist in planning activities for super bowl

Figure 11-9
Partial listing of tourism, sport and recreation career Websites. See page 185 for example of one Website.)

Tourism & Hospitality Career Sites

Casino Careers Online	www.casinocareers.com
Executive Placement Services	www.execplacement.com
Hospitality Net	www.hospitalitynet.org
Hotel Online	www.hotel-online.com/neo
Resort Jobs	www.resortjobs.com/index
American Hotel and Motel Management Association	www.ahma.com
American Society for Travel Agents	www.astanet.com
Casino/Hospitality and Travel Network	www.chat-network.com
Club Managers Association of America	www.cmaa.org
Cruise Line Jobs	www.cruiselinejobs.com
EHS & Associates-Restuarants and Hospitality	www.ehs-associates.com
Entry Jobs in Restaruants and Hospitality	www.entreejobbank.com
Food Service Industry Jobs	www.foodjobs.co.uk
Food Service Industry Jobs	www.foodservice.com/employment.htm
Hospitality Jobs	www.hospitalityonline.com
HSMAI	www.hsmai.org
Hyatt Regency Hilton Head Resort	www.hyatt.com
International Food Service Executives Association	www.ifsea.org/index.html
Meeting Industry	www.mim.com/jobboard/jobs
International Association of Conference Centers	www.iacconline.com/home
International Association of Exposition Management	www.iaem.org
Pacific Asia Travel Association	www.pata.org
Sharp Network - Hospitality Jobs	www.sharp-network.com
Sierra Club	www.sierraclub.org
Society for Food Service Management	www.sfm-online.org/welcome.html
Travel and Tourism Research Association	www.ttra.com

Sport & Recreation Career Sites

AAHPERD	www.aahperd.org
Action Jobs	www.actionjobs.com
American Camping Association	www.acacamps.org
Association of Amusement Parks & Attractions	www.iaapa.org
Associatoin of Collegiate Conference & Events Directors	www.acced-i.colostate.edu
Big Brothers Big Sisters of America	www.bbbsa.org/career/careers
Boys & Girls Clubs of America	www.nonprofitjobs.org
Boys Scouts of America	www.bsa.scouting.org
C.O.A.C.H.	www.coachhelp.com
Cool Works	www.coolworks.com
Disney Careers	www.disney.com
Fitness World's Job Fair	www.fitnessworld.com/pro/free/jobs
Girls Incorporated	www.girlsinc.org
Great Outdoor Recreation Pages	www.gorp.com/gorp/jobs
Jewish Community Centers	www.jcca.org
National Association of Recreation Resource Planners	www.narrp.org/jobs
National Federation of State High School Association	www.nfhs.org/home
National Intramural Recreation Sports Association	www.nirsa.org
Outdoor JobNet	www.outdoornetwork.com/jobnet/jobnet
Pennsylvania Recreation & Park Association	www.vicon.net/~prps/
Sport Link	www.sportlink.com
Sports Careers	www.sportscareers.com
The Fitness Professional's Center	www.fitnesslink.com/pro.htm
United States Golf Association	www.usga.org
United States Olympic Committee	www.usoc.org
United Way of America	www.unitedway.org/uwajobs
Universal Studios' Job Bank	www.universalstudios.com/jobs
VA Recreation and Park Society	www.vwc.edu/vrps.home
World Water Park Association	www.waterparks.com/w/index
YWCA	www.ywca.org

Figure 11-10
Opening page of Disney's Web site with general recruitment message.

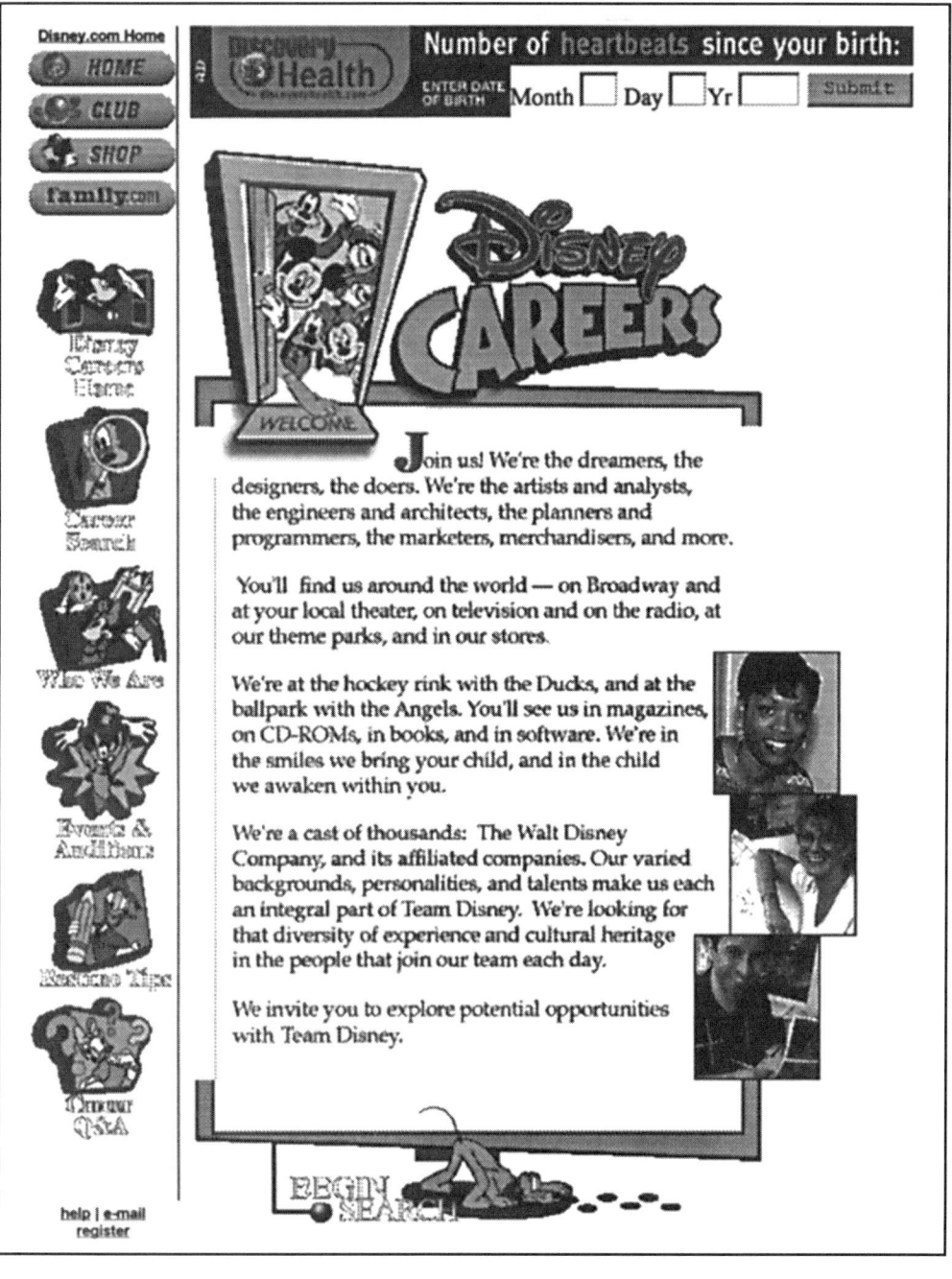

Figure 11-11
General recruitment Web page for Knott's Berry Farm in California.

Career Opportunities

From urban vivacity to seaside splendor to drowsy pastoral vistas, Southern California is the perfect environment for dreaming and doing. And from the beginning, Knott's Berry Farm, America's first themed amusement park, has always been the best place to do both.

Knott's Berry Farm proudly pledges equal access to employment, facilities, and programs without regard to race, color, creed, religion, sexual orientation, gender, age, disability, national origin, veteran or marital status.

We are seeking qualified men and women who desire to build a worthwhile career. We are a progressive company offering a variety of assignments and a competitive pay and benefits package.

An Equal Opportunity Employer

Professional Opportunities:
Knott's Berry Farm's success is rooted literally in those favorable elements produced by the temperate Southern California climate. The change and growth nourished by these conditions have defined our history and will also shape our future, so we take your personal and professional development very seriously at Knott's.

Figure 11-12
Dollywood Theme Park listing of employment opportunities, with specific details of job functions and skills needed for different positions.

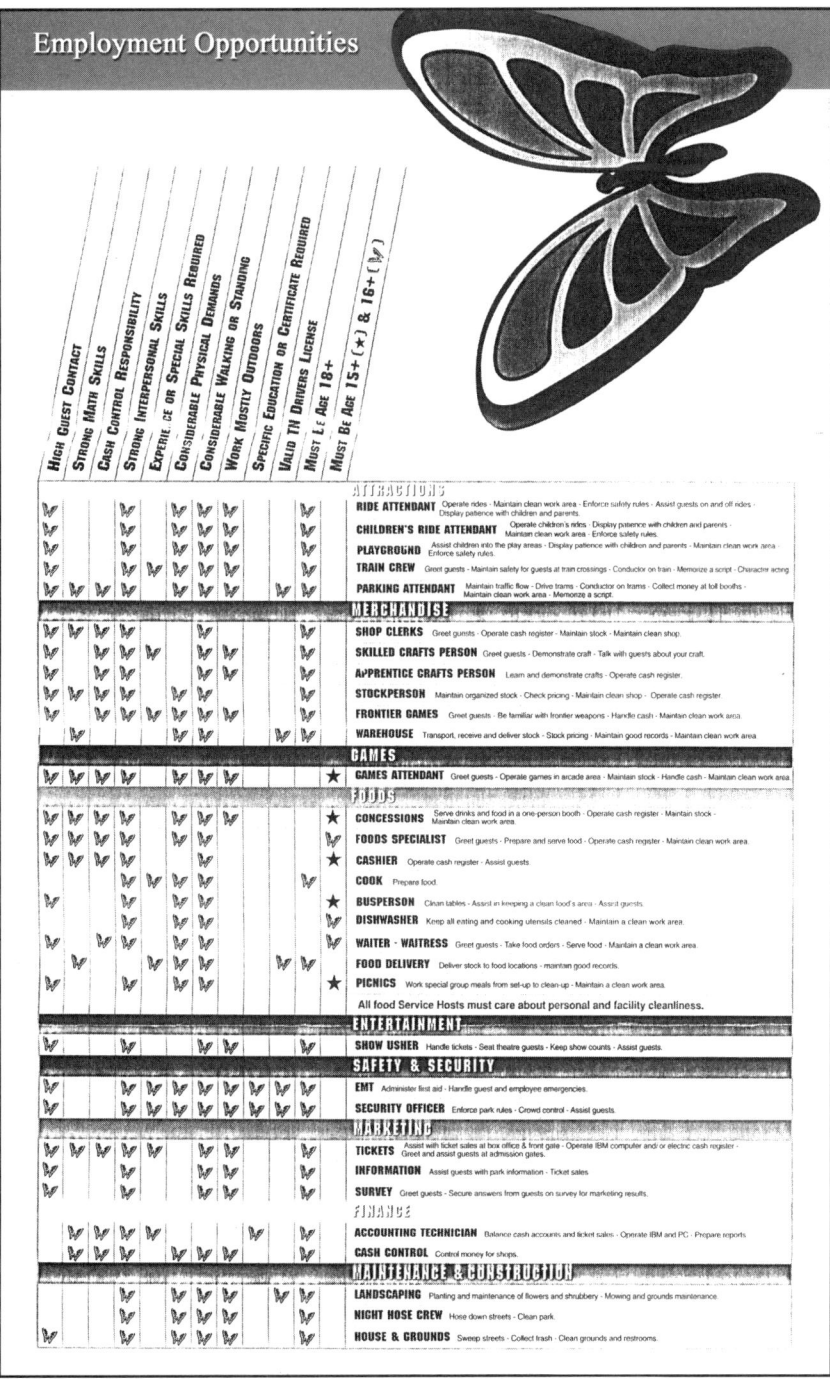

Career Development Planning

As a student in the leisure-service field, it is probably too early for you to be overly concerned with the job-search process, or with the services that list positions in your area of interest.

Instead, your emphasis should be on the kinds of self-assessment and exploration of various specialties in the fields that have just been outlined in this chapter. It would make sense for you to focus on building your own professional competence, developing needed leadership or management skills, taking the kinds of elective courses that will contribute to your overall ability and appeal to a prospective employer-and most of all, getting as much practical experience as possible during your college years.

Gaining Needed Experience

Such experience, whether gained in part-time, seasonal, or volunteer assignments, or in fieldwork or internship assignments taken for credit, will be an important part of your developing professional growth. It will not only give you confidence and needed knowledge in such practical areas as program leadership, staff relationships, facility operations, marketing, and community relations, but may very well lead to contacts that will result in job offers after graduation.

From this perspective, it is essential that you consider summer vacations or other "free" time during the year not simply as a chance to relax and make some needed income-but also as an important opportunity to prepare for your future career.

For the same reason, when you do get to the point of considering possible credit-yielding field work or internship assignments, it is critical that you analyze them carefully. Will you be doing real, meaningful work, or will your job be a routine, superficial set of petty tasks? Will your temporary employer have real expectations of you, or will you be seen just as a source of cheap, temporary labor? You will be fortunate to locate assignments at that point that really challenge you and that offer conscientious and helpful supervision on the job—amounting, if possible, to a mentoring kind of relationship.

To illustrate this point, the process of applying for an internship will represent an important early experience that will contribute to your professional growth. For example, in preparing for the interview stage of the screening procedure, you may be faced with the following kinds of questions that compel you to sharpen your own understanding of the field and of your own goals and personal qualities (Figure 11-14).

Job-Search Strategies

Looking ahead to the time when you will be ready to enter the field on a full-time, year-round basis, you will find many helpful resources. Numerous books and manuals deal with the job search process, particularly in the fields of sports management and travel, tourism, and hospitality. In some cases, organizations such as the National Therapeutic Recreation Society and the National Intramural and Recreational Sports Association have prepared publications designed to help people enter their fields professionally.

The *Occupational Outlook Handbook,* published by the U.S. Department of Labor, presents concise, up-to-date summaries of various sectors of the recreation, park, and leisure-service field, including employment prospects, working conditions, training and advancement opportunities, and future job outlooks.[4] It ranks varied human-service occupations,

Figure 11-13
Example of Internet job listing in outdoor recreation functions.

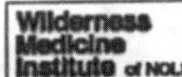

The Outdoor JobNet

Sample Job Titles found on Outdoor JobNet

Outdoor JobNet is the Internet's most popular site for serious jobs in outdoor education, outdoor recreation and adventure travel. As an example of the type of positions you'll find on our site, we present the following "sample" of position titles that were posted on Outdoor JobNet in just the last 90 days alone:

- Administrative Assistant
- Adventure Based Counseling Facilitator
- Adventure Programs Coordinator
- Adventure Sales Representative
- Adventure Trip Leader
- Assistant Coordinator Of School Program
- Assistant Director Of Administration
- Associate Director
- Backcountry Instructor
- Backcountry Operations Director
- Camp Assistant
- Caretaker
- Challenge Course Builder / Installer
- Climbing Programs Manager
- Conservation Crew Leader
- Contract Facilitator
- Intern
- Interpretive Naturalist
- Lead Instructor
- Logistics Coordinator
- Mountain Guide
- Naturalist
- Nordic Skiing Instructor
- Operations Manager
- Outdoor Educator/Instructor/Intern
- Outdoor Ministry Employee
- Park Ranger/Park Ranger Aide
- Parks And Recreation Director
- Planetarium Instructor
- Program Director
- Program Instructor
- Program Specialist
- Publication Coordinator
- Regional Manager
- Residential Dorm

Figure 11-14
Sample questions drawn from the Recreation Student Internship Manual of the Phoenix, Arizona, Department of Parks, Recreation and Library.

1. What are your short and long range career goals? How are you preparing to reach them?
2. Why did you choose a career in the leisure field?
3. What do you consider to be your strengths and your weaknesses?
4. How would you describe yourself professionally?
5. How do you think past employers would evaluate you and your performance?
6. How do you think your professors would describe your academic work?
7. Why do you feel you are qualified for an internship position with the department?
8. How do you function under pressure?
9. How will your education help you as an intern?
10. Why did you decide to seek an internship with this agency?
11. Describe past experiences that relate to your requested internship position.
12. How do you define success?
13. What qualities do you think a good internship supervisor should have?
14. What qualities do you think a good intern should have?
15. What are you doing to keep abreast of the current issues in the leisure field?
16. Describe a problem that you have faced and state how you solved it. What did you learn from this experience?

including recreation, among the fastest growing occupational fields and provides details of employment in such areas as therapeutic recreation and armed forces and employee services.

In addition, the *Occupational Outlook Handbook* presents helpful guidelines for the job-search process, including the use of personal contacts, classified advertisements, Internet networks and resources, public employment services, and college career planning and placement services. Along with other job manuals, it walks you through the process of making decisions about applying for jobs, preparing résumés, taking part in interviews, and evaluating job offers.

Career Advancement and Professional Development

Finally, as you view the recreation, park, and leisure-service field—or any specialized sector of it—from a career perspective, you will want to explore the personal strategies that will lead to long-term advancement for you on the job.

Very few occupational fields today reward employees with job promotion and higher pay strictly on the basis of seniority. Throughout your work life, you will therefore need to commit yourself to upgrading your skills and on-the-job performance. In part, this will depend on your personal commitment to excellence and conscientious acceptance of responsibility. However, it will also require an ongoing process of involvement in continuing professional education.

In-Service Training Experiences

Most leisure-service organizations today provide careful job orientation experiences for new employees, and many offer continuing-education programs at different levels of responsibility. Earlier chapters gave examples of such services in the YMCA and U.S. Navy Morale, Welfare and Recreation programs (see pages 82 and 118). Many theme parks and other tourism and hospitality organizations provide similar services.

For example, in such parks as the Old Country in Williamsburg, Virginia, job-training programs include such elements as practicing ride operations, operating cash registers, and learning basic food preparation and other practical tasks. At appropriate times, the Old Country may hold a practice day for employees. friends and families to serve as a dress rehearsal for park employees.

As employees gain experience in such roles as ride operators, zoo attendants, and food service workers, they may move on to managerial positions as unit or area supervisors. At this stage, they receive additional training in the form of several four-hour sessions, or leadership modules, which cover such elements as (1) the Old Country business philosophy, including leadership styles, supervisory responsibilities, and staff welfare; (2) communication skills; and (3) building employee motivation and a productive working climate.

In addition to such opportunities, there are numerous conferences, clinics, courses, and other educational services for practitioners that are offered by national organizations in the leisure-service field. The National Recreation and Park Association and its member branches and State affiliates offer many such programs, often in cooperation with other organizations or with leading colleges and universities. They focus on leadership and management skills, marketing and revenue-sources, risk management, and a host of other professional concerns. Figures 11-l5 shows a cross section of such educational programs that deal with a variety of professional concerns during a single month of the year.

Similarly, the World Waterpark Association sponsors an annual Symposium and Trade Show, which features major workshops such as a Certified Pool Operators Course, Lifeguard Instructor Training, and over 50 educational seminars.

The International Association of Amusement Parks and Attractions sponsors similar professional education programs that deal with financial management, human resource development, risk management and safety, successful merchandising, insurance coverage, and disability "etiquette"—in many cases, making use of training videotapes and other resources.

Certification Concerns. At an early point, you should learn whether one or more certifications by a professional society will be required in the leisure-service field that you plan to enter. Obviously, this would be the case in such fields as therapeutic recreation, aquatic program management, and fitness training services (see page 166).

However, certification requirements also apply in many other areas of leisure-service management, including employee services, varied categories of sports instruction and coaching, and outdoor recreation skills. The need for professional certification should therefore be determined and acted on, at an early stage of your professional development.

Figure 11-15
Examples of National Recreation and Park Association programs, state society-sponsored or cosponsored conferences, and continuing-education programs in a single month.

January 29-30. National Playground Safety Institute-Inspector Certification Course and Exam
Maryland Recreation and Park Association
Contact: Sheila Franklin, MRPA, 2000 Shorefield Road, Wheaton, MD 20902.
(301) 942-7203/ Fax (301) 942-7206

❖

January 29-31. 1st Annual National Recreation For Youth-At-Risk Environments Institute
Fort Worth, TX
Contact: Richard Horton, NRPA Western Service Center Regional Office, 619 Prospect Lake Drive, Colorado Springs, CO 80910.
(719) 632-7031/ Fax (719) 632-0709

❖

January 31-February 3. Kentucky Recreation and Park Society Conference and Trade Show
Lexington, KY
Contact: Ken DeGilio, KRPS, P.O. Box 708, Lexington, KY 40586.
(606) 269-8633/ Fax (same)
CEUs pending approval

❖

February

February. NRPA Pacific Risk Management School
Phoenix, AZ
Contact: Pam Earle, NRPA Pacific Service Center, 350 S. 333rd Street, #103, Federal Way, WA 98003.
(800) 796-6772/ Fax (253) 661-3929
CEU approved

❖

February. Youth Sports Conference
New York State Recreation and Park Society
2 days, Suffern, NY
Contact: Lee Serravillo, NYSRPS, Saratoga Spa State Park, 19 Roosevelt Drive, Suite 200, Saratoga Springs, NY 12866.
(518) 584-0321/ Fax (518) 584-5101
CEU approved

February 1-4. Michigan Recreation and Park Association Annual Conference/Trade and Travel Show
Detroit Westin Hotel
Contact: Michael J. Maisner, Executive Director, MRPA, 2722 E. Michigan Avenue, Suite 201, Lansing, MI 48912-4083.
(517) 485-9888/ Fax (517) 485-7932
CEUs pending approval

❖

February 7-11. NRPA 21st Annual Rocky Mountain Revenue and Management School
Estes Park, CO
Contact: Richard Horton, NRPA Western Service Center Regional Office, 619 Prospect Lake Drive, Colorado Springs, CO 80910.
(719) 632-7031/ Fax (719) 632-0709

❖

February 11-13. Minnesota Aquatic Conference
Minnesota Recreation and Park Association
Twin Cities (Chaska)
Contact: Jon Gurban, MRPA, 5005 W. 36th Street, St. Louis Park, MN 55416.
(612) 920-6906/ Fax (612) 920-6766
CEUs pending approval

❖

February 11-15. NRPA Mid-Year National Forum
Washington, DC
Contact: NRPA Headquarters, 22377 Belmont Ridge Road, Ashburn, VA 20148.
(703) 858-0784/ Fax (703) 858-0794

❖

February 15-19. Executive Development Program
National Recreation and Park Association/ University of Georgia
University of Georgia, Athens, GA
Contact: L. Steven Dempsey, University of Georgia, 1234 S. Lumpkin Street, Athens, GA 30602.
(706) 542-3350
CEU approved

February 15-19. School of Sports Management
Oglebay Continuing Education Department
Oglebay Park, Wheeling, WV
Contact: Sue Pelley, Oglebay Continuing Education Department, Route 88 North, Wheeling, WV 26003.
(888) OGLEBAY/ F: (304) 243-4106
CEU approved

❖

February 17-21. California/ NRPA Pacific Southwest Recreation and Park Training Conference
Santa Clara, CA
Contact: Leslie Fritz, CPRS, 7971 Freeport Blvd., Sacramento, CA 95832.
(916) 665-2777/ Fax (916) 665-9149
CEUs pending approval

❖

February 19-20. Maintenance Forum
Tennessee Recreation and Parks Association
Fall Creek Falls State Park
Contact: Dory Leff, Program Services Coordinator, TRPA, 226 Capitol Blvd., Suite 500, Nashville, TN 37219.
(615) 242-TRPA/ Fax (615) 255-2173
CEUs pending approval

❖

February 22-24. Southern Leisure Management and Trends Institute
South Carolina Recreation and Park Association
Springmaid Beach, Myrtle Beach, SC
Contact: James Headley, SCRPA, P.O. Box 1046, Lexington, SC 29071.
(803) 808-7753/ Fax (803) 808-7754
CEUs pending approval

❖

February 22-27. Pacific Northwest Maintenance Management School
Port Townsend, WA
Contact: Pam Earle, NRPA Pacific Service Center, 350 S. 333rd Street, #103, Federal Way, WA 98003.
(800) 796-6772/ Fax (253) 661-3929
CEU approved

❖

www.nrpa.org
Get up-to-date listings of meetings and workshops, policy issues, benefits, new information for each state, career information, *Parks & Recreation* Magazine, playground safety information, and more...

Professional Affiliation and Commitment

From the purely selfish point of view, becoming an active member of professional societies or trade associations will be an important step if you want to advance your own career.

Beyond this, affiliating with one or more such groups that represents your chosen occupational field is essential from a broader perspective. Such national professional societies and associations help to advance the effective delivery of leisure services through research, publications, training programs, and certification and accreditation processes. Often, they lobby for positive legislation affecting the field of service and carry on campaigns that strengthen its public image and clarify its identity.

For these reasons, it is important for all those planning to enter any of the specialized leisure-service fields described in this text to become professionally active at an early point. As part of one's career, this would mean being a member of a major students' club in one's college or university and a state professional society and, in time, a full member of the national organization that best represents your field. Taking this commitment seriously will pay generous dividends over the life of a professional career.

Suggested Questions for Class Discussions or Essay Examinations

1. As in any occupation or profession, it is important to examine the requirements of the leisure-service field before deciding on it as a career focus. What are some of the personal qualities and skills needed of people who enter this overall professional field?
2. Select any two of the 10 specialized sectors of the leisure-service field (examples: armed forces or therapeutic recreation). Discuss and contrast them from a career perspective, illustrating the kinds of entry-level jobs and career ladder possibilities they would present, the program-related or other responsibilities of employees in these fields, and the special attractions they might offer to young people entering them.
3. What are some useful strategies for examining your own strengths and weaknesses with respect to entering the leisure-service field? What would be some early actions you might take to explore the field and improve your own competences for potential employment in it?
4. This chapter presents several examples of employment in different leisure-service specializations in terms of general recruitment statements or specific job openings. How could you conduct a more comprehensive and systematic search of the overall field or of a particular type of agency?
5. What are the functions of professional organizations both with respect to strengthening leisure-service agencies and in assisting in the recruitment and hiring process? Why would it be important for you to become professionally active at an early point?

Footnotes

[1] Samuels, J.B., and Foucar-Szocki, R. (1999). *Guiding your entry into the hospitality, recreation, and tourism mega-profession.* Upper Saddle River, NJ: Prentice Hall, 7.

[2] Seagle, E.E., Smith, R.W., and Dalton, L. M. (1997), *Internships in recreation and leisure services: A practical guide for students.* State College, PA: Venture Publishing, 3.

[3] Ibid., 10-11.

[4] See *Occupational outlook handbook, 1998-1999.* U.S. Department or Labor, Bureau of Labor Statistics, Bulletin 2500.

Bibliography

Austin, David. (1999). *Therapeutic Recreation Proccesses and Techniques.* Champaign, IL: Sagamore Publishing.

Bannon, Joseph. (1999). *911 Management: A Comprehensive Guide for Leisure Service Managers.* Champaign, IL: Sagamore Publishing.

Barnett, Lynn. (1995. *Research about Leisure: Past, Present, and Future.* Champaign, IL: Sagamore Publishing.

Beck, Larry and Ted Cable. (1998). *Interpretation for the 21st Century.* Champaign, IL: Sagamore Publishing.

Brymer, Robert. (1998). *Hospitality and Tourism: An Introduction to the Industry.* Dubuque, IA: Kendall/Hunt Publishing.

Bryson, John. (1995). *Strategic Planning for Public and Nonprofit Organizations.* San Francisco: Joosey-Bass Publishers.

Bullock, Charles, and Michael Mahon. (1997). *Introduction to Recreation Services for People with Disabilities.* Champaign, IL: Sagamore Publishing.

Cordell, H. Ken. (1999). *Outdoor Recreation in American Life: A National Assessment of Demand and Supply Trends.* Champaign, IL: Sagamore Publishing

Crossley, John, and Lynn Jamieson. (1997). *Introduction to Commercial and Entrepreneurial Recreation.* Champaign, IL: Sagamore Publishing.

Dattilo, John. (1999). *Leisure Education Program Planning: A Systematic Approach.* State College, PA: Venture Publishing.

Dattilo, John. (1994). *Inclusive Leisure Services: Responding to the Rights of People with Disabilities.* State College, PA: Venture Publishing.

DeGraaf, Donald, Jordan, Debra, and Kathy DeGraaf. (1999). *Steps to Successful Programing.* State College, PA: Venture Publishing.

Dittmer, Paul, and Gerald Griffin. (1997). *Dimensions of the Hospitality Industry: An Introduction.* New York: Van Nostrand Reinhold.

Driver, B. L., Brown, Perry, and George Peterson, Eds. (1991). *Benefits of Leisure.* State College, PA: Venture Publishing.

Eberts, Marjorie, Brothers, Linda, and Ann Gisler. (1997). Careers in Travel, Tourism, and Hospitality. Lincolnwood, IL: VGM Career Horizons.

Edgell, David. (1999). *Tourism Policy: The Next Millennium.* Champaign, IL: Sagamore Publishing.

Edginton, Christopher, Hudson, Susan, and Phyllis Ford. (1999). *Leadership for Recreation and Leisure Programs and Settings.* Champaign, IL: Sagamore Publishing.

Edginton, Christopher, Jordan, Debra, DeGraaf, Donald, and Susan Edginton. (1995). *Leisure and Life Satisfaction: Foundational Perspectives.* Dubuque, IA: Brown and Benchmark.

Edginton, Susan, and Christopher Edginton. (1994). *Youth Programs: Promoting Quality Services.* Champaign, IL: Sagamore Publishing.

Field, Shelly. (1991. *Career Opportunities in the Sports Industry.* New York: Facts on File.

Godbey, Geoffrey. (1999). *Leisure in Your Life.* State College, PA: Venture Publishing.

Godbey, Geoffrey. (1997). *Leisure and Leisure Services in the 21st Century .* State College, PA: Venture Publishing.

Havitz, Mark, Ed. (1995). *Models of Change in Municipal Parks and Recreation: A Book of Innovative Case Studies.* State College, PA: Venture Publishing.

Henderson, Karla, Bialeschki, M. Deborah, Shaw, Susan, and Valeria Freysinger. (1996). *Both Gains and Gaps: Feminist Perspectives on Women's Leisure.* State College, PA: Venture Publishing.

Howard, Dennis, and John Crompton. (1995). *Financing Sports.* Morgantown, WV: Fitness Information Technology.

Jackson, Edgar, and Thomas Burton, Eds. (1999). Le*isure Studies: Prospects for the Twenty-first Century.* State College, PA: Venture Publishing.

Jordan, Debra. (1996). *Leadership in Leisure Services: Making a Difference.* State College, PA: Venture Publishing.

Jubenville, Alan, and Ben Twight. (1993. *Outdoor Recreation Management: Theory and Application.* State College, PA: Venture Publishing.

Kelly, John. (1996). *Leisure.* Boston: Allyn and Bacon.

Kelly, John, and Rodney Warnick. (1999). *Recreation Trends ad Markets: The Twenty-first Century.* Champaign, IL: Sagamore Publishing.

Kraus, Richard. 2000. *Leisure in a Changing America: Trends and Issues for the 21st Century.* Needham Heights, MA: Allyn and Bacon.

Kraus, Richard, (1997). *Recreation and Leisure in Modern Society.* Sudbury, MA: Jones and Bartlett.

Kraus, Richard, (1997). *Recreation Programming: A Benefits-Driven Approach.* Needham Heights, MA: Allyn and Bacon.

Kraus, Richard, and Joseph Curtis. 2000. *Creative Management in Recreation, Parks and Leisure Services.* St. Louis: McGraw-Hill.

McGuire, Francis, Boys, Rosangela, and Raymond Tedrick. (1999). *Leisure and Aging: Ulyssean Living in Later Life.* Champaign, IL: Sagamore Publishing.

McIntosh, Robert, Goeldner, Charles, and J. R. Brent Ritchie. (1995). *Tourism: Principles, Practices, Philosophies.* New York: John Wiley and Sons.

McLean, Daniel, Bannon, Joseph, and Howard Gray. (1999). *Leisure Resources: Its Comprehensive Planning.* Champaign, IL: Sagamore : Publishing.

Miller, Lori. (1997). *Sport Business Management.* Gaithersburg, MD: Aspen Publishing.

Mundy, Jean. (1998). *Leisure Education: Theory and Practice.* Champaign, IL: Sagamore Publishing.

Murphy, James, Niepoth, E. William, Jamieson, Lynn, and John Williams. (1991. *Leisure Systems: Critical Concepts and Applications.* Champaign, IL: Sagamore Publishing.

O'Morrow, Gerald, and Marcia Jean Carter. (1997). *Effective Management in Therapeutic Recreation Service.* State College, PA: Venture Publishing.

O'Sullivan, Ellen, and Kathy Spangler. (1998). *Experience Marketing: Strategies for the New Millennium.* State College, PA: Venture Publishing.

Parkhouse, Bonnie, Ed. (1996). *The Management of Sport: Its Foundation and Application.* St. Louis: Mosby and National Association for Sport and Physical Education.

Parks, Janet, Zanger, Beverly, and Jerome Quartmerman. (1998). *Contemporary Sport Management.* Champaign, IL: Human Kinetics.

Rossman, J. Robert. (1995). *Recreation Programming: Designing Leisure Experiences.* Champaign, IL: Sagamore Publishing.

Russell, Ruth. (1996). *Pastimes: The Context of Contemporary Leisure.* Dubuque, IA: Brown and Benchmark.

Samuels, Jack, and Reginald Foucar-Szocki. (1999). *Guiding Your Entry into the Hospitality, Recreation, and Tourism Mega-Profession.* Upper Saddle River, NJ: Prentice Hall.

Sawyer, Thomas, and Owen Smith. (1999). *The Management of Clubs, Recration and Sport: concepts and Applications.* Champaign, IL: Sagamore Publishing.

Schleien, Stuart, Ray, M. Tipton, and Frederick Green. (1997). *Community Recreation and People with Disabilities.* Baltimore, MD: Paul Brookes Publishing.

Seagle, Edward, Smith, Ralph, and Lola Dalton. (1997). *Internships in Recreation and Leisure Services: A Practical Guide for Students.* State College, PA: Venture Publishing.

Sessoms, H. Douglas, and Karla Henderson. (1994). *Introduction to Leisure Services.* State College, PA: Venture Publishing.

Starr, Nona. (1997). *Viewpoint: An Introduction to Travel, Tourism, and Hospitality.* Upper Saddle River, NJ: Prentice Hall.

Stumbo, Norma. (1999). *Intervention Activities for At-Risk Youth.* State College, PA: Venture Publishing.

Tedrick, Ted, and Elaine Green. (1995). *Activity Experiences and Programming within Long-Term Care.* State College, PA: Venture Publishing.

Walker, John. (1999). *Introduction to Hospitality.* Upper Saddle River, NJ: Prentice Hall.

Weston, Susan. (1996). *Commercial Recreation and Tourism: An Introduction to Business-Oriented Recreation.* Dubuque, IA: Brown and Benchmark.

Witt, Peter, and John Crompton, Eds. (1996). *Recreation Programs That Work for At-Risk Youth: The Challenge of Shaping the Future.* State College, PA: Venture Publishing.

Appendix A
Listing of Professional and Trade Associations

Association /Organization	*Address*
Association Travel Society (ATS)	6551 S. Revere Pky. Suite 160 Englewood, CO 80111
Amateur Softball Association of America	2801 N.E. 50th St. Oklahoma City, OK 73111
American Alliance for Health, Physical Education, Recreation and Dance (AAHPERD)	1900 Association Dr. Reston, VA 22091 www.aahperd.org
American Association for Leisure and Recreation (AALR)	1900 Association Dr. Reston, VA 22091 www.aahperd.org/aalr/aalrmain.html
American Association of Museums (AAM)	1575 Eye Street NW Suite 400 Washington, D.C. 20005 www.aam-us.org/services.htm
American Association of Zoological Parks & Aquariums (AAZPA)	Oglebay Park Wheeling, WV 26003
American Bass Association	P.O. Box 896 Gate City, FL 24251-0896
American Bowling Congress	5301 S. 76th St. Greendale, WI 53129-1127
American Boat and Yacht Council	3869 Solomons Island Rd. Edgewater, MD 21037-1416
American Camping Association (ACA)	Bradford Woods 5000 State Rd. 67N Martinsville, IN 46151-7902 www.acacamps.org/contact.htm
American Fitness Association	1945 Palo Verde Ave., Suite 202 Long Beach, CA 90815
American Gaming Association (AGA)	555 13th Street, NW Suite 1010 East Washington D.C. 20094 www.amercangaming.org
American Hotel & Management Association (AH&MA) www.ahma.com	1201 New York Avenue, NW #600 Washington, DC 20005-3931
American Sailing Association	13922 Marquesa Way Marina del Ray, CA 90292
American Ski Federation	10205 Cedar Pond Dr. Vienna, VA 22182-2906
American Society for Travel Agents (ASTA)	100 Second Street East Whitefish, MT 59937 ASTA Net www.astanet.com
American Spa and Health Resort Association	P.O. Box 585 Lake Forest, IL 60045
American Sports Casters Association (ASCA)	5 Beekman St. Ste. 814 New York, NY 10038 www.americansportscasters.com
American Therapeutic Recreation Association (ATRA)	P.O. Box 15215 Hattiesburg, MS 39402-5212 www.atra-tr.org/index.html

Armed Forces Recreation Society	22377 Belmont Ridge Road Ashburn, VA 20148-4501
Association of College Unions International	120 W. 7th St. Bloomington, IN 47404-3925
Association for Women in Sports Media (AWSM)	P.O. Box 17536
Athletic Institute	200 Castlewood Dr. N. Palm Beach, FL 33408-5697 www.pleiadesnet.com/org/AWSM.1.html
Bowling Proprietors Association of America	920 Airport Rd., Ste. 210 Chapel Hill, NC 27514
Black Women in Sports Foundation (BWSF)	P.O. Box 2610 Philadelphia, PA 19130
Club Managers Association of America (CMAA)	1733 King St. Alexandria, VA 22314 www.cmaa.org
Coalition of Americans to Protect Sports (CAPS)	200 Castlewood Drive N. Palm Beach, FL 33408 www.sportsafety.com
Corporate Hospitality and Event Association (CHA)	Firdene House Winsor Walk, Weybridge, Surrey KT13 9AP www.eventmanager.co.uk/cha.htm
Cruise Lines International Association (CLIA)	500 Fifth Ave. St. Suite 1407 New York, NY 10110 www.cruising.org/index.htm
Disabled Sports USA	451 Hungerford Dr., Ste. 100 Rockville, MD 20850
Dude Ranchers' Association (DRA)	P.O. Box F-471 LaPorte, CO 80535
Ecotourism Society (ES)	P.O. Box 755 North Bennington, VT 05257 www.ecotourism.org
Employee Services Management (ESM)	2211 York Road. Ste. 207 Oakbrook, IL 60523 www.nesra.org
Hospitality Sales & Marketing Association International (HSMAI)	1300 L. Street N.W. Suite 1020 Washington, DC 20005 www.hsmai.org
Hosteling International-AYH	733 15th St. N.W., No. 840 Washington, DC 20005
Ice Skating Institute	17120 Dallas Parkway Dallas, TX 75248
International Association of Amusement Parks and Attractions (IAAPA)	1448 Duke Street Alexandria, VA 22314 www.iaapaorg/about/9-cont.htm
International Association of Auditorium Managers (IAAM)	4425 W. Airport Freeway, Ste. 590 Irving, TX 75063-5835 www.iaam.org
International Association of Conference Centers	243 North Lindbergh Blvd. St. Louis, MO 63141 www.iacconline.com/home (IACC)
International Association of Convention & Visitors Bureaus (IACVB)	2000 L St. N.W. Ste. 702 Washington, DC 20036-4990 www.iacvb.org
International Association of Exposition Management (IAEM)	P.O. Box 802425 Dallas, TX 75380 www.iaem.org

International Association of Fairs and Expositions (IAFE)	P.O. Box 985 Springfield, MO 65801 www.iafenet.org
International Association of Tourism Professionals (IATP)	1218 Merry Oaks College Station, TX 77840-2609 www.actp.com
International Health, Racquet & Sports Club Association (IHRSCA)	263 Summer Street Boston, MA 02210 www.ihrsa.org
International Hotel and Resort Association (IHRA)	251 Rue Faubourg St. Martin, Paris, France 75010 www.ih-ra.com
International Paintball Players Association	864 Sconset Lane McLean, VA 22102-2120
International Spa and Fitness Association	113 S. West St., Ste. 400 Alexandria, VA 22314-2851
National Amusement Park Association	P.O. Box 83 Mt. Prospect, IL 60056
National Association for Campus Activities	13 Harbison Way Columbia, SC 29212
American Association for Leisure and Recreation	1900 Association Dr. Reston, VA 22091
National Association of County Park and Recreation Officials	5045 Stanley Rd. Flint, MI 48506
National Association of Girls and Women in Sport (NAGWS)	1900 Association Drive Reston, VA 20191 www.aahperd.org
National Association of Black Hospitality Professionals (NABHP)	P.O.Box 8132 Columbus, GA 31908 www.blackhospitality.com
National Association of State Park Directors	9894 E. Holden Place Tucson, AZ 85748-6531
National Association of RV Parks and Campgrounds	8605 Westwood Center Dr. Vienna, VA 22182
National Association of Sports Commissions (NASC)	300 Main St. 1st Floor Cincinnati, OH 45202 www.sportscommissions.org
National Association of Sports Officials (NASO)	2017 Lathrop Ave. Racine, WI 53405 www.naso.org
National Federation Interscholastic Coaches Association (NFICA)	11724 N.W. Plaza Circle Kansas City, MO 64153 www.nfhs.org
National Foundation of Wheelchair Tennis	122 S. El Camino Real, No. 140 San Clemente, CA 92672-4000
National Interscholastic Athletic Administrators Association (NIAAA)	11724 N.W. Plaza Circle Kansas City, MO 64153 www.nfhs.org
National Intramural Recreational Sports Association (NIRSA)	4185 SW Research Way Corvallis, OR 97333-1067 www.nirsa.org
National Recreation and Park Association (NRPA)	22377 Belmont Ridge Road Ashburn, VA 20148-4501 www.activeparks.org www.nrpa.org
National Shooting Sports Foundation	Flintlock Ridge Office Center, 11 Mile Hill Rd. Newtown, CT 06470-2359

National Ski Patrol System	133 S. Van Gordon St., Ste. 100
	Lakewood, CO 80228
National Therapeutic Recreation Society	22377 Belmont
	Ridge Road
	Ashburn, VA 20148-4501
National Wildlife Federation	8925 Leesburg Pike
	Vienna, VA 22184
North American Society for Sport Management (NASSM)	C/O Dr. Garth Paton
	U. of NB-Kinesiology
	PHYS. ED/REC
	Fredericton, NB E3B 5A3
	Canada
	www.unb.ca/sportmanagement
	www.nassm.org
Resort and Commercial Recreation Association (RCRA)	P.O. Box 1998
	Tarpon Springs, FL 34688
Roller Skating Association International	6905 Corporate Dr.
	Indianapolis, IN 46278-1927
Snow Sports Industries of America	8377-B Greensboro Dr.
	McLean, VA 22102-3587
Sport Fishing Institute	1033 N. Fairfax St.
	Alexandria, VA 22314-1540
Stadium Managers Association (SMA)	19 Mantua Rd.
	Mt. Royal, NJ 08061
	www.stadianet.com
Student Travel Association (STA)	University of Pennsylvania
	Philadelphia, PA
Trade Show Exhibitors Association (TSEA)	5501 Backlick Road
	Suite 105
	Springfield, VA 22151
	www.sta-travel.com
Travel Industry Association of America (TIA)	1100 New York Avenue, NW
	Suite 450
	Washington, DC 20005-3934
	http://www.tia.org/
United States Golf Association (USGA)	Golf House
	P.O. Box 746
	Far Hills, NJ 07931-9970
	www.usga.org/
USA Hockey	1775 Bob Johnson Dr.
	Colorado Springs, CO 80906-4090
Women's Sports Foundation	Eisenhower Park
	East Meadow, NY 11554
World Leisure and Recreation Association (WLRA)	WLRA Secretariat
	Suite 81C Compo
	Okanagan Falls, BC V0H
	1R0, Canada
	www.worldleisure.org/
World Travel and Tourism Council	20 Grosvenor Place
	London SW1X 7TT
	www.wttc.org
World Water Park Association (WWA)	P.O. Box 14826
	Lenexa, KS 66285
	www.waterparks.com/w/index.html

Appendix B

Class Enrichment Activities

In addition to class discussions or examinations based on this text, instructors and students may elect to undertake any of the following suggested assignments and special projects.

In some cases, they may involve the entire class in a shared task. In others, they may best be assigned to individual students or small groups. Before activities are undertaken, outlines should be prepared that specify the exact nature of the project, the oral or written reports to be prepared, and deadlines for completion or class presentation.

1. *Field Trips.* Through the semester, individuals or small groups of students may be scheduled to visit leisure-service agencies of different types in the community or nearby region, and to report to the class regarding their mission, program elements, funding practices, facilities, and staff makeup and personnel practices.

2. *Campus Leisure-Service Programs.* As a group assignment, students may analyze the overall college or university leisure-service programs and services, including organized sports clubs and intramurals, social and cultural activities, and other recreational programs. This analysis may simply be descriptive, or may involve a critical analysis leading to specific recommendations for strengthening campus leisure services.

3. *Professional Associations.* Students may select appropriate professional associations (national, regional, or state), contact them, and request membership information. They then may prepare reports dealing with each organization's mission, activities and services, membership, and benefits for the field and for future professionals.

4. *Conference Attendance.* Students may attend one or more professional conferences, workshops, or similar events, take part in as many sessions as possible, and report on them to the class. This attendance may be keyed to the individual student's exploration of future seasonal, part-time, or internship assignment, through contact with attending professionals.

5. *Convention and Visitors Bureau.* Students may contact nearby or regional convention and visitors bureaus, requesting information as if they were tourists planning a possible visit. They may then report to the class regarding the materials received and the effectiveness of the bureaus studied.

6. *Delivery Systems for Special Populations.* Class members may study and report on leisure opportunities or special services for individuals with physical or mental disabilities in the community or region. This study would involve both special, separate programs offered by public or nonprofit agencies and the availability of general community recreation opportunities—in terms of possible physical barriers to participation or adaptations made to encourage disabled persons to enter programs.

7. *Field Experiences.* Apart from general departmental requirements for supervised field work or internships, this course might include a specified period—possibly eight to 10 weeks—of assignment to a nearby community agency, recreation business, or other leisure-service organization, involving several hours each week, for varied leadership, clerical or other tasks. It may then be followed by a report to the class, summing up the student's experience and possible new insights into the field.

8. *News Notebook.* As a continuing assignment, students may be asked to monitor newpapers, magazines, television programs, or similar media sources to gather items related to recreation and leisure or to social and economic trends affecting this field. In a five- or 10-minute period at the beginning of class sessions for several weeks, they may then report briefly on the items they collected. This assignment may also be submitted in the form of notebooks presenting and commenting on the materials gathered.

9. *Group Video Project.* Small groups of students may prepare and submit a two-minute video promoting careers in separate areas of public, commercial or other types of leisure services, based on the taping of programs, interviews with agency managers or staff members, and other sources dealing with actual agencies.

10. *Internet Career Search.* Using Web sites suggested in the text or other sources, individual students may conduct preliminary job searches within selected areas of leisure services. They may then report their findings to the class. As suggested in Assignment No. 4, this search may be keyed to an individual student's exploration of possible internship or seasonal work assignments.

11. *Personal Career Plan.* Toward the close of the semester, students may be required to submit a two- or three-page paper outlining their evolving plans for a professional career and the steps they plan to take in terms of focusing on a specific employment area and preparing themselves for work in this field.

12. *Alphabet Jobs.* As a novel class activity, the class may be divided into several small groups. Each group is given 10–15 minutes to see which group can identify the greatest number of legitimate job titles or categories—one for each letter of the alphabet. This may cover all areas of leisure-service employment.

A

Adolescents, *see* Youth, programs for
Adult education, 138
Adventure recreation, 32, 89, 97, 193, 201-205
Advocacy function of leisure-service agencies, 26, 31-32, 157, 160
African-Americans, 14, 173-175, 192
    See also Race relations in recreation
Alcohol abuse services, 65, 113, 130
All-American Soap Box Derby, 77-78
American Academy of Park and Recreation Administration, 18, 32
American Bowling Congress, 176-177
American Camping Association, 77
American Park and Recreation Society, 32
Americans with Disability Act, 156
Aquatic recreation, 89, 95-97, 114, 134
    See also Boating, Fishing, Whitewater rafting
Armed forces recreation, 6, 26, 28, 32, 43, 107-118, 221, 228
Arts in recreation, 7, 46, 50, 53, 129, 139, 142, 161, 205-206
Asian-Americans, 14
At-risk youth, *see* Youth, programs for

B

Baseball, 18-19, 171, 175
    See also Little League
Basketball, 171-172
Benefits of recreation and leisure, 8-12, 26, 66, 71, 120, 129-131, 154-155, 182
Benefits-based management, 18-20
Biking, 97, 99
Black History Month, 51
Boating, 17, 37-38, 51, 95, 97, 114, 139
Bolla, P., 7
Boy Scouts, 4, 65, 69, 84, 160, 227
Boys and Girls Clubs, 4, 18, 65-68, 80, 84, 160
Bowling, 110, 171, 176
Brown, P., 8
Bullaro, J., 87-88
Bureau of Land Management, 43-44

C

California Park and Recreation Society, 18
Camp Fire Boys and Girls, 76
Camping, 17, 77, 83, 160, 171, 193
Campus recreation, 26, 28-29, 32, 35, 128-138, 221
Canada, recreation and parks in, 6, 8, 54, 58
    See also Kamloops, North York, Vancouver
Canadian Parks/Recreation Society, 6
Careers in recreation management, 6, 40-41, 184-186, 216-242
    See also Employment in leisure services professional development
Catholic Youth Organization, 71, 75, 170, 184
Central Park Conservancy, 37
Certification, 166, 239-240
Chase Corporate Challenge, 121-122
Chuck E. Cheese play centers, 101-102
Church groups, 76
    See also Religion-connected agencies
Civil Service, 58-62
Clinical therapeutic recreation, 148, 151-155
Cognitive values of recreation, 10
Colleges, *See* Professional preparation, Staff development
Commercial recreation, 6, 25-28, 33, 87-106, 163, 221
    See also Sports management, Tourism
Commodification of leisure services, 15-17
    See also Marketing approaches
Competition in leisure-service system, 35, 212-213
Computers in recreation management, 15-16, 57, 139
    See also Internet
Concordia University, 135-136
Conservation, *See* Environmental programs
Cooperation in leisure services, 35, 37-38
Country clubs, 138, 140
County recreation and park agencies, 49-50, 160
Coyle, C., 155
Crandall, R., 7

Credentialing of personnel, 99-100
    See also Certification, Job descriptions
Crompton, J., 18
Cruise lines, 200-201
Cultural programs, 11, 13, 46, 50, 53, 141
    See also Arts in recreation, dance

D

Dade County, Florida, 49
Dalton, L.M., 218-220
Dance, 53
Dawson, D., 7
Demographic changes, 192
Disability, *See* Therapeutic recreation service
Discretionary time, *See* Work week
Dollywood Theme Park, 104, 198-199, 234
Driver, B.L., 8
Drug abuse, 113
    See also Youth, programs for
Dunn, J.K., 131, 136

E

East Bay Park District, 47-48
Economic value of recreation, 10-13, 177, 179, 198
Ecotourism, 208
Edgell, D., 207
Edginton, C., 87-88
Efficacy research, 155
Elderhostel, 195, 197
Elderly, and recreation, 7, 206
    See also Demographic changes, retirement communities
Emotional benefits of recreation, 70
Employee services and recreation, 6, 26, 28, 58-62, 119-127, 221
Employment in leisure services, 6, 37-38, 80-82, 84-85, 97-100, 102-105, 108, 116-118, 135-136, 144, 163-167, 210-211
    See also Careers in recreation management
Enabling function, 26, 31, 157, 160
Environmental concerns and programs, 5, 11-12, 35-36, 43-47, 79, 91-93, 207-208

Ethical issues in sport, 184
Ewert, A., 208
Expenditures on recreation, 6, 10-13, 177, 179-181, 191, 198, 212-213

F

Family fun centers, 101-103
    services, 113-115
Federal role in recreation, 43- 45, 68, 193
    See also Forest Service, National Park Service
Fees in recreation and parks, 19, 110
Fish and Wildlife Service, 43-44, 79
Fishing, 17, 49, 57-58, 78-79, 95-96, 171
Fitness centers, 97, 99-100, 113, 120, 171
Football, 171-172, 176
Forest Service, 12, 43-44
Foucar-Szoki, R., 217
Four-H Clubs, 76
Functions of leisure-service agencies, 26, 31-32
Future trends, 20-21

G

Gambling, 36, 183, 208-210
Gardening, 24
Gender, *See* Sexual identity and recreation, Women and girls
Girl Scouts, 14, 65, 69, 71, 84, 160
Goeldner, C., 190, 194
Golf, 110, 171, 174
Government's local role, *See* Public recreation and park agencies

H

Harrington, M., 7
Hatboro-Horsham school district, 139
Health spas, *See* Fitness centers
Heritage tourism, 206
Hershey track-and-field program, 35, 178
Higher education, *See* Professional preparation
Hiring procedures in leisure services, 58-62
Hispanic-Americans, 14, 173-174
Hobbies, 11, 138

Hospitality management, *See* Tourism
Hosteling International, 206
Human-service programs, 50-54, 65-76, 114-115
Hunting, 17, 90-93, 171, 202-203

I

Ice hockey, 55, 94, 172
    skating, 94
Indians, *See* Native Americans
Indianapolis, 46
Information-referral function, 26, 31
Injuries in sport, 183
In-service training, 239
    See also Staff development
International Association of Amusement Parks and Attractions, 32-33, 239
Internet, impact on tourism, 193-194
    role in recruitment, 227-235
Internship programs, 117, 238
Intramurals and sport clubs, 131-134

J

Jazzercise, 101
Jewish community centers,
    See Young Men's and Young Women's Hebrew Associations
Job descriptions and notices, 59-61, 116-118, 163, 165-167, 225-235
Jones, R., 131, 13

K

Kamloops, British Columbia, Canada, 54-55, 195, 205
Kinney, W.B., 155
Knott's Berry Farm, 234

L

Lamke., G., 131, 136
Las Vegas, Nevada, 157-158
Legal basis of state and local agencies, 46-47
Leisurability therapeutic recreation model, 149-150
Leisure as free time, 13-14, benefits of, 8-12 motivations, 1-2, service system, 23-41 villages, 140-143

Lewis, J., 131, 136
Library services, 51
Little League, 19, 352 170, 175, 184
Local public departments, *See* Public recreation and park agencies
Long Beach, California, 51, 157, 159

M

Mainstreaming, 157-161, 163
Marinas, *See Boating*
Marketing trends in recreation management, 15-16, 57-58, 66-68, 71, 74, 80, 92, 94, 101-102, 182, 186, 193-194, 211
Martial arts, 101, 171
McIntosh, R., 190, 193
Models of leisure-service system, 25-26
Morale, Welfare and Recreation services, *See* Armed forces recreation
Motivations in recreation and tourism, 1-2, 7-8, 26, 194, 202-206
Multiculturalism, 14, 51
    See also Race relations in recreation
Municipal recreation, *See* Public recreation and park agencies
Music, 16

N

National Association for Sports and Physical Education, 182
National Employee Services and Recreation Association, 120, 122-125
National Endowment for the Arts, 46
National Intramural and Recreational Sports Association, 32, 135-136, 236
National Outdoor Leadership School, 35, 79, 81, 85
National Park Service, 12, 43-44, 226
National Recreation and Park Association, 6, 8, 37, 39, 118, 239-240
National Rifle Association, 14
National Therapeutic Recreation Society, 32, 149-150, 155, 167, 236
Native Americans, 14
Nonprofit leisure service agencies, 25-27, 64-86, 160-163, 221

North American Society for Sport Management, 182
North York, Ontario, Canada, 54

O

Old Country theme park, Virginia, 239
Ontario, Canada, Parks and Recreation Federation, 8
Open space developments, *See* Federal role in recreation
Organized leisure-service system, 23-41
Orlando, Florida, 198, 212
Outdoor recreation, 15, 17, 79, 89-97, 114, 287
    See also Environmental concerns and programs

P

Park districts, 47-49
Park rangers, 59-60
Park systems, value of, 11
Paintball, 92, 97
Partnerships, 36-39, 73, 116
    See also Cooperation in leisure services
Pelican Cove, Florida, 141, 145
PERA Club, Arizona, 119-120
Performing arts, 11, 53
Peterson, G., 8
Phoenix, Arizona, 50-52, 61, 238
Physical fitness, 7-9
    See also Fitness centers
Physical education, 129, 137, 179
Play, motivations for, 7-8
Pocono Whitewater Adventure, 97, 99
Police Athletic League, 66, 69, 170
Pop Warner Football, 170, 176, 231
Pricing policies, 57-58
Prince George's County, Maryland, 50
Private-membership organizations, 25-26, 29, 138-147, 221, 230
Privatization of leisure services, 36-37
Professional preparation, 35-36
Professionalism in leisure services, 26, 32, 123-121, 217-221, 238-241

Public recreation and park agencies, 15, 25-27, 42-68, 221

R

Race relations in recreation, 3, 14, 49, 51, 140, 173-174
RCH, Inc., San Francisco, 160-161
Recreation, benefits of, 8-12
    See Organized leisure-service system
Religion-connected agencies, 65, 71-76
Religion-linked tourism, 206
Retirement communities, 188
Riley, B., 155

S

Safari Club International, 90-92
Samuels, J., 217
San Diego State University, 135
San Mateo, California, 51, 53
Sarasota, Florida, 49-50
School-sponsored recreation, 137-139
Scottsdale, Arizona, 3, 224, 229
Seagle, E.E., 218-220
Self-assessment, 218-221, 223-224
Sexual identity and recreation, 7-8
    See also Women and girls
Shank, J., 155
Shooting sports, 171
Shultis, J., 208
Sierra Club, 12, 35
Six Flags theme park, 197
Skiing, 15, 54, 92, 94, 102-104, 114, 171
Smith, R.W., 218-220
Snowboarding, 92
Soccer, 170-171
Social development and recreation, 10, 51, 54-55, 65-66, 71-72
Societal benefits of recreation, 10
South Charleston, West Virginia, 34
South East Consortium, New York, 160-161, 164
Southern Illinois University, 131, 133
Special events, 35, 122, 125
Special-interest organizations, 76-79

Special Olympics, 32, 160-162
Special recreation, 118, 155-163
Spending on recreation, *See* Expenditures on recreation
Sports management, 6, 26, 30, 49-51, 54-56, 76-77, 113, 122-123, 131-134, 169-187, 193, 221, 229, 232
Staff development in recreation and parks, 62, 80-32, 84-85, 102, 104, 117-118, 239-240
State leisure-service agencies, 45-47
Sun City, Arizona, 141-143
Swimming, 171
See also Aquatic recreation
System, meaning of, 24-25

T
Technology, impact on leisure, 14-15, 57-58
Television and sport, 179
Temple University, 155
Tennis, 39, 171, 174, 177
Theme parks, 197-199, 211-213, 233-235
Therapeutic recreation service, 6, 8, 26, 29-30, 32, 148-168, 221
Title IX, 173
Tourism, 6, 11, 26, 30, 34, 44, 189-213, 222, 232

Trade associations and shows, 26, 32-33, 78-79, 95, 99-100, 230
Trail rides, 94, 995 202, 205
Travel, *See* Tourism
Treatment plans, 151-155

U
U.S. Air Force, 113
U.S. Army Corps of Engineers, 43-44
U.S. Army recreation, 114
U.S. Marine Corps, 113, 115
U.S. Navy recreation, 108-112, 224-225, 228
U.S. Tennis Association, 39, 177
University of Northern Colorado, 131, 133
University of New Mexico, 185

V
Vacation homes, 144
Vail, Colorado, 54-56
Valley Forge, Pennsylvania, 196
Vancouver, British Columbia, Canada, 58
Virginia Commonwealth University, 131-132
Volleyball, 56, 171
Voluntary organization, *See* Nonprofit leisure-service agencies
Volunteer leadership, 64, 66, 69

W
Walker, J.R., 200
Walt Disney Company, 197, 212-213
Water parks, 32, 200, 239
Web pages, *See* Internet role in recruitment
Westchester County, New York, 49, 160-161, 163
Wheelchair sports, 157, 160-161
Whitewater rafting, 97-98, 143
Winter sports, 93-95
Witt, P., 13
Women and girls, recreation for, 9, 39, 72, 140, 173-173, 202
Woodswomen, Inc., 202, 204
Workweek, 4, 13-14, 192

Y
Yoga, in fitness programs, 100
Young Men's Christian Association, 4. 18, 72-73, 80, 82, 160
Young Men's and Young Women's Hebrew Association, 71, 75-76, 78
Young Women's Christian Association, 4. 182 71-72, 160
Youth in society, 18, 54, 65, 114, 137-138
Youth, programs for, 51, 65-76, 114-115, 158-159